EXAM CRAM

The Network+ Cram Sheet

This Cram Sheet contains the distilled, key facts about the CompTIA Network+ exam. Review this information as the last thing you do before you enter the testing center, paying special attention to those areas in which you feel you need the most review. You can transfer any of these facts from your head onto a blank sheet of paper immediately before you begin the exam.

MEDIA AND TOPOLOGIES

- Peer-to-peer networks are useful for only relatively small networks. They are often used in small offices or home environments.
- Client/server networks, also called server-centric networks, have clients and servers. Servers provide centralized administration, data storage, and security. The client system requests data from the server and displays the data to the end user.
- The bus network topology is also known as a linear bus because the computers in such a network are linked together using a single cable called a trunk, or backbone.
- If a terminator on a bus network is loose, data communications might be disrupted. Any other break in the cable will cause the entire network segment to fail.
- In a star configuration, all devices on the network connect to a central device, and this central device creates a single point of failure on the network.
- In the physical ring topology, the network layout forms a complete ring. Computers connect to the network cable directly or, more commonly, through a specialized network device.
- Breaking the loop of a ring network disrupts the entire network.
- The mesh topology requires each computer on the network to be individually connected to every other device. This configuration provides maximum reliability and redundancy for the network.
- A wireless infrastructure network uses a centralized device known as a wireless access point (WAP). Ad hoc wireless topologies are a peer-to-peer configuration and do not use a wireless access point.
- 802.2, the LLC sublayer, defines specifications for the Logical Link Control (LLC) sublayer in the 802 standard series.
- 802.3 defines the carrier-sense multiple-access with collision detection (CSMA/CD) media access method used in Ethernet networks. This is the most popular networking standard used today.
- 802.5 defines Token Ring networking.
- 802.11 defines standards for wireless LAN communication.
- Many factors cause EMI, including computer monitors and fluorescent lighting fixtures.
- Copper-based media are prone to EMI, whereas fiber-optic cable is immune to it.
- Data signals might also be subjected to something commonly referred to as *crosstalk*, which occurs when signals from two cables, or from wires within a single cable, interfere with each other.
- The weakening of data signals as they traverse the media is referred to as *attenuation*.
- Half-duplex mode enables each device to both transmit and receive, but only one of these processes can occur at a time.
- Full-duplex mode enables devices to receive and transmit simultaneously. A 100Mbps network card in full-duplex mode can operate at 200Mbps.
- 802.11b/g uses 2.4 GHz RF for transmissions, whereas 802.11a uses 5GHz RF.
- Infrared and Bluetooth are short range wireless technologies often used to connect peripheral devices to a computer.

CABLES AND CONNECTORS

- Thin coax is only .25 inches in diameter and has a maximum cable length of 185 meters (approximately 600 feet).

- An extranet is an application or system made available to users outside of an organization. Access to the extranet is tightly controlled and secure.
- Protocols associated with intranets and extranets include HTTP and FTP.

BACKUPS

- In a full backup, all data is backed up. Full backups do not use the archive bit, but do clear it.
- Incremental backups back up all data that has changed since the last full or incremental backup. They use and clear the archive bit.
- Differential backups back up all data since the last full or differential backup. They use the archive bit but do not clear it.

VLANS AND NAS

- VLANs are used to segment networks. This is often done for organizational or security purposes.

CLIENT CONNECTIVITY

- To log on to a NetWare server, you might need a username, password, tree, server name, and context.
- UNIX and Linux use the Network File System (NFS) protocol to provide file-sharing capabilities between computers.

SECURITY: PHYSICAL, LOGICAL, PASSWORDS, AND FIREWALLS

- A password that uses eight case-sensitive characters, with letters, numbers, and special characters, often makes a strong password.
- Windows 2000/2003 permissions include Full Control, Modify, Read & Execute, List Folder Contents, Read, Write.
- On a Windows system, NTFS provides a higher level of security, including file and folder level security.
- When a user can't access files that other users can, verify that the correct permissions are set.
- A firewall is a system or group of systems that controls the flow of traffic between two networks. A firewall often provides such services as NAT, proxy services, and packet filtering.
- A proxy server allows Internet access to be controlled. Having a centralized point of access allows for a great deal of control over the use of the Internet.

NETWORK SUPPORT

- You can ping the local loopback adapter by using the command `ping 127.0.0.1`. If this command is successful, you know that the TCP/IP protocol suite is installed correctly on your system and functioning.
- `Tracert` reports the amount of time it takes to reach each router in the path. It's a useful tool for isolating bottlenecks in a network. The `Tracert` command performs the same task on UNIX and Linux systems.
- ARP is the part of the TCP/IP suite whose function is to resolve IP addresses to MAC addresses.
- `netstat` is used to view both inbound and outbound TCP/IP network connections.
- `nbtstat` is used to display protocol and statistical information for NetBIOS over TCP/IP connections.
- `ipconfig` shows the IP configuration information for all NICs installed within a system.
- `ipconfig /all` is used to display detailed TCP/IP configuration information.
- `ipconfig /renew` is used to renew the system's DNS information.
- When looking for client connectivity problems using `ipconfig`, you should ensure that the gateway is correctly set.
- The `ifconfig` command is the Linux equivalent of the `ipconfig` command.
- `winipcfg` is the Windows 95, Windows 98, and Windows Me equivalent of the `ipconfig` command.
- The `nslookup` command is a TCP/IP diagnostic tool used to troubleshoot DNS problems. Dig can be used for the same purpose on UNIX and Linux systems.

MEDIA TOOLS AND LEDS

- A wire crimper is a tool that you use to attach media connectors to the ends of cables.
- Media testers, also called cable testers, are used to test whether a cable is working properly.
- An optical cable tester performs the same basic function as a wire media tester, but on optical media.
- The hardware loopback tests the outgoing signals of a device such as a network card.
- If the LED on a network card is constantly lit, you might have a chattering network card.

- UTP cabling is classified by category. Category 5/5e and 6 offer transmission distances of 100 meters.
- Fiber-optic cabling is immune to interference and can be used over great distances. It comes in two varieties—single mode and multimode.
- F-type connectors are used with coaxial cable, most commonly to connect Cable modems and TVs.
- SC, ST, LC, and MT-RJ connectors are associated with fiber cabling. ST connectors offer a twist-type attachment and SC, LC, and MTRJ connectors are push-on.
- RJ-45 connectors are used with UTP cable and are associated with networking applications. RJ-11 connectors are used with telephone cables.
- FireWire connectors come in 4-pin and 6-pin versions.

10BASE-X, 100BASE-X, 1000BASE-X, and 10GbE Standards

- 10Mbps networking standards include 10BASE-T (twisted pair) and 10BASE-FL (fiber optic).
- The 10BASE-T standard specifies a limit of 100 meters between a computer and a switch or hub.
- 100Mbps networking standards include 100BASE-TX (twisted pair) and 100BASE-FX (fiber optic).
- 1000Mbps (gigabit) networking standards include 1000BASE-T (twisted pair) and 1000BASE-CX (twisted pair), 1000BASE-SX and 1000BASE-LX (fiber optic).
- 10GbE is the common term used to describe the 802.3ae 10 gigabit Ethernet networking standards. Current standards all use fiber-optic cabling.

NETWORK DEVICES

- Token Ring networks use special devices called multistation access units (MSAUs) to create the network.
- A straight-through cable is used to connect systems to the switch or hub using the MDI-X ports.
- In a crossover cable, wires 1 and 3 and wires 2 and 6 are crossed.
- Switches introduce microsegmentation, by which each connected system effectively operates on its own dedicated network connection.
- Routing Information Protocol (RIP) is a distance-vector routing protocol used for both the TCP/IP and IPX/SPX protocol suites.
- A MAC address is a 6-byte address that lets a NIC be uniquely identified on the network. The first three bytes (`00:D0:59`) identify the manufacturer of the card; the last three bytes (`09:07:51`) are the Universal LAN MAC address, which makes the interface unique.

OSI MODEL

- As data is passed up or down through the OSI model structure, headers are added (going down) or removed (going up) at each layer—a process called *encapsulation* (when added) or *decapsulation* (when removed).
- The application layer provides access to the network for applications and certain end-user functions. It displays incoming information and prepares outgoing information for network access.
- The presentation layer converts data from the application layer into a format that can be sent over the network. It converts data from the session layer into a format that can be understood by the application layer. It also handles encryption and decryption of data and provides compression and decompression functionalities.
- The session layer synchronizes the data exchange between applications on separate devices. It handles error detection and notification to the peer layer on the other device.
- The transport layer establishes, maintains, and breaks connections between two devices. It determines the ordering and priorities of data. It also performs error checking and verification and handles retransmissions, if necessary.
- The network layer provides mechanisms for the routing of data between devices across single or multiple network segments and handles the discovery of destination systems and addressing.
- The data-link layer has two distinct sublayers: LLC and MAC. It performs error detection and handling for the transmitted signals. It also defines the method by which the medium is accessed and defines hardware addressing through the MAC sublayer.
- The physical layer defines the physical structure of the network. It also defines voltage/signal rates and the physical connection methods, as well as the physical topology.
- Mapping network devices to the OSI model:

Hub	Physical (Layer 1)
Switch	Data-link (Layer 2)
Bridge	Data-link (Layer 2)
Router	Network (Layer 3)
NIC	Data-link (Layer 2)
WAP	Data-link (Layer 2)

PROTOCOLS

- A Class A TCP/IP address uses only the first octet to represent the network portion, a Class B address uses two octets, and a Class C address uses three octets.
- Class A addresses span from 1 to 126, with a default subnet mask of 255.0.0.0.
- Class B addresses span from 128 to 191, with a default subnet mask of 255.255.0.0.
- Class C addresses span from 192 to 223, with a default subnet mask of 255.255.255.0.
- The 127 network ID is reserved for the local loopback.
- Application protocols map to the application, presentation, and session layers of the OSI model. Application protocols include AFT, FTP, SFTP, TFTP, NCP, NTP, NNTP, SSH, Telnet, SCP, LDAP, and SNMP.
- Transport protocols map to the transport layer of the OSI model and are responsible for transporting data across the network. Transport protocols include ATP, NetBEUI, SPX, TCP, and UDP.
- The NetBEUI protocol uses names as addresses.
- Network protocols are responsible for providing the addressing and routing information. Network protocols include IP, IPX, and DDP.
- The TCP/IP protocol suite is used by all major operating systems and is a routable protocol.
- IPX/SPX protocol is associated with NetWare network and is routable.
- NetBEUI is used on Windows networks and is not routable.
- DHCP/BOOTP is a network service that automatically assigns IP addressing information.
- APIPA is a system used on Windows to automatically self assign an IP address in the absence of a DHCP server.
- DNS resolves hostnames to IP addresses.
- NAT translates private network addresses into public network addresses.
- WINS resolves NetBIOS names to IP addresses.
- SNMP provides network-management facilities on TCP/IP-based networks.
- Samba is a service that runs on UNIX/Linux systems to allow Windows clients to access the file/print services of that server without additional client software.
- NFS is the native file access protocol for UNIX/Linux. SMB is the native file access protocol for Windows. AFP is the native file access protocol for Macintosh systems.
- In a network that does not use DHCP, you need to watch for duplicate IP addresses that prevent a user from logging on to the network.
- Subnetting is a process in which parts of the host ID portion of an IP address is used to create more network IDs.

REMOTE ACCESS AND SECURITY PROTOCOLS

- The underlying technologies that enable the RAS process are dial-up protocols such as PPP and SLIP.
- SLIP protocol is used to establish remote connection. SLIP doesn't provide error checking or packet addressing, so it can be used only in serial communications.
- PPP provides several security enhancements compared to SLIP. The most important of these is the encryption of usernames and passwords during the authentication process.
- The RDP protocol allows client systems to access and run applications on a server, using the resources of the server, with only the user interface, keystrokes, and mouse movement being transferred between the client and server computers.
- IPSec is designed to encrypt data during communication between two computers. IPSec operates at the Network layer of the OSI model and provides security for protocols that operate at higher layers.
- SSL is a security protocol used on the Internet. Secure website URLs begin with `https://` instead of `http://`. HTTPS connections require a browser to establish a secure connection. Secure SSL connections for web pages are made through port 443 by default.
- The security tokens used in Kerberos are known as *tickets*.
- SOHO routers are used to share broadband Internet connectivity on small office and home networks.

RAID

- RAID 0 offers no fault tolerance and improves I/O performance. It requires a minimum of two disks.
- RAID 1, disk mirroring, provides fault tolerance and requires two hard disks. Separate disk controllers can be used—a strategy known as *disk duplexing*.
- RAID 5, disk striping with distributed parity, requires a minimum of three disks—the total size of a single disk being used for the parity calculation.

INTRANETS AND EXTRANETS

- An intranet is typically a Web server–hosted application made available only to users within an organization.

EXAM CRAM™ 2

Network+ Certification Practice Questions

Charles Brooks

Que® CERTIFICATION

Network+ Certification Practice Questions Exam Cram 2

International Standard Book Number: 0-789-73352-8

Library of Congress Catalog Card Number: 2004118398

Printed in the United States of America

First Printing: May 2005

08 07 06 05 4 3 2 1

Trademarks

All terms mentioned in this book that are known to be trademarks or service marks have been appropriately capitalized. Que Publishing cannot attest to the accuracy of this information. Use of a term in this book should not be regarded as affecting the validity of any trademark or service mark.

Warning and Disclaimer

Every effort has been made to make this book as complete and as accurate as possible, but no warranty or fitness is implied. The information provided is on an "as is" basis. The author and the publisher shall have neither liability nor responsibility to any person or entity with respect to any loss or damages arising from the information contained in this book or from the use of the CD or programs accompanying it.

Bulk Sales

Que Publishing offers excellent discounts on this book when ordered in quantity for bulk purchases or special sales. For more information, please contact

U.S. Corporate and Government Sales

1-800-382-3419

corpsales@pearsontechgroup.com

For sales outside the U.S., please contact

International Sales

international@pearsoned.com

Publisher
Paul Boger

Executive Editor
Jeff Riley

Acquisitions Editor
Jeff Riley

Development Editor
Pamalee Nelson

Managing Editor
Charlotte Clapp

Project Editor
Seth Kerney

Proofreader
Tracy Donhardt

Technical Editor
Rob Shimonski

Publishing Coordinator
Pamalee Nelson

Multimedia Developer
Dan Scherf

Interior Designer
Gary Adair

Cover Designer
Anne Jones

Page Layout
Michelle Mitchell

QUE® CERTIFICATION

Que Certification • 800 East 96th Street • Indianapolis, Indiana 46240

A Note from Series Editor Ed Tittel

You know better than to trust your certification preparation to just anybody. That's why you, and more than 2 million others, have purchased an Exam Cram book. As Series Editor for the new and improved Exam Cram 2 Series, I have worked with the staff at Que Certification to ensure you won't be disappointed. That's why we've taken the world's best-selling certification product—a two-time finalist for "Best Study Guide" in CertCities' reader polls—and made it even better.

As a two-time finalist for the "Favorite Study Guide Author" award as selected by CertCities readers, I know the value of good books. You'll be impressed with Que Certification's stringent review process, which ensures the books are high quality, relevant, and technically accurate. Rest assured that several industry experts have reviewed this material, helping us deliver an excellent solution to your exam preparation needs.

Exam Cram 2 books also feature a preview edition of MeasureUp's powerful, full-featured test engine, which is trusted by certification students throughout the world.

As a 20-year-plus veteran of the computing industry and the original creator and editor of the Exam Cram Series, I've brought my IT experience to bear on these books. During my tenure at Novell from 1989 to 1994, I worked with and around its excellent education and certification department. At Novell, I witnessed the growth and development of the first really big, successful IT certification program—one that was to shape the industry forever afterward. This experience helped push my writing and teaching activities heavily in the certification direction. Since then, I've worked on nearly 100 certification related books, and I write about certification topics for numerous Web sites and for *Certification* magazine.

In 1996, while studying for various MCP exams, I became frustrated with the huge, unwieldy study guides that were the only preparation tools available. As an experienced IT professional and former instructor, I wanted "nothing but the facts" necessary to prepare for the exams. From this impetus, Exam Cram emerged: short, focused books that explain exam topics, detail exam skills and activities, and get IT professionals ready to take and pass their exams.

In 1997 when Exam Cram debuted, it quickly became the best-selling computer book series since "*...For Dummies*," and the best-selling certification book series ever. By maintaining an intense focus on subject matter, tracking errata and updates quickly, and following the certification market closely, Exam Cram established the dominant position in cert prep books.

You will not be disappointed in your decision to purchase this book. If you are, please contact me at etittel@jump.net. All suggestions, ideas, input, or constructive criticism are welcome!

Ed Tittel

About the Author

Charles J. Brooks is currently the president of Marcraft International Corporation, located in Kennewick, Washington, and is in charge of research and development. He is the author of several books, including *A+ Training Guide*, *A+ Concepts and Practices*, and *Microcomputer Systems—Theory and Service*. Other titles produced by Mr. Brooks include: *Speech Synthesis*, *Pneumatic Instrumentation*, *The Complete Introductory Computer Course*, *Radio-Controlled Car Project Manual*, and *IBM PC Peripheral Troubleshooting and Repair*.

A former electronics instructor and technical writer with the National Education Corporation, Charles has taught and written on post-secondary EET curriculum, including introductory electronics, transistor theory, linear integrated circuits, basic digital theory, industrial electronics, microprocessors, and computer peripherals.

About Marcraft International Corporation

Marcraft International Corporation has been producing IT training products for 30 years, supplying the hardware, software, and courseware materials for numerous technical training curricula. Marcraft sells its products worldwide from its headquarters in Kennewick, Washington. Marcraft's mission is to develop exceptional products for effectively teaching and training people the IT skills in demand both today and in the future.

Contents at a Glance

Table of Contents

We Want to Hear from You!

As the reader of this book, *you* are our most important critic and commentator. We value your opinion and want to know what we're doing right, what we could do better, what areas you'd like to see us publish in, and any other words of wisdom you're willing to pass our way.

As an executive editor for Que Publishing, I welcome your comments. You can email or write me directly to let me know what you did or didn't like about this book—as well as what we can do to make our books better.

Please note that I cannot help you with technical problems related to the topic of this book. We do have a User Services group, however, where I will forward specific technical questions related to the book.

When you write, please be sure to include this book's title and author as well as your name, email address, and phone number. I will carefully review your comments and share them with the author and editors who worked on the book.

Email: feedback@quepublishing.com

Mail: Jeff Riley
Executive Editor
Que Publishing
800 East 96th Street
Indianapolis, IN 46240 USA

For more information about this book or another Que Certification title, visit our website at www.examcram2.com. Type the ISBN (excluding hyphens) or the title of a book in the Search field to find the page you're looking for.

Introduction

What Is this Book About?

Welcome to the *Network+ Practice Questions Exam Cram 2*, Second Edition! The aim of this book is solely to provide you with practice questions, complete with answers and explanations that will help you learn, drill, and review for the Network+ certification exam.

Who Is this Book For?

If you have studied the Network+ exam's content and feel you are ready to put your knowledge to the test, but not sure you want to take the real exam yet, this book is for you! Maybe you have answered other practice questions or unsuccessfully taken the real exam, reviewed, and want to do more practice questions before going to take the real exam; this book is for you, too!

What Will You Find in this Book?

As mentioned before, this book is all about practice questions. This book is separated according to the topics you will find in the Network+ exam. Each chapter represents an exam topic, and in the chapter you will find three elements:

- *Practice Questions*—These are the numerous questions that will help you learn, drill, and review.
- *Quick Check Answer Section*—Once you have finished answering the questions, you can quickly grade your exam from this section. Only correct answers are given here. No explanations are offered yet.

- *Answers and Explanations*—This section offers you the correct answers as well as further explanation about the content posed in that question. Use this information to learn why an answer is correct and to reinforce the content in your mind for exam day.

You will also find a *CramSheet* at the beginning of this book specifically written for this exam. This is a very popular element that is also found in the corresponding *Network+ Exam Cram 2*, Second Edition study guide (ISBN 0-7897-3254-8). This item condenses all the necessary facts found in this exam into one easy-to-handle tear card. The CramSheet is something you can carry with you to the exam location and use as a last-second study aid. Be aware that you can't take it into the exam room, though!

Hints for Using this Book

As this book is a paper practice product, you might want to complete your questions on a separate piece of paper so you can reuse the exams over and over without having previous answers in your way. Also, a general rule of thumb across all practice question products is to make sure you are scoring well into the high 80 to 90 percent range in all topics before attempting the real exam. The higher percentages you score on practice question products, the better your chances for passing the real exam. Of course, we can't guarantee a passing score on the real exam, but we can offer you plenty of opportunities to practice and assess your knowledge levels before entering the real exam.

Need Further Study?

Are you having a hard time correctly answering these questions? If so, you probably need further review. Be sure to see the sister product to this book, the *Network+ Exam Cram 2*, Second Edition, by Que Publishing (ISBN 0-7897-3254-8) for further review. If you need even further study, check out Que's *Network+ Exam Prep 2* (ISBN 0-7897-3255-6).

1

Media and Topologies

Quick Check

Domain 1.0: Media and Topologies

Objective 1.1: Recognize Logical or Physical Topologies, Given a Schematic Diagram or Description

1. Which of the following types of topology has at least two network connections on every device on the network?
   - ❑ A. Bus
   - ❑ B. Mesh
   - ❑ C. Ring
   - ❑ D. Star

Quick Answer: **28**
Detailed Answer: **31**

2. When describing the structure of a network, which term is used to describe the physical layout?
   - ❑ A. Physical map
   - ❑ B. Backbone
   - ❑ C. Network
   - ❑ D. Topology

Quick Answer: **28**
Detailed Answer: **31**

3. Which of the following network topologies is the most fault tolerant?
   - ❑ A. Mesh
   - ❑ B. Hierarchical star
   - ❑ C. Ring
   - ❑ D. Star

Quick Answer: **28**
Detailed Answer: **31**

4. The most widely used _______ topology are the Internet and the telephone network.
   - ❑ A. star
   - ❑ B. bus
   - ❑ C. mesh
   - ❑ D. token ring

Quick Answer: **28**
Detailed Answer: **31**

Quick Check

5. Which of the following is a key benefit to implementing a token ring topology?
   - ❑ A. IP addressing is eliminated.
   - ❑ B. Workstations don't contend for network access.
   - ❑ C. Token ring is always implemented in full duplex.
   - ❑ D. Nodes are added without interrupting the network.

Quick Answer: **28**
Detailed Answer: **31**

6. Nodes connected in a star topology _____
   - ❑ A. must have TCP/IP installed
   - ❑ B. must be assigned an IP address
   - ❑ C. may only use Ethernet
   - ❑ D. connect to a central hub

Quick Answer: **28**
Detailed Answer: **31**

7. What is the hub used in a token ring network called?
   - ❑ A. Patch Panel
   - ❑ B. AUI
   - ❑ C. Switch
   - ❑ D. MSAU

Quick Answer: **28**
Detailed Answer: **31**

8. Which of the following IEEE 802 standards pertain to token ring?
   - ❑ A. IEEE 802.3
   - ❑ B. IEEE 802.5
   - ❑ C. IEEE 802.2
   - ❑ D. IEEE 802.11

Quick Answer: **28**
Detailed Answer: **31**

9. Which of the following represents the best solution for connecting three computers in a LAN?
   - ❑ A. Peer-to-peer
   - ❑ B. Server-based
   - ❑ C. Direct connect
   - ❑ D. Router-based

Quick Answer: **28**
Detailed Answer: **32**

10. A disadvantage of a ring topology is that _____.
    - ❑ A. nodes must be connected in a point-to-point manner
    - ❑ B. a shorted bus will crash the network
    - ❑ C. the ring has to be opened to add a new node
    - ❑ D. it requires an excessive number of connections

Quick Answer: **28**
Detailed Answer: **32**

Quick Check

11. Which of the following network types is easiest to add new nodes to?

 - ❑ A. Ring
 - ❑ B. Star
 - ❑ C. Bus
 - ❑ D. Mesh

Quick Answer: **28**
Detailed Answer: **32**

12. Which of the following is not an advantage of the star topology compared to the mesh topology?

 - ❑ A. Easy to manage
 - ❑ B. Easy to add nodes
 - ❑ C. Low overhead
 - ❑ D. High fault-tolerant

Quick Answer: **28**
Detailed Answer: **32**

13. Which of the following is not a common logical topology?

 - ❑ A. Bus
 - ❑ B. Ring
 - ❑ C. Star
 - ❑ D. Mesh

Quick Answer: **28**
Detailed Answer: **32**

14. A star topology consists of a central ____.

 - ❑ A. gateway
 - ❑ B. router
 - ❑ C. brouter
 - ❑ D. hub

Quick Answer: **28**
Detailed Answer: **32**

15. In a bus topology _______.

 - ❑ A. nodes connect to a hub in a point-to-point arrangement
 - ❑ B. each end of the bus must be properly terminated
 - ❑ C. nodes are connected through redundant links
 - ❑ D. fiber-optic cable is the predominate media

Quick Answer: **28**
Detailed Answer: **32**

16. What is the formula for determining the number of connections that must be maintained in a full mesh network?

 - ❑ A. Connections = Nodes+1
 - ❑ B. Connections = Nodes-1
 - ❑ C. Connections = Nodes*2
 - ❑ D. Connections = Nodes(Nodes-1)/2

Quick Answer: **28**
Detailed Answer: **32**

Quick Check

Objective 1.2: Specify the Main Features of the 802.2 (LLC), 802.3 (Ethernet), 802.5 (Token Ring), 802.11 (Wireless), and FDDI Networking Technologies

1. Which IEEE specification does CSMA/CD map to?

   - ❑ A. IEEE 802.5
   - ❑ B. IEEE 802.2
   - ❑ C. IEEE 802.3
   - ❑ D. IEEE 802.11b

Quick Answer: **28**
Detailed Answer: **32**

2. Which of the following IEEE standards describes the LLC sublayer?

   - ❑ A. IEEE 802.5
   - ❑ B. IEEE 802.12
   - ❑ C. IEEE 802.3
   - ❑ D. IEEE 802.2

Quick Answer: **28**
Detailed Answer: **32**

3. What is the maximum number of stations permitted on an IEEE 802.3 network?

   - ❑ A. 16
   - ❑ B. 1,024
   - ❑ C. 100
   - ❑ D. 1,500

Quick Answer: **28**
Detailed Answer: **33**

4. Which IEEE 802 standard contains specifications for 100BASE-T?

   - ❑ A. IEEE 802.3
   - ❑ B. IEEE 802.4
   - ❑ C. IEEE 802.8
   - ❑ D. IEEE 802.14

Quick Answer: **28**
Detailed Answer: **33**

5. Which of the following statements is true?

   - ❑ A. The token in a token ring network is a 2-byte data stream passed from node to node.
   - ❑ B. Token ring networks are less reliable than Ethernet networks.
   - ❑ C. Token ring networks offer a higher degree of reliability than Ethernet networks.
   - ❑ D. The data delivery time in a token ring network is not predictable.

Quick Answer: **28**
Detailed Answer: **33**

Quick Check

6. Which of the following IEEE 802 standards describes Token Ring networks?
   - ❑ A. IEEE 802.5
   - ❑ B. IEEE 802.12
   - ❑ C. IEEE 802.2
   - ❑ D. IEEE 802.3

Quick Answer: **28**
Detailed Answer: **33**

7. Of the following, which is a valid data rate for token ring?
   - ❑ A. 12Mbps
   - ❑ B. 16Mbps
   - ❑ C. 8Mbps
   - ❑ D. 28Mbps

Quick Answer: **28**
Detailed Answer: **33**

8. A user equipped with an IEEE 802.11b card is unable to connect to an access point. Which of the following is true?
   - ❑ A. The user's IEEE 802.11b card can only connect to a wireless router.
   - ❑ B. The user's IEEE 802.11b card needs to have an RJ-45 connection.
   - ❑ C. The user's IEEE 802.11b card needs to be first connected to a 10BASE-T hub.
   - ❑ D. The user's IEEE 802.11b card is too far away from the access point.

Quick Answer: **28**
Detailed Answer: **33**

9. To exchange files between workstations equipped with IEEE 802.11b cards, what type of device is needed?
   - ❑ A. An MSAU
   - ❑ B. An access point
   - ❑ C. A hub
   - ❑ D. A router

Quick Answer: **28**
Detailed Answer: **33**

10. What is the maximum data rate of an IEEE 802.11a network device?
    - ❑ A. 54Mbps
    - ❑ B. 4Mbps
    - ❑ C. 100Mbps
    - ❑ D. 11Mbps

Quick Answer: **28**
Detailed Answer: **33**

11. Which connection type is the most reliable?
    - ❑ A. Connection-oriented
    - ❑ B. Connectionless
    - ❑ C. UDP
    - ❑ D. SMTP

Quick Answer: **28**
Detailed Answer: **33**

Quick Check

12. What is not an example of a bit-oriented protocol?
    - ❑ A. SDLC
    - ❑ B. LAPB
    - ❑ C. HDLC
    - ❑ D. BCS

Quick Answer: 28
Detailed Answer: 34

13. At what speed does FDDI work?
    A.10Mbps
    B.100Mbps
    C.1000Mbps
    D.1Gbps

Quick Answer: 28
Detailed Answer: 34

14. At what speeds do token ring networks operate?
    A.4/16Mbps
    B.10/100Mbps
    C.4/28Mbps
    D.100/1000Mbps

Quick Answer: 28
Detailed Answer: 34

Objective 1.3: Specify the Characteristics (e.g., Speed, Length, Topology, Cable Type, etc.) of the Following Cable Standards: 10BASE-T, 10BASE-FL, 100BASE-TX, 100BASE-FX, 1000BASE-T, 1000BASE-CX, 1000BASE-SX, 1000BASE-LX, 10GBASE-SR, 10GBASE-LR, and 10GBASE-ER

1. Which of the following is the expected data rate on a 10BASE-T network?
    - ❑ A. 100Mbps
    - ❑ B. 10Mbps
    - ❑ C. 500Mbps
    - ❑ D. 1000Mbps

Quick Answer: 28
Detailed Answer: 34

2. The segment length from hub port to workstation NIC on a 10BASE-T network should be no longer than ______.
    - ❑ A. 100 meters
    - ❑ B. 185 meters
    - ❑ C. 200 meters
    - ❑ D. 10 meters

Quick Answer: 28
Detailed Answer: 34

Quick Check

3. In a 100BASE-T network, the distance of cable from hub to workstation should not exceed ______.

   - ❑ A. 25 meters
   - ❑ B. 50 meters
   - ❑ C. 100 meters
   - ❑ D. 200 meters

Quick Answer: **28**
Detailed Answer: **34**

4. You have a workstation that is 153 meters from the server, there is no repeater and it uses 10BASE-T wiring. You cannot connect to the network.

   Required Objective: Connect to the server.

   Optional Objectives: Faster connection, easier access for users.

   Proposed Solution: Replace the old NIC with a 100BASEFX NIC.

   - ❑ A. This meets only the required objective.
   - ❑ B. This meets the optional objectives.
   - ❑ C. This meets the required and one of the optional objectives.
   - ❑ D. This does not meet the required or optional objectives.

Quick Answer: **28**
Detailed Answer: **34**

5. IEEE 802.5 refers to _____.

   - ❑ A. Token Bus
   - ❑ B. Token ring
   - ❑ C. Ethernet
   - ❑ D. MAN

Quick Answer: **28**
Detailed Answer: **34**

6. Which of the following networking standards specifies a maximum segment length of 100 meters?

   - ❑ A. 10BASE-T
   - ❑ B. 10BASE5
   - ❑ C. 10BASEYX
   - ❑ D. 10BASE2

Quick Answer: **28**
Detailed Answer: **34**

7. Which of the following technologies uses Category 5 cable?

   - ❑ A. 100BASE-TX
   - ❑ B. Fiber-optic
   - ❑ C. 10BASE5
   - ❑ D. 10BASE2

Quick Answer: **28**
Detailed Answer: **34**

Quick Check

8. What kind of connector would you use to make a patch cable for a 10BASE-T network?

- ❑ A. RJ-11
- ❑ B. RJ-45
- ❑ C. RJ-T
- ❑ D. BNC

Quick Answer: **28**
Detailed Answer: **35**

9. If you increase the resistance on a wire, what happens to the signal energy loss?

- ❑ A. There is no change.
- ❑ B. The signal energy loss decreases.
- ❑ C. The signal energy loss increases.
- ❑ D. The signal energy change fluctuates wildly between very high increases and very high decreases.

Quick Answer: **28**
Detailed Answer: **35**

10. What is the proper termination for unshielded twisted-pair network cable?

- ❑ A. 150 ohms
- ❑ B. 50 ohms
- ❑ C. 93 ohms
- ❑ D. 100 ohms

Quick Answer: **28**
Detailed Answer: **35**

11. What causes intersymbol interference?

- ❑ A. Ohms
- ❑ B. Crosstalk
- ❑ C. Adaptive equalizers
- ❑ D. Reactive components of cables

Quick Answer: **28**
Detailed Answer: **35**

12. What does an adaptive equalizer do?

- ❑ A. It increases intersymbol interference.
- ❑ B. It samples and evaluates data for intersymbol interference.
- ❑ C. It promotes crosstalk in wires.
- ❑ D. It prevents crosstalk in wires.

Quick Answer: **28**
Detailed Answer: **35**

13. How does an equalizer lower ISI?

- ❑ A. It increases the twists in the copper cabling.
- ❑ B. It increases crosstalk.
- ❑ C. It incorporates phase shifts to counter the effects of the channel.
- ❑ D. An equalizer normally increases ISI.

Quick Answer: **28**
Detailed Answer: **35**

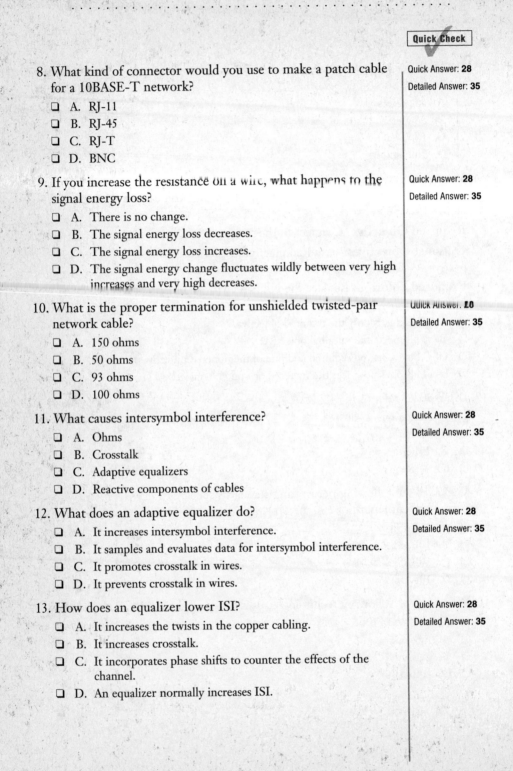

Quick Check

14. Which of the following types of noise results from sunspot activity?
   - ❑ A. Impulse noise
   - ❑ B. Atmospheric noise
   - ❑ C. Frequency noise
   - ❑ D. Crosstalk

Quick Answer: **28**
Detailed Answer: **35**

15. What cable type is used with the IEEE 100BASE-FX standard?
   - ❑ A. Coaxial
   - ❑ B. Fiber-optic
   - ❑ C. STP
   - ❑ D. UTP

Quick Answer: **28**
Detailed Answer: **35**

16. Which of the following types of noise is caused by engine ignition systems?
   - ❑ A. Sunspots
   - ❑ B. Crosstalk
   - ❑ C. Impulse noise
   - ❑ D. Twists in the cabling

Quick Answer: **28**
Detailed Answer: **35**

17. Which of the following types of noise originates from carrier frequencies?
   - ❑ A. Atmospheric noise
   - ❑ B. Impulse noise
   - ❑ C. Crosstalk
   - ❑ D. Frequency noise

Quick Answer: **28**
Detailed Answer: **35**

18. Crosstalk occurs when you lay unshielded cables _____.
   - ❑ A. in parallel
   - ❑ B. in perpendicular
   - ❑ C. in right angles
   - ❑ D. end-to-end

Quick Answer: **28**
Detailed Answer: **36**

19. In early days, you could hear another conversation while talking on the telephone. What caused this problem?
   - ❑ A. Attenuation
   - ❑ B. Signal loss
   - ❑ C. Crosstalk
   - ❑ D. Parity

Quick Answer: **28**
Detailed Answer: **36**

Quick Check

20. Distortion is expressed using what kind of measurement?
    - ❑ A. Watts
    - ❑ B. Decibels
    - ❑ C. Amps
    - ❑ D. Meters

Quick Answer: **28**
Detailed Answer: **36**

21. If the power of the noise is 5 mW, and the power of the desired signal is 50 mW, what is the SNR, in decibels?
    - ❑ A. 18 dB
    - ❑ B. 10 dB
    - ❑ C. 5 dB
    - ❑ D. 1 dB

Quick Answer: **28**
Detailed Answer: **36**

22. What is an acceptable SNR for digital communications?
    - ❑ A. 60 dB
    - ❑ B. 50 dB
    - ❑ C. 40 dB
    - ❑ D. 70 dB

Quick Answer: **29**
Detailed Answer: **36**

23. What is the maximum segment length of a 100BASE-FX Ethernet connection?
    - ❑ A. 100m
    - ❑ B. 265m
    - ❑ C. 412m
    - ❑ D. 1000m

Quick Answer: **29**
Detailed Answer: **36**

24. What is the standard speed for an IEEE 100BASE-TX network?
    - ❑ A. 100Mbps
    - ❑ B. 200Mbps
    - ❑ C. 10Mbps
    - ❑ D. 100bps

Quick Answer: **29**
Detailed Answer: **36**

25. Thinnet is also referred to as ______.
    - ❑ A. 10BASE-T
    - ❑ B. 10BASE5
    - ❑ C. Cheapernet
    - ❑ D. Thin UTP

Quick Answer: **29**
Detailed Answer: **36**

26. What is the topic of the IEEE 802.10 standard?
    - ❑ A. LAN security
    - ❑ B. Broadband technology
    - ❑ C. Wireless LANs
    - ❑ D. 100VG-AnyLAN

Quick Answer: **29**
Detailed Answer: **36**

Quick Check

27. Which of the IEEE 802 standards describes Ethernet?

- ❑ A. IEEE 802.2
- ❑ B. IEEE 802.12
- ❑ C. IEEE 802.3
- ❑ D. IEEE 802.5

Quick Answer: **29**
Detailed Answer: **36**

28. A client in a 10BASE-T LAN using category 5 UTP is unable to access the server. The hub is located 80 meters from a patch panel. The distance from the patch panel to wall outlet is 15 meters. The patch cable from wall outlet to client is 10 meters. Which of the following statements best describes the proposed solution?

Required Results: To provide access to the server from the client workstation.

Optional Desired Results: To improve data rates on the LAN and to reduce the amount of logged downtime.

Proposed Solution: Reduce the length of the patch cable from wall outlet to client workstation to 5 meters.

- ❑ A. The proposed solution produces the required result and one of the optional desired results.
- ❑ B. The proposed solution produces the required result and both of the optional desired results.
- ❑ C. The proposed solution produces the required result but neither of the optional desired results.
- ❑ D. The proposed solution does not produce the required result but produces both of the optional desired results.

Quick Answer: **29**
Detailed Answer: **37**

29. What is the maximum segment length of 10BASE-T STP cable?

- ❑ A. 50 meters
- ❑ B. 100 meters
- ❑ C. 75 meters
- ❑ D. 200 meters

Quick Answer: **29**
Detailed Answer: **37**

30. What is the maximum data rate of a 10BASE-T network?

- ❑ A. 100Mbps
- ❑ B. 500Mbps
- ❑ C. 10Mbps
- ❑ D. 1000Mbps

Quick Answer: **29**
Detailed Answer: **37**

Quick Check

31. In a 100BASE-T4 network, the distance of cable from hub to workstation should not exceed _____.
- ❑ A. 200 meters
- ❑ B. 50 meters
- ❑ C. 25 meters
- ❑ D. 100 meters

Quick Answer: **29**
Detailed Answer: **37**

32. Which of the following cable types is recommended for 100BASE-TX networks?
- ❑ A. Thinnet
- ❑ B. Thicknet
- ❑ C. Category 5 UTP
- ❑ D. Category 3 UTP

Quick Answer: **29**
Detailed Answer: **37**

33. Which of the following uses only two conductors?
- ❑ A. 100BASEFX
- ❑ B. 100BASE-T
- ❑ C. 10BASE-T
- ❑ D. 10BASE5

Quick Answer: **29**
Detailed Answer: **37**

34. What is the maximum segment length of 100BASE-TX?
- ❑ A. 100 meters
- ❑ B. 200 meters
- ❑ C. 50 meters
- ❑ D. 75 meters

Quick Answer: **29**
Detailed Answer: **37**

35. Which 100Mbps standard uses all eight wires in a category 5 cable?
- ❑ A. 10BASE-T
- ❑ B. 100BASE-T4
- ❑ C. 100BASEFX
- ❑ D. 100BASE-TX

Quick Answer: **29**
Detailed Answer: **37**

36. What type of network media is used with 100BASEFX?
- ❑ A. UTP
- ❑ B. Coaxial
- ❑ C. Fiber optic
- ❑ D. Microwave

Quick Answer: **29**
Detailed Answer: **37**

Quick Check

37. You are connecting a network storage system to a LAN using 1000BASE-SX connections. What type of cabling are you using?

Quick Answer: **29**
Detailed Answer: **37**

❑ A. Single mode fiber-optic cabling
❑ B. CAT6 cabling
❑ C. Multimode fiber-optic cabling
❑ D. iSCSI cabling

38. Which of the following IEEE standards specifies a 1300nm laser beam to drive data across the network media?

Quick Answer: **29**
Detailed Answer: **37**

❑ A. 1000BASE-LX
❑ B. 10GBASE-LR
❑ C. 1000BASE-CX
❑ D. 1000BASE-SX

Objective 1.4: Recognize the Following Media Connectors and Describe Their Uses: RJ-11, RJ-45, F-Type, ST, SC, IEEE-1394, Fiber LC, MT-RJ, and USB

1. You are making some category 5 twisted-pair cables and have run out of connectors. What type of connector should you order from your supplier?

Quick Answer: **29**
Detailed Answer: **37**

❑ A. RJ-45
❑ B. RJ-11
❑ C. BNC
❑ D. ST

2. You are configuring a router. According to the manual, you will need a transceiver to connect to the LAN ports of the router. What kind of physical interface does the router have?

Quick Answer: **29**
Detailed Answer: **38**

❑ A. MSAU
❑ B. AUI
❑ C. RJ-11
❑ D. BNC

Quick Check

3. In a hardware loopback plug, which two wire numbers are connected?

Quick Answer: 29
Detailed Answer: 38

- ❑ A. 3 and 4
- ❑ B. 1 and 3
- ❑ C. 1 and 2
- ❑ D. 2 and 6
- ❑ E. 3 and 5

4. Which of the following uses an RJ-45 connector?

Quick Answer: 29
Detailed Answer: 38

- ❑ A. Coaxial cable
- ❑ B. UTP cable
- ❑ C. Fiber-optic cable
- ❑ D. Thinnet cable

5. What type of connector is used for the cable that connects the DSL modem to the computer?

Quick Answer: 29
Detailed Answer: 38

- ❑ A. RJ-45 connector
- ❑ B. BNC connector
- ❑ C. F-Type connector
- ❑ D. Fiber LC connector

6. An RJ-45 connector is comprised of ______ pins.

Quick Answer: 29
Detailed Answer: 38

- ❑ A. 4
- ❑ B. 8
- ❑ C. 16
- ❑ D. 25

7. What type of connector would you expect to find in a 1000BASE-SX network?

Quick Answer: 29
Detailed Answer: 38

- ❑ A. RJ-45 connector
- ❑ B. MT-RJ connector
- ❑ C. SC connector
- ❑ D. Fiber LC connector

8. What sort of connector would you expect to be working with in a 1000BASE-FX network?

Quick Answer: 29
Detailed Answer: 38

- ❑ A. RJ-45 connector
- ❑ B. MT-RJ connector
- ❑ C. SC connector
- ❑ D. BNC connector

Quick Check

Objective 1.5: Recognize the Following Media Types and Describe Their Use: Cat 3,5,5e, and 6, UTP, STP, Coax, Single-Mode Fiber, and Multimode Fiber

1. What is the advantage of fiber-optic cable over copper-based media?

    - ❑ A. It's immune to EMI interference.
    - ❑ B. It interfaces easily to other media types.
    - ❑ C. It's cheaper.
    - ❑ D. It uses conventional radio waves for a carrier.

    Quick Answer: **29**
Detailed Answer: **38**

2. Select the best networking media for a new installation in which 10 clients are connected to a hub in a 100BASE-T network.

    - ❑ A. Category 3 UTP
    - ❑ B. RG-58
    - ❑ C. Fiber optic
    - ❑ D. Category 5 UTP

    Quick Answer: **29**
Detailed Answer: **38**

3. While troubleshooting a network connectivity problem, you notice that the network card in your system is operating at 10Mbps in half-duplex mode. At what speed is the network link operating?

    - ❑ A. 10Mbps
    - ❑ B. 5Mbps
    - ❑ C. 2.5Mbps
    - ❑ D. 20Mbps

    Quick Answer: **29**
Detailed Answer: **38**

4. You are tasked with specifying a way to connect two buildings across a parking lot. The distance between the two buildings is 78 meters. An underground wiring duct exists between the two buildings, although there are concerns about using it because it also houses high-voltage electrical cables. The budget for the project is very tight, but your manager wants you to specify the most suitable solution. Which of the following cable types would you recommend?

    - ❑ A. UTP
    - ❑ B. Fiber-optic
    - ❑ C. Thin coax
    - ❑ D. STP

    Quick Answer: **29**
Detailed Answer: **38**

Quick Check

5. Which two of the following connectors would you use when working with fiber-optic cable?
   - ❑ A. ST
   - ❑ B. RJ-45
   - ❑ C. SC
   - ❑ D. RJ-11

Quick Answer: **29**
Detailed Answer: **39**

6. Which of the following may be a disadvantage of using shielded twisted-pair cabling?
   - ❑ A. It requires an AUI connector on each end.
   - ❑ B. It can only be used in token ring networks.
   - ❑ C. It must be properly grounded.
   - ❑ D. Data rates are limited to 4Mbps.

Quick Answer: **29**
Detailed Answer: **39**

7. Which of the following is an advantage of fiber-optic cable?
   - ❑ A. It's comparatively easy to install.
   - ❑ B. It's immune to EMI interference.
   - ❑ C. It's comparatively inexpensive.
   - ❑ D. It requires little specialized training to install.

Quick Answer: **29**
Detailed Answer: **39**

8. Which of the following IEEE standards specifies fiber-optic technology?
   - ❑ A. IEEE 802.12
   - ❑ B. IEEE 802.8
   - ❑ C. IEEE 802.3
   - ❑ D. IEEE 802.5

Quick Answer: **29**
Detailed Answer: **39**

9. What kind of cable is totally immune from EMI interference?
   - ❑ A. Fiber-optic cable
   - ❑ B. Category 3
   - ❑ C. Category 5
   - ❑ D. Coaxial Cable

Quick Answer: **29**
Detailed Answer: **39**

10. What is *not* usually a factor that can be attributed to losses in fiber optic cable?
    - ❑ A. Improper splices
    - ❑ B. Misaligned connectors
    - ❑ C. Too many twists
    - ❑ D. Severe bends

Quick Answer: **29**
Detailed Answer: **39**

Quick Check

11. Why is a bent cable in fiber optics undesirable in terms of signal loss?

❑ A. It does not matter.

❑ B. Bent cable reacts with the twists to create more crosstalk.

❑ C. The cable is susceptible to atmospheric noise when it is bent.

❑ D. The energy will refract into the cladding and be lost.

Quick Answer: **29**
Detailed Answer: **39**

12. An amplifier has an input power of 20 mW (milliwatts) and a power output of 200 mW. What is the gain in decibels?

❑ A. 10 dB

❑ B. 5 dB

❑ C. 2 dB

❑ D. 1 dB

Quick Answer: **29**
Detailed Answer: **40**

13. What does a negative dB mean when evaluating the performance of a line?

❑ A. Your server needs to be replaced.

❑ B. Gain of signal strength.

❑ C. Nothing.

❑ D. Loss of signal strength.

Quick Answer: **29**
Detailed Answer: **39**

14. A particular advantage of category 5 UTP is that it eliminates ________.

❑ A. all EMI

❑ B. a maximum data rate

❑ C. crosstalk

❑ D. the need for NICs

Quick Answer: **29**
Detailed Answer: **40**

15. What UTP communication and data media is rated for 100MHz operation?

❑ A. Cat 3 cabling

❑ B. Cat 4 cabling

❑ C. Cat 5 cabling

❑ D. Cat 6 cabling

Quick Answer: **29**
Detailed Answer: **40**

Quick Check

Objective 1.6: Identify the Purpose, Features, and Functions of the Following Network Components: Hubs, Switches, Bridges, Routers, Gateways, CSU/DSU, NICs, ISDN, WAPs, Modems, Transceivers, and Firewalls

1. What type of connection is required at a hub port that's marked MDI?

Quick Answer: **29**
Detailed Answer: **40**

- ❑ A. Straight-through pinning at the port connector is required.
- ❑ B. Use an AUI cable at the port.
- ❑ C. A crossover cable is required at the port.
- ❑ D. A BNC connector must be used.

2. In addition to workstations, a 10BASE-T hub has a router connected to it. Which of the following is a good indicator that the router is connected to the hub?

Quick Answer: **29**
Detailed Answer: **40**

- ❑ A. The 10BASE-T link light on the router
- ❑ B. The self-test lights on the hub
- ❑ C. The power-on light on the router
- ❑ D. NIC link lights

3. A bridge is used to ______.

Quick Answer: **29**
Detailed Answer: **40**

- ❑ A. replace multiple repeaters
- ❑ B. interconnect network segments using of the same access protocol
- ❑ C. reroute data around LANs
- ❑ D. interconnect networks of different access protocols

4. Consider the following description of a network and choose the best connection component for it from those listed. An Ethernet LAN consists of 10 clients, a standalone server, and two printers. The media used is category 5 UTP.

Quick Answer: **29**
Detailed Answer: **40**

- ❑ A. Gateway
- ❑ B. MAU
- ❑ C. Hub
- ❑ D. Transceiver

Quick Check

5. A large LAN has been segmented into two separate LANs. Which network element is the best choice for connecting the two LANs?

- ❑ A. A gateway
- ❑ B. A hub
- ❑ C. A router
- ❑ D. A NIC

Quick Answer: 29
Detailed Answer: 40

6. A hub port is marked MDI-X. What does this mean?

- ❑ A. The port is unavailable.
- ❑ B. A crossover cable is required at the port.
- ❑ C. A coaxial cable is required at the port.
- ❑ D. A separate transceiver is required at the port.

Quick Answer: 29
Detailed Answer: 40

7. You want to connect two networks that are using different protocols. What type of device should you use?

- ❑ A. Bridge
- ❑ B. Router
- ❑ C. Repeater
- ❑ D. Gateway

Quick Answer: 29
Detailed Answer: 40

8. By using network monitoring tools, you determine that your Ethernet network is suffering performance degradation from too many collisions. Which of the following devices could you use to divide the network into multiple segments and therefore reduce the number of collisions?

- ❑ A. Source-route bridge
- ❑ B. Hub
- ❑ C. MSAU
- ❑ D. Switch

Quick Answer: 29
Detailed Answer: 40

9. For many years, the design department and the marketing department have operated separate networks. The design department uses AppleTalk and the marketing department uses token ring. Now, the two departments have decided that they want to be able to access files from each other's servers. What network device or service would you implement to facilitate this?

- ❑ A. Router
- ❑ B. Source-route bridge
- ❑ C. Gateway
- ❑ D. Transparent bridge

Quick Answer: 29
Detailed Answer: 40

Quick Check

10. You are the network administrator for a token ring network. A NIC in a system fails, and you replace it with a new one. However, the system is unable to connect to the network. What is the most likely cause of the problem?

- ❑ A. The card is a 100Mbps card, and the ring is configured for only 10Mbps.
- ❑ B. The card is set to the wrong ring speed.
- ❑ C. The card is set to full-duplex, and the ring is running at only half-duplex.
- ❑ D. The card is faulty.

Quick Answer: **30**
Detailed Answer: **41**

11. While troubleshooting a network connectivity problem, you notice that the network card in your system is operating at 10Mbps in half-duplex mode. At what speed is the network link operating?

- ❑ A. 2.5Mbps
- ❑ B. 5Mbps
- ❑ C. 10Mbps
- ❑ D. 20Mbps

Quick Answer: **30**
Detailed Answer: **41**

12. A server has two modems installed. The first is configured for COM 2, IRQ 11, and I/O of 03E8-03EF. The second is configured for COM 3, IRQ 9, and I/O of 03E8-03EF. What action should be taken in regard to the configuration settings?

- ❑ A. Change the IRQ setting of the first modem.
- ❑ B. Change the IRQ setting of the second modem.
- ❑ C. No action is required.
- ❑ D. Change the I/O address of the first modem.

Quick Answer: **30**
Detailed Answer: **41**

13. Which device is used to convert from one protocol to another?

- ❑ A. A hub
- ❑ B. A gateway
- ❑ C. A router
- ❑ D. A switch

Quick Answer: **30**
Detailed Answer: **41**

14. The hub used in a token ring network is called a(n) ______.

- ❑ A. AUI
- ❑ B. MAU
- ❑ C. Concentrator
- ❑ D. Transceiver

Quick Answer: **30**
Detailed Answer: **41**

Quick Check

15. A ______ is used to provide a centralized connection point for network access.

- ❑ A. modem
- ❑ B. RJ-45
- ❑ C. hub
- ❑ D. NIC

Quick Answer: **30**
Detailed Answer: **41**

16. Two stackable hubs are connected with category 5 UTP that uses straight-through pinning at the RJ-45 connectors. The connectors are inserted into hub ports labeled MDI-X. Which of the following is true?

- ❑ A. The straight-through UTP must be replaced with a crossover.
- ❑ B. Only the hubs will communicate, but not the workstations connected to them.
- ❑ C. The hubs cannot be connected.
- ❑ D. The hubs are properly connected.

Quick Answer: **30**
Detailed Answer: **41**

17. Which of the following devices is used to pass data between different network access protocols?

- ❑ A. Gateway
- ❑ B. Router
- ❑ C. Hub
- ❑ D. Bridge

Quick Answer: **30**
Detailed Answer: **41**

18. Which of the following contains a transceiver that is used to send and receive data frames on and off the network?

- ❑ A. Gateway
- ❑ B. Hub
- ❑ C. Router
- ❑ D. NIC

Quick Answer: **30**
Detailed Answer: **41**

19. An Ethernet network and a token ring LAN may be interconnected using a ______.

- ❑ A. repeater
- ❑ B. transceiver
- ❑ C. bridge
- ❑ D. hub

Quick Answer: **30**
Detailed Answer: **41**

Quick Check

20. Which device is used to transfer packets between different networks?

Quick Answer: **30**
Detailed Answer: **42**

- ❑ A. Bridge
- ❑ B. Router
- ❑ C. Repeater
- ❑ D. MAU

21. A node on an Ethernet LAN at IP 196.168.50.50 needs to send a message to a node on a token ring LAN at IP 172.16.24.72. Which of the following components will handle the task?

Quick Answer: **30**
Detailed Answer: **42**

- ❑ A. Bridge
- ❑ B. Repeater
- ❑ C. Router
- ❑ D. Hub

22. Which of the following is an advantage of using a dynamic router?

Quick Answer: **30**
Detailed Answer: **42**

- ❑ A. It requires manual intervention.
- ❑ B. It requires more administrative time.
- ❑ C. It's easier to set up and configure.
- ❑ D. It requires less administrative time.

23. An Ethernet frame is to be transported across the Internet using TCP/IP. Which of the following is true?

Quick Answer: **30**
Detailed Answer: **42**

- ❑ A. IP addresses are discarded at each router.
- ❑ B. IP addresses are updated at each router.
- ❑ C. TCP is discarded at each router.
- ❑ D. MAC addresses are updated at each router.

24. By interpreting baselines, you determine that the volume of traffic on your network is reaching unacceptable levels. The network is a 10BASE-T system with hubs. Which of the following upgrade paths are you most likely to recommend?

Quick Answer: **30**
Detailed Answer: **42**

- ❑ A. Implement 100BASE-T by replacing all the network cards and hubs with 100Mbps devices.
- ❑ B. Implement switches in place of the hubs.
- ❑ C. Install a router to divide the network into two segments, thereby reducing the overall amount of network traffic.
- ❑ D. Implement a bridge.

Quick Check

25. Which of the following is an end-to-end digital communication path?
    - ❑ A. ISDN
    - ❑ B. PSTN
    - ❑ C. POTS
    - ❑ D. PPTP

Quick Answer: **30**
Detailed Answer: **42**

26. A standalone computer may connect to an ISP using a ______.
    - ❑ A. patch panel
    - ❑ B. repeater
    - ❑ C. bridge
    - ❑ D. modem

Quick Answer: **30**
Detailed Answer: **42**

27. In an ISDN channel, signaling information is contained in the ______.
    - ❑ A. BRI
    - ❑ B. bearer channel
    - ❑ C. data channel
    - ❑ D. PRI

Quick Answer: **30**
Detailed Answer: **43**

28. Which of the following best describes active hubs and repeaters?
    - ❑ A. Repeaters link network segments while active hubs do not.
    - ❑ B. Both active hubs and repeaters restore signals.
    - ❑ C. Repeaters restore signal integrity while active hubs do not.
    - ❑ D. Neither active hubs nor repeaters link network segments.

Quick Answer: **30**
Detailed Answer: **43**

29. To directly connect the NIC cards in two personal computers, what's needed?
    - ❑ A. Hub
    - ❑ B. Crossover cable
    - ❑ C. Router
    - ❑ D. Bridge

Quick Answer: **30**
Detailed Answer: **43**

30. What is the function of a repeater?
    - ❑ A. To boost the signal strength and restore its shape.
    - ❑ B. To reconcile MAC and IP addresses.
    - ❑ C. To connect different networks.
    - ❑ D. To connect Ethernet and token ring LANs.

Quick Answer: **30**
Detailed Answer: **43**

Quick Check

31. Which of the following statements best describes dynamic routing?

Quick Answer: **30**
Detailed Answer: **43**

- ❑ A. Established Routing paths cannot be changed.
- ❑ B. The IEEE 802.2 protocol stipulates that routers will be dynamic.
- ❑ C. Routers send and receive advertisements that automatically update the router database table.
- ❑ D. The network administrator must periodically update the router database tables.

32. Which of the following devices will not pass network broadcasts?

Quick Answer: **30**
Detailed Answer: **43**

- ❑ A. Hub
- ❑ B. Switch
- ❑ C. Router
- ❑ D. Repeater

33. You have been tasked with connecting two computers together to transfer data from one to the other so that the older of the two can be decommissioned. You have 2 straight-through networking cables available. Which of the following devices can be used to make this connection work?

Quick Answer: **30**
Detailed Answer: **43**

- ❑ A. Router
- ❑ B. Switch
- ❑ C. Modem
- ❑ D. USB Hub

Objective 1.7: Specify the General Characteristics (For Example: Speed, Carrier Speed, Frequency, Transmission Type and Topology) of the Following Wireless Technologies: 802.11 (Frequency Hopping Spread Spectrum), 802.11x (Direct Sequence Spread Spectrum), Infrared, and Bluetooth

1. For a device to be compatible with the 802.11a standard, what is the minimum connection speed at which it must be able to operate?

Quick Answer: **30**
Detailed Answer: **43**

- ❑ A. 9Mbps
- ❑ B. 5.5Mbps
- ❑ C. 2Mbps
- ❑ D. 11Mbps

Quick Check

2. What type of spread spectrum technique is used where the radio carrier frequency is shifted in selected increments across a given frequency band?
   - ❑ A. FHSS
   - ❑ B. THSS
   - ❑ C. DSSS
   - ❑ D. Pulsed/FM

Quick Answer: **30**
Detailed Answer: **43**

3. What is the maximum data rate for Bluetooth communications?
   - ❑ A. 11Mbps
   - ❑ B. 54Mbps
   - ❑ C. 2Mbps
   - ❑ D. 5.5Mbps

Quick Answer: **30**
Detailed Answer: **43**

4. Bluetooth operates in the ______ ISM band.
   - ❑ A. 902MHz
   - ❑ B. 5.15GHz
   - ❑ C. 5.725GHz
   - ❑ D. 2.4GHz

Quick Answer: **30**
Detailed Answer: **43**

5. DSSS supports data rate up to ______ Mbps.
   - ❑ A. 11
   - ❑ B. 5
   - ❑ C. 2
   - ❑ D. 1

Quick Answer: **30**
Detailed Answer: **43**

6. What is the maximum data rate of an IrDA 1.1 infrared device?
   - ❑ A. 5Mbps
   - ❑ B. 4Mbps
   - ❑ C. 3Mbps
   - ❑ D. 2Mbps

Quick Answer: **30**
Detailed Answer: **43**

7. What is the maximum transmission range specified by IrDA1.1?
   - ❑ A. 1 meter
   - ❑ B. 10 meters
   - ❑ C. 20 meters
   - ❑ D. 100 meters

Quick Answer: **30**
Detailed Answer: **43**

Quick Check

8. DSSS operates in the ______ ISM band.

Quick Answer: **30**
Detailed Answer: **44**

- ❑ A. 902MHz
- ❑ B. 5.15GHz
- ❑ C. 5.725GHz
- ❑ D. 2.4GHz

9. Which of the following wireless techniques is used by Bluetooth?

Quick Answer: **30**
Detailed Answer: **44**

- ❑ A. Infrared
- ❑ B. FHSS
- ❑ C. DSSS
- ❑ D. OFDM

Objective 1.8: Identify Factors That Affect the Range and Speed of Wireless Service (For Example: Interference, Antenna Type and Environmental Factors)

1. You have prepared a new notebook computer for your employer. When you walk upstairs to the boss' office to deliver it, you cannot establish the network connection. What is the most likely cause of this failure?

Quick Answer: **30**
Detailed Answer: **44**

- ❑ A. You failed to activate the multiple AP selection option.
- ❑ B. You attempted to log in using the boss' account, which has not been enabled.
- ❑ C. You moved out of the AP's range.
- ❑ D. The fluorescent lights in the boss' office are interfering with the wireless connection.

2. Which antenna type provides the longest range for wireless networking?

Quick Answer: **30**
Detailed Answer: **44**

- ❑ A. Yagi-v
- ❑ B. Parabolic
- ❑ C. Yagi-h
- ❑ D. Dipole

Quick Check

3. You have installed a wireless AP in the auditorium of a church that also operates a radio station in another area of the building. The radio station broadcasts at 106MHz. After you have the AP installed, you find that you cannot make connections with wireless clients in any of the church offices. What is the most likely cause of this problem?

- ❑ A. Interference from fluorescent lights in the auditorium.
- ❑ B. FM transmissions from the radio station are creating a harmonic that interferes with the transmission band of the AP.
- ❑ C. EMI being generated by the equipment in the radio station.
- ❑ D. The auditorium is too large for the range of the AP.

Quick Answer: **30**
Detailed Answer: **44**

4. Which antenna type provides omni directional broadcasting?

- ❑ A. Yagi
- ❑ B. Vertical
- ❑ C. Parabolic
- ❑ D. Log Periodic

Quick Answer: **30**
Detailed Answer: **44**

Quick Check Answer Key

Objective 1.1: Recognize Logical or Physical Topologies, Given a Schematic Diagram or Description

1. B
2. D
3. A
4. C
5. B
6. D
7. D
8. B
9. A
10. C
11. B
12. D
13. C
14. D
15. B
16. D

Objective 1.2: Specify the Main Features of the 802.2 (LLC), 802.3 (Ethernet), 802.5 (Token Ring), 802.11 (Wireless), and FDDI Networking Technologies

1. C
2. D
3. B
4. A
5. C
6. A
7. B
8. D
9. B
10. A
11. A
12. D
13. B
14. A

Objective 1.3: Specify the Characteristics (For Example, Speed, Length, Topology, Cable Type, and so on) of the Following Cable Standards: 10BASE-T, 10BASE-FL, 100BASE-TX, 100BASE-FX, 1000BASE-T, 1000BASE-CX, 1000BASE-SX, 1000BASE-LX, 10GBASE-SR, 10GBASE-LR, and 10GBASE-ER

1. B
2. A
3. C
4. D
5. B
6. A
7. A
8. B
9. C
10. D
11. D
12. B
13. C
14. B
15. B
16. C
17. D
18. A
19. C
20. B
21. B

Quick Check Answer Key

22. C
23. C
24. A
25. C
26. A
27. C
28. A
29. D
30. C
31. D
32. C
33. A
34. A
35. B
36. C
37. C
38. A

Objective 1.4: Recognize the Following Media Connectors and Describe Their Uses: RJ-11, RJ-45, F-Type, ST, SC, IEEE-1394, Fiber LC, MT-RJ, and USB

1. A
2. B
3. D, B
4. B
5. A
6. B
7. C
8. C

Objective 1.5: Recognize the Following Media Types and Describe Their Use: Cat 3,5,5e, and 6, UTP, STP, Coax, Single-Mode Fiber, and Multimode Fiber

1. A
2. D
3. A
4. B
5. A, C
6. C
7. B
8. B
9. A
10. C
11. D
12. A
13. D
14. C
15. C

Objective 1.6: Identify the Purpose, Features, and Functions of the Following Network Components: Hubs, Switches, Bridges, Routers, Gateways, CSU/DSU, NICs, ISDN, WAPs, Modems, Transceivers, and Firewalls

1. A
2. A
3. B
4. C
5. C
6. B
7. D
8. D
9. C

Quick Check Answer Key

10. B
11. C
12. D
13. B
14. B
15. C
16. A
17. A
18. D
19. C
20. B
21. C
22. D
23. D
24. B
25. A
26. D
27. C
28. B
29. B
30. A
31. C
32. C
33. B

Objective 1.7: Specify the General Characteristics (For Example: Speed, Carrier Speed, Frequency, Transmission Type and Topology) of the Following Wireless Technologies: 802.11 (Frequency Hopping Spread Spectrum), 802.11x (Direct Sequence Spread Spectrum), Infrared, and Bluetooth

1. C
2. A
3. C
4. D
5. A
6. B
7. A
8. D
9. B

Objective 1.8: Identify factors That Affect the Range and Speed of Wireless Service (For Example: Interference, Antenna Type, and Environmental Factors)

1. C
2. B
3. D
4. B

Answers and Explanations

Objective 1.1

1. **Answer: B.** In a mesh topology, each device is connected directly to every other device on the network. Such a structure requires that each device have at least two network connections. The mesh topology is not commonly implemented. In a bus topology, each device is connected to the network through a single connection. In a ring topology, each device is connected to the network through a single connection. In a star topology, each device is connected to the network through a single connection.

2. **Answer D.** The layout of the network is referred to as the topology. The logical topology defines how the devices connected to the network see it, and the physical topology defines how the network is actually laid out. The term backbone is used to describe a segment of the network that acts as a connection point for other segments. Network is a generic term used to describe the network as a whole. The term physical map is not commonly used.

3. **Answer: A.** In a mesh topology, all devices are connected directly to every other device on the network. If one link fails, there is always another available. It is the most fault-tolerant network topology. A hierarchical star is a variation of the standard star and is not considered a fault-tolerant implementation. A ring topology is not considered fault tolerant. In a star topology, each device is normally connected to one central device and therefore is not fault tolerant.

4. **Answer C.** The most widely implemented mesh topologies are the Internet and the telephone network.

5. **Answer B.** Because workstations don't contend for access to the network, access is guaranteed with a token ring network. IP addressing is a Network layer concept and isn't dependent on a Data Link layer protocol or topology. Token ring may be implemented in full-duplex, but at the workstation level, it isn't common. A ring must be broken to add a new workstation.

6. **Answer: D.** A star topology consists of a central hub that is a common connection point for all nodes. The nodes connect to ports on the hub.

7. **Answer: D.** The hub used in a token ring network is called a Multi-Station Access Unit, or MSAU. It may also be called a Multistation Access Unit, or MAU. An AUI is used in Ethernet coaxial networks. A switch is used to provide the full bandwidth of the network to each node. A patch panel provides a modular connection for extension of the wall cabling into the hub.

8. **Answer: B.** Token ring is specified in the IEEE 802.5 standard. IEEE 802.11 describes wireless LANs. IEEE 802.3 describes CSMA/CD Ethernet. IEEE 802.2 describes the LLC sublayer of the Data Link layer.

9. **Answer: A.** This is a small LAN and unless there is reason to believe it will grow drastically, a peer-to-peer arrangement should meet the needs of the three users.

10. **Answer: C.** A ring must be broken to add a new node. This is a disadvantage of a ring topology. Having an excessive number of connections is a disadvantage of a large mesh network. Problems with a shorted bus may occur on a bus network. A point-to-point connection is made in a star topology.

11. **Answer: B.** Each node on a star network uses its own cable, making it easy to add users without disrupting current users. Adding a node to a bus network will involve breaking the segment, which makes it inaccessible to all other nodes on the network. A ring network topology will require that the ring be broken to add a new device. A mesh topology requires that every device be connected to every other device on the network. It is, therefore, quite difficult to expand a mesh network.

12. **Answer: D.** All that's required to expand a star topology is to add another node to a hub port. Star topologies usually have low overhead and high throughput.

13. **Answer: C.** The most common logical topologies are the Ring, Bus, and mesh.

14. **Answer: D.** A star topology consists of a central hub with spokes that connect to nodes.

15. **Answer: B.** The topology of a network may affect your decision on the type of media. Bus networks, for example, require that the ends of the bus be terminated with a proper resistance so that data signals aren't reflected back through the wire thereby creating distortion.

16. **Answer: D.** The number of links (connections) required to service a specific number of nodes in a mesh network is found using the formula: L*n* = N*n*(N*n*-1)/2, where N*n* is the number of nodes and L*n* is the number of connections.

Objective 1.2

1. **Answer: C.** Carrier Sense Multiple Access/Collision Detection (CSMA/CD) is a media access method defined by the 802.3 standard. The 802.2 standard defines Logical Link Control functions. The 802.5 standard defines token ring networking. The 802.11b standard defines wireless networking for LAN systems.

2. **Answer: D.** The Logical Link Control (LLC) describes the conventions a sender and receiver follow to ensure the data flow is orderly. The conventions correspond to the IEEE 802.2 standards. The LLC is a software interface situated between the software that controls network interface hardware, such as that found on the Network Interface Card (NIC), and the communication software running on a network, such as Windows NT/2000 or NetBIOS.

3. **Answer: B.** The maximum number of stations permitted on an IEEE 802.3 network is 1,024.

4. **Answer: A.** IEEE 802.3 is the standard specification for 100BASE-T.

5. **Answer: C.** Because the transmission times of nodes can be predicted, token ring has a huge advantage over Ethernet. Token ring has a huge advantage over CSMA/CD networks in that it's deterministic. This means that the nodes transmit at specific, predictable times. Because the transmission times of nodes can be predicted, so can the delivery times. Without contention on the network, there are no collisions. Ultimately, this has led to a general consensus that token ring networks offer a higher degree of reliability, and integrity than Ethernet networks.

6. **Answer: A.** The IEEE 802.5 standard was adapted from token ring access methods developed by IBM in the early 1970s. Token ring networks are specified for 4Mbps and 16Mbps operation, with the latter being used in all modern networks.

7. **Answer: B.** A CSMA/CD, Ethernet LAN has a bandwidth of 10Mbps, while a token ring network operates at 4 or 16Mbps. Ethernet is available at 1000Mbps, but only with a contention access method. 100VG-AnyLAN operates on ring topologies, but isn't widely deployed. Although token ring only runs at 16Mbps, the good thing about it is that node access can be made deterministic, an option not available with Ethernet. What's needed is a technology that offers the access advantages of token ring, and the speed of Ethernet.

8. **Answer: D.** The farther a workstation is moved away from an AP, the lower the data rate. The minimum data rate is 1Mbps. The maximum distance at any data rate varies with the material that the radio waves must pass through between workstation and AP. Commercial cards can transmit up to about a quarter mile at the lowest data rates in an open-air setting.

9. **Answer: B.** A wireless network is implemented with a wireless card installed into an expansion slot of a computer, and that communicates with an access point.

10. **Answer: A.** In 2000, the IEEE approved the IEEE 802.11a standard. This standard offers even higher data rates, peaking at 54Mbps. Commercial products began shipping for 802.11a later in 2001.

11. **Answer: A.** A connection-oriented protocol assigns sequence numbers to frames passed into the LLC, and tracks them at the receiving node. At the Data Link layer, it's the same as Type II LLC. Because the frames are tracked, connection-oriented protocols are also called reliable.

12. **Answer: D.** Bit-oriented protocols have high efficiency and low overhead. SDLC (Synchronous Data Link Control), HDLC (High-Level Data Link Control), and LAPB (Link Access Protocol-Balanced) are bit-oriented protocols. Conversely, character-oriented protocols, such as IBM Binary Synchronous Communication (BCS), frame and send blocks of characters at a time.

13. **Answer: B.** FDDI Networks operate at 100Mbps on rings of up to 100 kilometers.

14. **Answer: A.** Token Ring networks operate at 4 and 16Mbps. More recent Token Ring cards run at 16Mbps, but have the capability to fall back to 4Mbps operation to remain compatible with older Token Ring equipment.

Objective 1.3

1. **Answer: B.** A 10BASE-T network has a maximum data rate of 10Mbps. The 10 in 10BASE-T indicates the data rate. 100Mbps refers to 100BASE-T. 500Mbps doesn't apply to any standard data rate. 1000Mbps refers to 1000BASE-T.

2. **Answer: A.** The maximum segment length is 100 meters for 10BASE-T networks. Because the cable media is UTP and a hub is being used, a segment refers to the media length from hub port to NIC card of a workstation. 10BASE2 networks have a maximum segment length of 185 meters. 10BASE5 networks have a maximum segment length of 500 meters. 10 meters doesn't apply to any standard segment lengths.

3. **Answer: C.** 100BASE-TX suffers from the same 100-meter distance limitations as other UTP-based networks.

4. **Answer: D.** A 100BASE-FX fiber-optic NIC will not work with 10BASE-T copper cabling.

5. **Answer: B.** 802.5 defines token ring networking.

6. **Answer: A.** 10BASE-T has a maximum segment length of 100 meters. The maximum length of a 10BASE2 segment is 185 meters. The maximum length of a 10BASE5 segment is 500 meters. 10BASEYX is not a valid networking standard.

7. **Answer: A.** 100BASE-TX uses Category 5 cabling. Fiber optic is a type of cable. 10BASE5 is an Ethernet networking standard that uses thick coaxial cable. 10BASE2 is an Ethernet networking standard that uses thin coaxial cable.

8. **Answer: B.** 10BASE-T networks use twisted-pair cable and RJ-45 connectors. RJ-11 connectors are associated with telephone cabling. RJ-T is not a valid type of connector. A BNC connector is associated with coaxial cabling, not twisted-pair cabling.

9. **Answer: C.** It's important to make a distinction between how frequency affects signal loss, and how the resistance of copper cable affects signal loss. Losses due to frequency changes are the result of line inductance and capacitance. Resistance has a negligible impact when the frequency changes. However, the resistance of the wiring dissipates electrical energy in the form of heat. The higher the resistance, the greater the signal energy loss. Resistance is directly proportional to the length of the wire.

10. **Answer: D.** The proper termination for unshielded twisted-pair network cable is 100 ohms.

11. **Answer: D.** The reactive components of cables cause Intersymbol Interference (ISI).

12. **Answer: B.** Adaptive equalization adds expense and complexity to a data communication system. A signal that has been conditioned with an adaptive equalizer is also difficult to evaluate from a troubleshooting standpoint, because it may have very little resemblance to the square waves associated with digital logic. An adaptive equalizer constantly samples and evaluates data for ISI.

13. **Answer: C.** An equalizer separates signal frequencies through filtering and incorporates phase shifts to counter the effects of the channel.

14. **Answer: B.** In addition to lightning, sunspot activity creates atmospheric noise. On the sun, a sunspot is an explosion that releases a tremendous amount of energy that travels through the solar system, striking the earth, and creating noise in a way similar to lightning strikes. Sunspots are cyclical, occurring about every 11 years, and can therefore be anticipated.

15. **Answer: B.** 100BASE-FX uses a fiber-optic cable and has a segment length of 412 meters.

16. **Answer: C.** Impulse noise is sporadic and of short duration, usually caused by periodic use of electromechanical equipment or from a glitch that occasionally appears. Mechanical switches, motors, generators, and engine ignition systems all contribute to the distortion of data bits, and are collectively called "impulse noise." It's generally of short duration and in close proximity to the affected data system.

17. **Answer: D.** Frequency noise originates from 60 Hz wire, system clocks, or carrier frequencies. Frequency noise is of a constant time but of variable amplitude. The most common type of frequency noise is the 60 Hz radiated from fluorescent lights and the associated wiring.

18. **Answer: A.** Crosstalk is the electromagnetic induction (transmitted noise) that results from unshielded cables laying in parallel.

19. **Answer: C.** You may have been talking on the telephone and have heard another conversation. Crosstalk is a frequent problem in the telephone system because hundreds of cables may run in parallel. The energy from a cable radiates and cuts across adjacent cables, inducing a signal into them. Although crosstalk in a telephone conversation is annoying, it generally doesn't prevent you from continuing your own conversation. But crosstalk between data signals can blur the distinction between logic levels and introduce a considerable error component into data.

20. **Answer: B.** Noise and distortion are expressed in decibels. The decibel results from the ratio of an actual value to a reference value. Reference values for data communications are 1 mW and 6 mW.

21. **Answer: B.** The signal-to-noise ratio is a measure of the desired signal power relative to the noise signal power at the same point in a circuit. It's expressed mathematically as: SNR = *Ps*/*Pn* where *Ps* = the power of the desired signal and *Pn* = the power of the noise. It's often expressed in decibels as:

 SNR =10 log (*P* s/*P* n) dB

 By replacing *Ps* and *Pn* with the given numbers, we can rewrite the expression as

 SNR =10 log (50 mW/5 mW) dB

 SNR =10 log (10) dB

 SNR =10 (1) dB

 SNR =10 dB

22. **Answer: C.** An acceptable SNR for digital communications is 40 dB.

23. **Answer: C.** The maximum segment length of a 100BASE-FX network is 412 meters. The maximum number of nodes for this type of network is 1024 and the maximum length of the network is 5 kilometers.

24. **Answer: A.** The IEEE 100BASE-TX standard speed is 100Mbps.

25. **Answer: C.** Thinnet (also called cheapernet, RG-58A/U, 10BASE2 or thin coaxial) coaxial cable has less shielding than thicknet, and consequently, smaller permissible segment lengths in a LAN.

26. **Answer: A.** The standard is 802.10 and covers LAN Security.

27. **Answer: C.** The 802.3 standard for bus networks is based on the joint efforts of Digital Equipment Corporation, Intel, and Xerox. The original standard was

called Ethernet, and the name has been retained although the current versions are not the same as the original. The original is now called Ethernet I, or simply "the DIX standard" after the founding companies.

28. **Answer: A.** The maximum length of a 10BASE-T segment is 100 meters. The segment length in the question is 105 meters. By reducing the length of the NIC to wall outlet patch cable, the total segment length meets the standard. This reduces the number of service calls to this particular workstation because the connection should no longer be intermittent. It's not likely to have an effect on collisions because network collisions are more affected by the volume of network traffic than by segment length.
29. **Answer: D.** The maximum cable length for a 10BASE-T (STP) is 200 meters.
30. **Answer: C.** A 10BASE-T network operates at a maximum of 10Mbps.
31. **Answer: D.** The maximum segment length for 10BASE-T4 is 100 meters.
32. **Answer: C.** 100BASE-TX uses the full bandwidth capabilities of category 5 cable to achieve 100Mbps data rates.
33. **Answer: A.** 100BASEFX is the fiber-optic version 100Mbps Ethernet. The connection between devices includes only two fiber strands: a transmit strand and a receive strand. Both are running at 100Mbps.
34. **Answer: A.** The maximum segment length for 10BASE-TX is 100 meters.
35. **Answer: B.** 100BASE-T4 is an alternate version of 100BASE-TX. It uses category 3 (or better), voice-grade twisted pairs for cable links to hubs. Unlike 100BASE-TX, T4 will use all eight wires (4 pairs) that are attached to an RJ-45 connector.
36. **Answer: C.** 100BASEFX is the fiber-optic version 100Mbps Ethernet. It uses any of the common fiber-optic connectors. The connection between devices includes only two fiber strands - one transmit strand and a receive strand. Both are running at 100Mbps.
37. **Answer: C.** The 1000BASE-SX specification provides gigabit transfers across multimode fiber using 850nm light.
38. **Answer: A.** The 1000BASE-LX specification calls for a 1300nm laser to drive the light signal over multimode fiber. The other specification that calls for 1300nm light is the 100BASE-FX technology.

Objective 1.4

1. **Answer: A.** Category 5 UTP cables use RJ-45 connectors. RJ-11 connectors are used to connect phone wires. BNC connectors are associated with thin coaxial cabling. ST connectors are associated with fiber-optic cabling.

2. **Answer: B.** An AUI port is typically used to connect an external transceiver to a device such as a router. An MSAU is a type of network device used on token ring networks. RJ-11 is a connector type associated with telephone cabling. BNC is a type of network connector used on coaxial networks.

3. **Answers: D, B.** A hardware loopback plug connects the 2 and 6 wires and 1 and 3 wires to simulate a live network connection. The remaining possible answers are not correct for the cabling in a hardware loopback adapter.

4. **Answer: B.** UTP and STP cabling is commonly used with RJ-45 connectors.

5. **Answer: A.** Typically, the connection from the DSL modem to the NIC card in the computer is mad through a UTP cable that terminates in an RJ-45 connector.

6. **Answer: B.** An RJ-45 connector is a eight-pin connector that can be used with any UTP category.

7. **Answer: C.** 1000BASE-SX networks use multimode fiber optic cables, which terminate in SC (or ST) connectors.

8. **Answer: C.** 1000BASE-FX networks use fiber optic cables, which terminate in SC (or ST) connectors.

Objective 1.5

1. **Answer: A.** Fiber cable is immune to EMI because it propagates light signals rather than electrical signals. Fiber-optic cable requires specialized training and tools to install. The cost of fiber cable is higher than UTP and coaxial. Fiber uses light waves and not microwaves.

2. **Answer: D.** Category 5 UTP cable is the most appropriate media for a small 100BASE-T network. RG-58 coaxial and category 3 UTP cannot carry the data throughput required by a 100BASE-T network. Fiber-optic cable is too expensive for a small implementation.

3. **Answer: A.** Because the card is functioning at half-duplex 10Mbps, the transfer rate is going to be 10Mbps.

4. **Answer: B.** Fiber-optic cable provides the most resistance to EMI and therefore is often used in environments where there is a risk of interference. Although cheap, UTP cabling has a very low resistance to EMI. Therefore, it is unsuitable for running near high voltage electric cables. Thin coax has a low resistance to EMI. Therefore, it is unsuitable for running near high-voltage electric cables. STP has a good level of resistance to EMI, but is still not as resistant as fiber optic. Not factoring in the cost, fiber optic is the most suitable solution.

5. **Answers: A, C.** Fiber-optic cable can either use SC or ST type connectors. An RJ-45 connector is used with copper UTP cable. An RJ-11 connector is used with standard copper telephone wire.

6. **Answer: C.** When grounded properly, the shielding carries an interference-induced current that generates electromagnetic flux, which in turn induces an opposite polarity current into the twisted pairs. Because the two noise signals are of opposite polarities, they cancel each other, thereby eliminating the interfering noise.

7. **Answer: B.** Even though it's an expensive choice, there are several reasons to install fiber in a network. Because no copper is used in the cable, data bits won't be corrupted by electromagnetic interference (EMI), crosstalk, or other external noise that may garble bits in a UTP or coaxial system.

8. **Answer: B.** The 802.8 is the standard for fiber-optic cable.

9. **Answer: A.** Fiber optics has been hailed as the transmission media totally immune from EMI interference. Fiber-optic cable can be run side-by-side with industrial-grade motors and not be affected by radiated noise. However, fiber remains an expensive option when compared to alternative, copper-based media. In addition, there are problems created during the installation of fiber-optic cable that affect signal integrity.

10. **Answer: C.** Connection losses contribute to signal degradation. Connection losses result from fiber splices, the interface of light source to fiber, and of fiber to light detector. The actual amount of signal attenuation is measured with a photometer.

11. **Answer: D.** When injected into a perfectly straight fiber cable, the rays travel as axial beams through the cable, neither reflecting nor refracting. In a bent cable, the axial rays will strike the core/cladding interface and reflect along the remaining distance to the receiver. Some of the energy will refract into the cladding and be lost. A bind in a fiber-optic cable will produce losses and signal attenuation. This is true of all optical cable types, so cable runs should be kept as straight as possible.

12. **Answer: A.** dB = 10 log (*Po*/*Pi*)

    dB = 10 log (200 mW/20 mW)

    dB = 10 log (10)

    dB = 10 (1)

    dB = 10

13. **Answer: D.** A loss of signal strength is indicated by a negative dB.

14. **Answer: C.** The wires are twisted together to reduce noise and, in particular, crosstalk. Recall that crosstalk is the magnetic induction of a signal from wires lying in a parallel plane. The twisting of the wires causes the unwanted crosstalk signals to cancel. Twisted pair is the most widely installed media. Unshielded twisted pair (UTP) is the preferred cabling for LANs. UTP is classified by the EIA/TIA according to categories. Use category 5 UTP cable whenever possible.

15. **Answer: C.** Category 5 cable is rated for data up to 100Mbps using 100 ohm impedance 22 or 24 AWG wire.

Objective 1.6

1. **Answer: A.** MDI (Media Dependent Interface) means that a cable connected to the port should be wired using straight-through pinning. An IEEE-compliant hub labels ports with MDI-X if the hub does not perform the crossover internally. A BNC connector is used with coaxial cable. AUI refers to a 15-pin connector.

2. **Answer: A.** The router link light can be checked at a glance to determine whether there's a connection to the hub. The self-test lights on the hub and the power-on lights on the router provide information about the operation of the hub and router, but not about the connection between router and hub. A NIC is associated with servers and workstations.

3. **Answer: B.** Bridges specifically interconnect LAN segments that use the same access protocols. Bridges aren't routinely used for either rerouting data around LANs or replacing multiple repeaters.

4. **Answer: C.** A simple hub can be used for this network. The Gateway represents too much power for this size of LAN. MAU and transceiver are associated with coaxial cabled networks.

5. **Answer: C.** A router is used to connect networks.

6. **Answer: B.** MDI-X, or Media Dependent Interface-Crossover, is an indication that a crossover cable must be used between the hub port and connected workstation or another hub.

7. **Answer: D.** A gateway is any device, system, or software application that can perform the function of translating data from one protocol/format to another.

8. **Answer: D.** The switch is the only device listed that can be used to divide up an Ethernet network to reduce collisions.

9. **Answer: C.** A gateway is used to translate between networks using dissimilar protocols. In this question it is used to translate between an AppleTalk and a token ring network. A source-route bridge is used on token ring networks. A

router is use to connect two networks. Strictly speaking a router does not perform translational tasks, though the gateway functionality can be implemented on some routers. A transparent bridge is used to segregate Ethernet networks.

10. **Answer: B.** When a new card is installed on a token ring network, the speed of the card has to be set to match the speed used by the network. Token ring networks operate at either 4 or 16Mbps. Full-duplex connections are not used on token ring networks. Although it is possible, it is not most likely that the card is faulty.

11. **Answer: C.** Because the card is functioning at half-duplex 10Mbps, the transfer rate is going to be 10Mbps.

12. **Answer: D.** The base I/O port is a hexadecimal number used by the system microprocessor to identify the destination of data sent to a peripheral device. Because the bus in a computer is shared by all peripherals, the base I/O port identifies where data is to be sent within the computer. The base I/O port for all devices must be unique. Common 32-bit base I/O ports are 0300 and 031F.

13. **Answer: B.** A gateway is a device that converts one communication system to another or from one protocol to another.

14. **Answer: B.** The hub used in a token ring network is called a Multi-Station Access Unit, or MSAU. It may also be called a Multistation Access Unit, or MAU. An AUI is used in Ethernet coaxial networks. A switch is used to provide the full bandwidth of the network to each node. A patch panel provides a modular connection for extension of the wall cabling into the hub.

15. **Answer: C.** A hub is a device used to provide centralized access to the network. Hubs are used in a physical star topology. The network nodes connect to ports in the hub via a cable such as UTP or coaxial. One end of the cable plugs into the node NIC card while the other end plugs into a port on a hub.

16. **Answer: A.** MDI-X (Media Independent Interface-Crossover) requires a crossover cable because the port does not perform this function.

17. **Answer: A.** A gateway is used to connect networks that use different network access protocols. For example, a gateway is used to connect users on an Ethernet LAN and users on a Token Ring LAN. Wireless access points that have an Ethernet port employ a gateway to connect the IEEE 802.11b users and the Ethernet users.

18. **Answer: D.** A network interface card (NIC) contains a transceiver that sends and receives data frames on and off the network.

19. **Answer: C.** A bridge is primarily used to connect networks that use different network access protocols. For example, a bridge is used to connect users on an Ethernet LAN and users on a token ring LAN.

20. **Answer: B.** A router is used to connect different networks and, occasionally, different network segments. A "network" in this context refers to a group of nodes that share the same network portion of an IP address. If two groups of nodes don't have the same network portion of an IP address, they are located on different networks. The router interconnects data packets across a network running TCP/IP. The network consists of an Ethernet, a token ring, and a Token Bus LAN. Notice that the router allows computers on all three LANs to communicate, regardless of the topology and access protocols.

21. **Answer: C.** A router is used to connect different networks and, occasionally, different network segments. A "network" in this context, refers to a group of nodes that share the same network portion of an IP address. Routers operate at the Network layer of the OSI model. A router isn't concerned if the data it receives originated from a token ring LAN or an Ethernet LAN. The router is only concerned with getting the data to the correct destination network.

22. **Answer: D.** A dynamic router learns addressing information automatically, without intervention from the network administrator. Dynamic routers broadcast the addressing information in their tables in the form of advertisements.

23. **Answer: D.** At each router hop, the router will compare its list of MAC addresses to the destination IP address. If they aren't the same, it will reframe the MAC addresses and pass it on.

24. **Answer: B.** Replacing hubs with switches is a practical, economical, and very effective way to improve performance on twisted-pair networks. It is the accepted upgrade path in hub-based networks. Although implementing switches is a valid approach, the cost of doing so may be prohibitive and it is not the best option of those given. Implementing a router is not the most likely approach and would require extensive reconfiguration of the network. Implementing a bridge is not the most likely approach.

25. **Answer: A.** Integrated Services Digital Network (ISDN) is a set of digital services that are available over telephone lines. ISDN is a complete digital solution from end-user to end-user. Because the connection is all digital, data rates can be much higher than on an analog telephone connection--as high as 128 kbps.

26. **Answer: D.** A modem provides a computer user with a tremendous amount of access. Literally, a good modem makes the difference in working at an isolated PC and accessing the great, wide-open spaces of the Internet. Nearly all data communications utilize modems--from the single user at home with a PC, to internationally distributed networks of conglomerate corporations.

27. **Answer: C.** As ISDN frame carries data in a Bearer channel (B channel) that has a 64 kbps bandwidth. On older telephone systems, B channels may drop to 56 kbps. A Data channel (D channel) carries supervisor and signaling information at 16 kbps (and sometimes at 64 kbps).
28. **Answer: B.** An active hub operates under its own power supply. Data signals may be amplified in an active hub to restore signal losses, or to remove noise. Active hubs are also called repeaters.
29. **Answer: B.** A crossover cable may be necessary to troubleshoot NICs or hub ports. A crossover allows you to directly connect two stations, without a hub. A crossover is merely a means of connecting the proper transmit pins of one NIC card to the corresponding receive pins of another NIC card, and vice versa.
30. **Answer: A.** The regenerator, or repeater, is an in-line amplifier that boosts the signal level and restores the square wave to its original shape.
31. **Answer: C.** The routing tables in a dynamic router are updated automatically.
32. **Answer: C.** Hubs, switches, and repeaters will pass network broadcasts. However, a router will not pass broadcast packets.
33. **Answer: B.** A switch can be used to link two computers together using straight-through cables.

Objective 1.7

1. **Answer: C.** For a device to be compatible with the 802.11a standard, it must be able to operate at a minimum connection speed of 2Mbps.
2. **Answer: A.** Frequency-Hopping Spread Spectrum (FHSS) is a method in which the radio carrier frequency is shifted in selected increments across a given frequency band.
3. **Answer: C.** Bluetooth has a transmission speed up to 2Mbps.
4. **Answer: D.** The Bluetooth wireless technology supports both point-to-point and point-to-multipoint connections. The radio interface operates in the 2.4GHz ISM band and employs Frequency Hopped Spread Spectrum (FHSS) modulation.
5. **Answer: A.** Direct Sequence Spread Spectrum (DSSS) supports data rate up to 11Mbps. With increases in range from card to AP, the data rates fall back to about 2Mbps.
6. **Answer: B.** An IrDA 1.1-compliant device can send data through its infrared port up to 4Mbps.
7. **Answer: A.** The maximum transmission range for IrDA 1.1 devices is 1 meter.

8. **Answer: D.** Direct Sequence Spread Spectrum (DSSS) is the most widely deployed system used with commercial 802.11b products. It supports a data rate up to 11Mbps and operates in the 2.4GHz range.

9. **Answer: B.** FHSS is a technique used by wireless technologies such as Bluetooth to reduce interference and snooping.

Objective 1.8

1. **Answer: C.** The first items to check with an 802.11 wireless network connection are the range and line-of-sight path between the clients and the AP. The IEEE specifications for 802.11b provide a clear line-of-sight range of 150 feet (50 meters) before the signal strength becomes too low and the connection becomes unreliable. Fluorescent lights do not interfere with 2.4GHz 802.11b operations (although cell/wireless phones might). All 802.11 networks can handle multiple-AP situations—Windows finds all available APs and provides connection options for them. If you try to log in with the wrong account information, you will have connectivity but no permissions to access anything.

2. **Answer: B.** The parabolic (dish) antenna is the highest-gain antenna type listed, but it's also highly directional. The dipole antenna provides the lowest gain of these antenna types. The vertical (perpendicular to the earth) and horizontal (parallel to the earth) yagi antenna orientations, although highly directional, do not provide the gain of the parabolic dish antenna.

3. **Answer: D.** The best choice is that the auditorium is too large for the AP's range. The IEEE specifications for 802.11b provide a clear line-of-sight range of 150 feet (50 meters) before the signal strength becomes too low and the connection becomes unreliable. Fluorescent lights do not interfere with 2.4GHz 802.11b operations (although cell/wireless phones might). The 106MHz band used to broadcast the radio signal shouldn't interfere with the 2.4GHz signal—the two frequencies don't have a direct harmonic relationship. Although EMI could cause some interference, it's unlikely that it would completely corrupt communication between the network nodes, especially as the radio transmitter isn't located in the auditorium.

4. **Answer: B.** The vertical antenna produces a donut-shaped output pattern with equal transmissions in all directions (omnidirectional). The other antenna options are all highly directional.

2

Protocols and Standards

Domain 2.0: Protocols and Standards

Objective 2.1: Given an Example, Identify a Media Access Control (MAC) Address and its Parts

Quick Check

1. Which of the following is a valid MAC address?
   - ❑ A. 00-D0-59-09-07-51
   - ❑ B. A7-D3-45-2D-3F
   - ❑ C. 199.221.34.10
   - ❑ D. 00-GA-34-T1-F8-92

Quick Answer: **93**
Detailed Answer: **99**

2. Which of the following best describes the function of a MAC address?
   - ❑ A. It's used to physically locate a device on a network.
   - ❑ B. It's used to logically locate a device on a network.
   - ❑ C. It's used to route packets between networks.
   - ❑ D. It's used to assign workstations to specific hub ports.

Quick Answer: **93**
Detailed Answer: **99**

3. Which of the following statements related to a MAC address is not always correct?
   - ❑ A. MAC addresses are displayed in the hexadecimal numbering system.
   - ❑ B. A MAC address is hard-wired into the circuitry of a device.
   - ❑ C. MAC addresses are physically printed on devices.
   - ❑ D. MAC addresses are also called physical addresses.

Quick Answer: **93**
Detailed Answer: **99**

4. Which utility can you use to find out the MAC address of your workstation?
   - ❑ A. Ipconfig
   - ❑ B. Ping
   - ❑ C. Arp
   - ❑ D. Tracert

Quick Answer: **93**
Detailed Answer: **99**

Quick Check

5. An Ethernet frame is to be transported across the Internet using TCP/IP. Which of the following is true?
   - ❑ A. MAC addresses are checked at each router.
   - ❑ B. IP addresses are updated at each router.
   - ❑ C. TCP is discarded at each router.
   - ❑ D. IP addresses are discarded at each router.

Quick Answer: **93**
Detailed Answer: **99**

6. What do the first three sections of the MAC address 00-80-48-C5-2A-CB represent?
   - ❑ A. The Network layer address
   - ❑ B. Individual node addresses
   - ❑ C. Ethernet addresses
   - ❑ D. Unique vendor-specific addresses

Quick Answer: **93**
Detailed Answer: **99**

Objective 2.2: Identify the Seven Layers of the OSI Model and Their Functions

1. Which layer of the OSI model is responsible for encryption and decryption?
   - ❑ A. Network
   - ❑ B. Presentation
   - ❑ C. Session
   - ❑ D. Physical

Quick Answer: **93**
Detailed Answer: **99**

2. Which of the following OSI layers establishes, manages, and breaks communication sessions between applications?
   - ❑ A. Session
   - ❑ B. Application
   - ❑ C. Presentation
   - ❑ D. Network

Quick Answer: **93**
Detailed Answer: **99**

3. Which layer of the OSI model determines whether the communication between nodes will be full or half duplex?
   - ❑ A. Presentation
   - ❑ B. Session
   - ❑ C. Application
   - ❑ D. Physical

Quick Answer: **93**
Detailed Answer: **100**

Quick Check

4. Which layer of the OSI model is responsible for establishing a reliable connection?
   - ❑ A. Network
   - ❑ B. Session
   - ❑ C. Transport
   - ❑ D. Data Link

Quick Answer: 93
Detailed Answer: 100

5. Which layer of the ISO OSI model determines which route data will take across a complex network?
   - ❑ A. Network
   - ❑ B. Data Link
   - ❑ C. Transport
   - ❑ D. Session

Quick Answer: 93
Detailed Answer: 100

6. At what layer of the OSI model are logical addresses (IP addresses) assigned?
   - ❑ A. Data Link
   - ❑ B. Application
   - ❑ C. Physical
   - ❑ D. Network

Quick Answer: 93
Detailed Answer: 100

7. What layer of the OSI model is involved in translating data to codes such as ASCII?
   - ❑ A. Session
   - ❑ B. Presentation
   - ❑ C. Physical
   - ❑ D. Transport

Quick Answer: 93
Detailed Answer: 100

8. Which layer of the OSI model is responsible for placing the signal on the network media?
   - ❑ A. Data Link
   - ❑ B. Physical
   - ❑ C. MAC
   - ❑ D. LLC

Quick Answer: 93
Detailed Answer: 100

9. At which of the following OSI layers does TCP operate?
   - ❑ A. Presentation
   - ❑ B. Network
   - ❑ C. Session
   - ❑ D. Transport

Quick Answer: 93
Detailed Answer: 100

Quick Check

10. Email and FTP work at which layer of the OSI model?
    - ❑ A. Application
    - ❑ B. Session
    - ❑ C. Presentation
    - ❑ D. User

Quick Answer: **93**
Detailed Answer: **100**

11. You are conducting a data transfer over a direct connection between two RS-232 serial ports. At what level of the OSI model do these ports operate?
    - ❑ A. Data Link
    - ❑ B. Session
    - ❑ C. Presentation
    - ❑ D. Physical

Quick Answer: **93**
Detailed Answer: **100**

12. At which OSI layer does the 802.3 Ethernet protocol operate?
    - ❑ A. Session
    - ❑ B. Data Link
    - ❑ C. Transport
    - ❑ D. Physical

Quick Answer: **93**
Detailed Answer: **100**

13. Which layer of the OSI model is associated with network services and applications?
    - ❑ A. Data Link
    - ❑ B. Network
    - ❑ C. Application
    - ❑ D. Session

Quick Answer: **93**
Detailed Answer: **100**

14. The Simple Network Management Protocol operates at the ______ layer of the ISO OSI model.
    - ❑ A. Data Link
    - ❑ B. Application
    - ❑ C. Network
    - ❑ D. Transport

Quick Answer: **93**
Detailed Answer: **100**

15. Which layer of the OSI model is responsible for the dialog in the connection between two network hosts?
    - ❑ A. Session
    - ❑ B. Application
    - ❑ C. Transport
    - ❑ D. Data Link

Quick Answer: **93**
Detailed Answer: **100**

Quick Check

16. What Session layer tool is used to maintain a connection between client and server on clients running Windows 9x?
    - ❑ A. SMB
    - ❑ B. Requestor
    - ❑ C. Redirector
    - ❑ D. Client

Quick Answer: 93
Detailed Answer: 101

17. To allow a Windows 9x client to display a file that's located on a server, what tool is used?
    - ❑ A. Requester
    - ❑ B. Redirector
    - ❑ C. Checkpoint
    - ❑ D. Client

Quick Answer: 93
Detailed Answer: 101

18. At which layer of the OSI model is the protocol HTTP associated?
    - ❑ A. Session
    - ❑ B. Application
    - ❑ C. Network
    - ❑ D. Presentation

Quick Answer: 93
Detailed Answer: 101

19. A server redirector is handled at which layer of the OSI model?
    - ❑ A. Presentation
    - ❑ B. Application
    - ❑ C. Network
    - ❑ D. Session

Quick Answer: 93
Detailed Answer: 101

20. Which layer of the ISO OSI model contains classes of service?
    - ❑ A. Transport
    - ❑ B. Data Link
    - ❑ C. Network
    - ❑ D. Physical

Quick Answer: 93
Detailed Answer: 101

21. At which layer of the OSI model is UDP placed?
    - ❑ A. Session
    - ❑ B. Network
    - ❑ C. Transport
    - ❑ D. Presentation

Quick Answer: 93
Detailed Answer: 101

Quick Check

22. Which layer of the OSI model is responsible for routing?
    - ❑ A. Transport
    - ❑ B. Presentation
    - ❑ C. Network
    - ❑ D. Data Link

Quick Answer: 93
Detailed Answer: 101

23. Which of the following statements is true regarding IP addresses?
    - ❑ A. They can only be used with TCP.
    - ❑ B. All NIC cards contain an IP address.
    - ❑ C. They are examined at the Network layer to determine where the data is going.
    - ❑ D. They specify the physical location of a node.

Quick Answer: 93
Detailed Answer: 101

24. Which layer of the OSI model is responsible for translating Internet domain names to IP addresses?
    - ❑ A. Data Link
    - ❑ B. Network
    - ❑ C. Transport
    - ❑ D. Presentation

Quick Answer: 93
Detailed Answer: 101

25. Which of the following provides for an interface to the Network layer?
    - ❑ A. Transport layer
    - ❑ B. MAC sublayer
    - ❑ C. Physical layer
    - ❑ D. LLC sublayer

Quick Answer: 93
Detailed Answer: 101

26. Which layer of the OSI model contains the MAC and LLC sublayers?
    - ❑ A. Transport
    - ❑ B. Application
    - ❑ C. Data Link
    - ❑ D. Physical

Quick Answer: 93
Detailed Answer: 102

27. Which layer of the OSI model is responsible for electrical and mechanical specifications?
    - ❑ A. Physical
    - ❑ B. Application
    - ❑ C. Data Link
    - ❑ D. Session

Quick Answer: 93
Detailed Answer: 102

Quick Check

28. Which layer of the ISO OSI model contains the parameters of bits?
    - ❑ A. Presentation
    - ❑ B. Data Link
    - ❑ C. Physical
    - ❑ D. Network

Quick Answer: 93
Detailed Answer: 102

29. What do the following have in common: OSI, SNA, and DNA?
    - ❑ A. They all describe Ethernet.
    - ❑ B. They all describe networking models.
    - ❑ C. They all describe a cabling infrastructure.
    - ❑ D. They all describe a network protocol.

Quick Answer: 93
Detailed Answer: 102

30. A node sends several data packets but receives no indication from a receiving node if packets were received. This is an example of _____.
    - ❑ A. ISDN
    - ❑ B. connectionless transport
    - ❑ C. connection-oriented transport
    - ❑ D. dynamic routing

Quick Answer: 93
Detailed Answer: 102

31. Ping is a TCP/IP networking utility that sends network packets to specific IP addresses to determine whether they are accessible. At what layer of the OSI model does this utility work?
    - ❑ A. Data Link
    - ❑ B. Network
    - ❑ C. Presentation
    - ❑ D. Session

Quick Answer: 93
Detailed Answer: 102

32. Which OSI layer handles format and code conversion functions?
    - ❑ A. Session
    - ❑ B. Network
    - ❑ C. Presentation
    - ❑ D. Physical

Quick Answer: 93
Detailed Answer: 102

33. Which layer of the OSI model is responsible for encryption and decryption?
    - ❑ A. Session
    - ❑ B. Network
    - ❑ C. Presentation
    - ❑ D. Physical

Quick Answer: 93
Detailed Answer: 102

Quick Check

Objective 2.3: Identify the OSI Layers at Which the Following Network Devices Operate: Hubs, Switches, Bridges, Routers, NICs, and WAPs

1. Which of the following devices operates at the Network layer of the OSI model?
   - ❑ A. Router
   - ❑ B. Repeater
   - ❑ C. Hub
   - ❑ D. Switch

Quick Answer: **93**
Detailed Answer: **102**

2. Which of the following devices is used to pass data between different Network layer protocols?
   - ❑ A. Brouter
   - ❑ B. Router
   - ❑ C. Hub
   - ❑ D. Bridge

Quick Answer: **93**
Detailed Answer: **103**

3. Which of the following devices operates at the Data Link as well as the Network layer?
   - ❑ A. Hub
   - ❑ B. Brouter
   - ❑ C. Bridge
   - ❑ D. Router

Quick Answer: **93**
Detailed Answer: **103**

4. Which of the following network devices operates at the Physical layer of the OSI model?
   - ❑ A. Hub
   - ❑ B. Router
   - ❑ C. Bridge
   - ❑ D. NIC

Quick Answer: **93**
Detailed Answer: **103**

5. A NIC card is replaced with a NIC card that has jumper switches for configuring IRQ, DMA, and I/O Base address. Which of the following should you do when configuring these settings?
   - ❑ A. Manually configure them with the jumpers.
   - ❑ B. Let Plug-and-Play configure them.
   - ❑ C. Download the latest software version.
   - ❑ D. Locate a software patch and install it on the card.

Quick Answer: **93**
Detailed Answer: **103**

Quick Check

6. Which of the following devices is not associated with the Data Link layer?
   - ❑ A. Router
   - ❑ B. NIC card
   - ❑ C. Switch
   - ❑ D. Bridge

Quick Answer: 93
Detailed Answer: 103

7. Which of the following devices is associated with the Physical layer?
   - ❑ A. Switch
   - ❑ B. NIC card
   - ❑ C. Fiber optic cable
   - ❑ D. Router

Quick Answer: 93
Detailed Answer: 103

8. At which OSI level does a router function?
   - ❑ A. Network
   - ❑ B. Transport
   - ❑ C. Session
   - ❑ D. Physical

Quick Answer: 93
Detailed Answer: 103

9. Why are NIC cards classified at the Data Link layer?
   - ❑ A. They contain IP addresses.
   - ❑ B. They contain TCP addressing.
   - ❑ C. They contain MAC addresses.
   - ❑ D. They connect directly to the network media.

Quick Answer: 93
Detailed Answer: 103

10. Which type of device processes information at the OSI Network layer?
    - ❑ A. Hub
    - ❑ B. Switch
    - ❑ C. Bridge
    - ❑ D. Router

Quick Answer: 93
Detailed Answer: 103

Quick Check

Objective 2.4: Differentiate Between the Network Protocols in Terms of Routing, Addressing Schemes, Interoperability, and Naming Conventions for IPX/SPX, NetBEUI, AppleTalk, and TCP/IP

1. Which three of the following protocols are parts of the TCP/IP protocol suite?

   - ❑ A. DHCP
   - ❑ B. TCP
   - ❑ C. HTTP
   - ❑ D. SPX
   - ❑ E. NLSP

Quick Answer: 94
Detailed Answer: 104

2. As network administrator for Timeleigh Solutions, you are given the task of integrating the existing network with a new network that will be located in another building. In total, there will be three network segments. The systems on the network are Windows 2000 and Novell NetWare servers and Windows 2000 workstations. You want to confine the network to a single protocol. Which two of the following network protocols might you consider using for the entire network?

   - ❑ A. PPP
   - ❑ B. NetBEUI
   - ❑ C. IPX
   - ❑ D. TCP/IP

Quick Answer: 94
Detailed Answer: 104

3. Which of the following is a valid NetBIOS computer name?

   - ❑ A. janesworkstation
   - ❑ B. server 4
   - ❑ C. 00-0C-D1-E4-C3-F4
   - ❑ D. ADE4:DC34:0800:4C32:B003

Quick Answer: 94
Detailed Answer: 104

4. What advantage does IPX offer over NetBEUI?

   - ❑ A. It doesn't require specialized client software.
   - ❑ B. It's a routable protocol.
   - ❑ C. It's not proprietary.
   - ❑ D. It performs with no collisions.

Quick Answer: 94
Detailed Answer: 104

Quick Check

5. Which of the following is associated with the proprietary protocol IPX?
   - ❑ A. TCP/IP
   - ❑ B. Windows NT
   - ❑ C. UNIX
   - ❑ D. NetWare

Quick Answer: 94
Detailed Answer: 104

6. To implement a network that doesn't use IP or IPX addressing, which of the following should be used?
   - ❑ A. TCP/IP
   - ❑ B. NetWare
   - ❑ C. NetBEUI
   - ❑ D. UNIX

Quick Answer: 94
Detailed Answer: 104

7. Which of the following protocols cannot be routed?
   - ❑ A. UDP
   - ❑ B. NetBEUI
   - ❑ C. IP
   - ❑ D. TCP

Quick Answer: 94
Detailed Answer: 104

8. What is the difference between routable and nonroutable protocols?
   - ❑ A. Routable protocols include a logical address that contains a network number and a host number.
   - ❑ B. Nonroutable protocols can accommodate only logical addressing schemes.
   - ❑ C. A routable protocol is guaranteed delivery, whereas a non-routable protocol isn't.
   - ❑ D. Routable protocols have preplanned routes mapped before they're sent.

Quick Answer: 94
Detailed Answer: 104

9. Which two of the following protocols are responsible for network addressing?
   - ❑ A. IP
   - ❑ B. TCP
   - ❑ C. SPX
   - ❑ D. IPX

Quick Answer: 94
Detailed Answer: 104

Quick Check

10. On an AppleTalk network, what is the function of the AARP protocol?
   - ❑ A. It allows the resolution of MAC addresses to AppleTalk addresses.
   - ❑ B. It is a distance vector routing protocol.
   - ❑ C. It allows the resolution of AppleTalk addresses to MAC addresses.
   - ❑ D. It is a link state routing protocol.

Quick Answer: **94**
Detailed Answer: **105**

11. Which of the following doesn't use IP or IPX addressing?
   - ❑ A. TCP/IP
   - ❑ B. NetBEUI
   - ❑ C. NetWare
   - ❑ D. IP

Quick Answer: **94**
Detailed Answer: **105**

12. Of the following protocols, which is not routable?
   - ❑ A. UDP
   - ❑ B. TCP
   - ❑ C. IP
   - ❑ D. NetBEUI

Quick Answer: **94**
Detailed Answer: **105**

13. IPX is a proprietary protocol utilized in _______ networks.
   - ❑ A. Windows NT
   - ❑ B. UNIX
   - ❑ C. Netware
   - ❑ D. TCP/IP

Quick Answer: **94**
Detailed Answer: **105**

14. What advantage does Novell IPX offer over Microsoft NetBEUI?
   - ❑ A. It can be routed.
   - ❑ B. It doesn't require specialized client addressing.
   - ❑ C. It can't be routed.
   - ❑ D. It doesn't require error checking.

Quick Answer: **94**
Detailed Answer: **105**

15. To set up a small, Microsoft, peer-to-peer LAN, without a server and using computer names as the addressing scheme, which of the following is most likely to be used?
   - ❑ A. NetBEUI
   - ❑ B. TCP
   - ❑ C. TCP/IP
   - ❑ D. Ethernet

Quick Answer: **94**
Detailed Answer: **105**

Quick Check

16. To assign a static IP address to a workstation, which of the following must you do?
    - ❑ A. Choose to obtain an IP address automatically.
    - ❑ B. Specify the IP address and subnet mask.
    - ❑ C. Specify only an IP address.
    - ❑ D. Choose to obtain the subnet mask automatically.

Quick Answer: **94**
Detailed Answer: **105**

17. To resolve a NetBIOS name to IP address on a Windows workstation, which local file do you manually change?
    - ❑ A. Hwinfo
    - ❑ B. WINS
    - ❑ C. Grpconv
    - ❑ D. LMHOSTS

Quick Answer: **94**
Detailed Answer: **105**

18. A protocol that guarantees the delivery of a packet is said to be ___________.
    - ❑ A. connection-oriented
    - ❑ B. connectionless
    - ❑ C. Type I
    - ❑ D. subnetted

Quick Answer: **94**
Detailed Answer: **105**

19. Which of the following protocols is associated with the Internet?
    - ❑ A. TCP/IP
    - ❑ B. NetBEUI
    - ❑ C. Token ring
    - ❑ D. IEEE 802.3

Quick Answer: **94**
Detailed Answer: **105**

20. What are the minimum configuration requirements for a TCP/IP connection to the Internet?
    - ❑ A. IP address and Subnet Mask
    - ❑ B. IP address, Gateway and DNS setting
    - ❑ C. IP address only
    - ❑ D. IP address, Subnet mask and Gateway setting

Quick Answer: **94**
Detailed Answer: **106**

Quick Check

Objective 2.5: Identify the Components and Structure of IP Addresses (Ipv4, Ipv6) and Required Settings for Connections Across the Internet

1. Which of the following is a valid Ipv6 address?

   Quick Answer: 94
   Detailed Answer: 106

   - ❑ A. 00-DC-45-F2-C3-04
   - ❑ B. 192.168.45.15.212.211.16.7
   - ❑ C. 3FF1:D501:C308:221F:0260:97DE:ED42:032C
   - ❑ D. 3FF1;D501;H308;221G;0260;97DH;ED42;032C

2. Which of the following protocols enables you to access and manipulate email messages on a server?

   Quick Answer: 94
   Detailed Answer: 106

   - ❑ A. IMAP
   - ❑ B. IMAP4
   - ❑ C. POP3
   - ❑ D. SMTP

3. Which of the following is an important feature of IMAP4?

   Quick Answer: 94
   Detailed Answer: 106

   - ❑ A. Faster mail retrieval
   - ❑ B. Faster Internet access
   - ❑ C. Encrypted instant message
   - ❑ D. Simultaneous accesses to a single mailbox

Objective 2.6: Identify Classful IP Address Ranges and Their Default Subnet Masks

1. Given the IP address of 212.16.175.24 and a subnet mask of 255.255.0.0, what is the network address of the segment to which this node is connected?

   Quick Answer: 94
   Detailed Answer: 106

   - ❑ A. 212.16.175
   - ❑ B. 212.16
   - ❑ C. 212.16.24
   - ❑ D. 212.16.175.24

2. Which of the following is a valid Class C IP address?

   Quick Answer: 94
   Detailed Answer: 106

   - ❑ A. 12.17.221.6
   - ❑ B. 211.261.145.16
   - ❑ C. 191.23.145.16
   - ❑ D. 192.168.1.1

Quick Check

3. Which of the following is an example of a class C IP address?
   - ❑ A. 192.168.20.1
   - ❑ B. 176.56.20.1
   - ❑ C. 183.24.20.1
   - ❑ D. 21.134.20.1

Quick Answer: 94
Detailed Answer: 106

4. Which of the following is an example of a Class B IP address?
   - ❑ A. 192.168.22.1
   - ❑ B. 10.15.13.1
   - ❑ C. 172.16.32.1
   - ❑ D. 127.0.0.1

Quick Answer: 94
Detailed Answer: 106

5. Which of the following is an example of a Class A IP address?
   - ❑ A. 192.168.20.1
   - ❑ B. 192.176.20.1
   - ❑ C. 10.124.20.1
   - ❑ D. 176.150.20.1

Quick Answer: 94
Detailed Answer: 106

6. A node has been assigned the IP address 129.168.34.25 255.255.0.0. What is the host address of this node?
   - ❑ A. 168.34
   - ❑ B. 129.168
   - ❑ C. 255.255
   - ❑ D. .34.25

Quick Answer: 94
Detailed Answer: 106

Objective 2.7: Identify the Purpose of Subnetting

1. What term is used to describe the process of using parts of the node address range of an IP address as network IDs?
   - ❑ A. Supernetting
   - ❑ B. Subnetting
   - ❑ C. Subnet masking
   - ❑ D. Super routing

Quick Answer: 94
Detailed Answer: 107

2. How do you ensure that the testing of a new server will not affect everyone else on a large network?
   - ❑ A. Install a router to create a new network subnet segment.
   - ❑ B. Set up a subnet to test the server.
   - ❑ C. Install the new server in a test network until it has been proven.
   - ❑ D. Change the subnet so that a private network is created.

Quick Answer: 94
Detailed Answer: 107

Quick Check

3. 255.255.0.0 is the default subnet mask for a ______ IP address.

Quick Answer: **94**
Detailed Answer: **107**

- ❑ A. Class C
- ❑ B. Class A
- ❑ C. Class B
- ❑ D. Class D

4. Which of the following is the default subnet mask for a Class B IP address?

Quick Answer: **94**
Detailed Answer: **107**

- ❑ A. 255.255.0.0
- ❑ B. 255.255.255.0
- ❑ C. 255.0.0.0
- ❑ D. 255.255.255.0

5. Which of the following is the default subnet mask for a Class A IP address?

Quick Answer: **94**
Detailed Answer: **107**

- ❑ A. 255.0.0.0
- ❑ B. 255.255.255.255
- ❑ C. 255.255.255.0
- ❑ D. 255.255.0.0

6. Which of the following is the default subnet mask for a Class C IP address?

Quick Answer: **94**
Detailed Answer: **107**

- ❑ A. 255.255.255.255
- ❑ B. 255.255.255.0
- ❑ C. 255.0.0.0
- ❑ D. 255.255.0.0

7. Which of the following protocols must use a subnet mask?

Quick Answer: **94**
Detailed Answer: **107**

- ❑ A. IPX/SPX
- ❑ B. TCP/IP
- ❑ C. NWLink
- ❑ D. Appletalk

Objective 2.8: Identify the Differences Between Public vs. Private Network Addressing Schemes

1. Which of the following represents the best method for protecting data sent across the Internet?

Quick Answer: **95**
Detailed Answer: **107**

- ❑ A. Password protection
- ❑ B. Share-level access
- ❑ C. User-level access
- ❑ D. Encryption

Quick Check

2. Which of the following is not one of the private address ranges?
   - ❑ A. 10.x.x.x
   - ❑ B. 224.181.x.x
   - ❑ C. 172.16.x.x
   - ❑ D. 192.168.x.x

Quick Answer: 95
Detailed Answer: 107

3. Your company has two offices in different locations. You need to establish a secure link between the two. You want to use the Internet as a communication mechanism to keep the costs down. Which of the following technologies is best suited for your needs?
   - ❑ A. VPN
   - ❑ B. 802.11b
   - ❑ C. VLAN
   - ❑ D. TDR

Quick Answer: 95
Detailed Answer: 107

4. If you contacted the IANA, what would you be trying to do?
   - ❑ A. Get an IP address to connect a system to a private network.
   - ❑ B. Get a new telephone number.
   - ❑ C. Get an Internet domain name reassigned.
   - ❑ D. Get an IP address to connect a system to a public network.

Quick Answer: 95
Detailed Answer: 108

5. What class of IP address is 172.16.0.1?
   - ❑ A. Reserved
   - ❑ B. Class B
   - ❑ C. Class C
   - ❑ D. Private

Quick Answer: 95
Detailed Answer: 108

6. What class of IP address is 127.9.0.3?
   - ❑ A. Reserved
   - ❑ B. Class B
   - ❑ C. Class C
   - ❑ D. Private

Quick Answer: 95
Detailed Answer: 108

Quick Check

Objective 2.9: Identify and Differentiate Between the Following IP Addressing Methods: Static, Dynamic, and Self-Assigned (APIPA)

1. What is the first action a DHCP client performs when it starts up?

   Quick Answer: 95
   Detailed Answer: 108

   - ❑ A. It checks its internal IP address lease to see that it is still valid.
   - ❑ B. It checks with the DHCP server to determine whether there are any IP addresses available.
   - ❑ C. It requests an IP address and subnet mask from the DHCP server.
   - ❑ D. It contacts the nearest router to determine the location of the nearest DHCP server.

2. Which of the following is true of Private IP addresses?

   Quick Answer: 95
   Detailed Answer: 108

   - ❑ A. They require a subnet mask of 255.255.255.0.
   - ❑ B. They require a subnet mask of 255.0.0.0.
   - ❑ C. Private IP addresses are only provided by ISPs for certain applications.
   - ❑ D. ISPs cannot provide or access Private IP addresses.

3. Which of the following statements concerning APIPA is correct?

   Quick Answer: 95
   Detailed Answer: 108

   - ❑ A. APIPA uses DHCP to temporarily assign an IP address to a client.
   - ❑ B. A workstation can communicate with others outside its network using an APIPA address.
   - ❑ C. When the APIPA server is not available, DHCP can be used to assign IP address to a client.
   - ❑ D. APIPA can be useful for identifying problems with DHCP.

Quick Check

Objective 2.10: Define the Purpose, Function, and Use of the Following Protocols Within the TCP/IP Suite: TCP, UDP, FTP, SFTP, TFTP, SMTP, HTTP, HTTPS, POP3/IMAP4, Telnet, SSH, ICMP, ARP, NTP, NNTP, SCP, LDAP, IGMP, and LPR

1. Which of the following network protocols offer guaranteed delivery, error correction, and the capability to recover lost network packets?

   ❑ A. TCP
   ❑ B. IPX
   ❑ C. ARP
   ❑ D. IP

   Quick Answer: **95**
   Detailed Answer: **108**

2. Which of the following protocols can be used to synchronize time information across servers on a network?

   ❑ A. NTP
   ❑ B. NDPS
   ❑ C. NTPS
   ❑ D. NFS

   Quick Answer: **95**
   Detailed Answer: **108**

3. At which layer of the OSI model does UDP operate?

   ❑ A. Session
   ❑ B. Transport
   ❑ C. Connection
   ❑ D. Network

   Quick Answer: **95**
   Detailed Answer: **108**

4. Your manager asks you to look into a solution for the following problem: Your company wants to make it possible for clients to upload graphics files to a Linux system to incorporate them into marketing material that your company produces. Some of the files are quite large. Which of the following technologies are you most likely to suggest?

   ❑ A. Samba
   ❑ B. Telnet
   ❑ C. FTP
   ❑ D. Squid

   Quick Answer: **95**
   Detailed Answer: **108**

5. Which protocol is used to send email?

   ❑ A. NTP
   ❑ B. IMAP4
   ❑ C. POP3
   ❑ D. SMTP

   Quick Answer: **95**
   Detailed Answer: **109**

Quick Check

6. Which two of the following protocols use a connection-oriented transport protocol as opposed to a connectionless transport?
   - ❑ A. FTP
   - ❑ B. RGP
   - ❑ C. TFTP
   - ❑ D. HTTP

Quick Answer: **95**
Detailed Answer: **109**

7. Which of the following best describes TCP?
   - ❑ A. Nonroutable
   - ❑ B. Connection-oriented
   - ❑ C. Connectionless
   - ❑ D. Unreliable

Quick Answer: **95**
Detailed Answer: **109**

8. Which of the following protocols is best suited for connectionless transport?
   - ❑ A. IPX
   - ❑ B. TCP
   - ❑ C. UDP
   - ❑ D. NetBEUI

Quick Answer: **95**
Detailed Answer: **109**

9. You are managing a network that uses both a UNIX server and a Windows 2000 server. Which of the following protocols can you use to transfer files between the two servers?
   - ❑ A. PPP
   - ❑ B. FTP
   - ❑ C. Telnet
   - ❑ D. PPTP

Quick Answer: **95**
Detailed Answer: **109**

10. Which three of the following protocols are parts of the TCP/IP protocol suite?
    - ❑ A. HTTP
    - ❑ B. FTP
    - ❑ C. AFP
    - ❑ D. DHCP

Quick Answer: **95**
Detailed Answer: **109**

11. Which three of the following are connectionless protocols?
    - ❑ A. SPX
    - ❑ B. UDP
    - ❑ C. IPX
    - ❑ D. IP

Quick Answer: **95**
Detailed Answer: **109**

Quick Check

12. You are attempting to configure a client's email program. They can receive mail, but are unable to send any. In the mail server configuration screen of the mail application, you notice that the Type Of Outgoing Mail Server field is blank. This explains why the client is unable to send mail. Which of the following protocols are you most likely to enter as a value in the outgoing mail server type field?

Quick Answer: **95**
Detailed Answer: **109**

- ❑ A. IMAP
- ❑ B. POP3
- ❑ C. NMP
- ❑ D. SMTP

13. Which three of the following protocols are included in the TCP/IP protocol suite?

Quick Answer: **95**
Detailed Answer: **110**

- ❑ A. HTTP
- ❑ B. FTP
- ❑ C. AFP
- ❑ D. SMTP
- ❑ E. NCP

14. Which of the following protocols is best suited for "live" Internet radio?

Quick Answer: **95**
Detailed Answer: **110**

- ❑ A. UDP
- ❑ B. TCP
- ❑ C. IPX
- ❑ D. NetBEUI

15. You are managing a network that uses both a UNIX server and a Windows 2000 server. Which of the following protocols would be best utilized to transfer files between the two servers?

Quick Answer: **95**
Detailed Answer: **110**

- ❑ A. PPP
- ❑ B. FTP
- ❑ C. Telnet
- ❑ D. PPTP

16. SMTP is used to _______.

Quick Answer: **95**
Detailed Answer: **110**

- ❑ A. send email
- ❑ B. map the physical address of a node to the logical address
- ❑ C. encode data
- ❑ D. check the network connectivity

Quick Check

17. Which of the following is responsible for outgoing email?

- ❑ A. SNMP
- ❑ B. SMTP
- ❑ C. POP3
- ❑ D. Telnet

Quick Answer: **95**
Detailed Answer: **110**

18. Which protocol holds email until the client retrieves it?

- ❑ A. POP3
- ❑ B. WINS
- ❑ C. DNS
- ❑ D. SMTP

Quick Answer: **95**
Detailed Answer: **110**

19. Which of the following is responsible for receiving email?

- ❑ A. POP3
- ❑ B. SNMP
- ❑ C. ARP
- ❑ D. Telnet

Quick Answer: **95**
Detailed Answer: **110**

20. Which protocol is used to access the World Wide Web portion of the Internet?

- ❑ A. PPP
- ❑ B. MIME
- ❑ C. FTP
- ❑ D. HTTP

Quick Answer: **95**
Detailed Answer: **110**

21. Which TCP/IP utility is used for terminal emulation?

- ❑ A. ARP
- ❑ B. Telnet
- ❑ C. FTP
- ❑ D. NetSTAT

Quick Answer: **95**
Detailed Answer: **110**

22. What feature does SSH offer?

- ❑ A. A secure connection between client and server
- ❑ B. Faster Internet access
- ❑ C. Remote network access
- ❑ D. A table to convert IP addresses to physical MAC addresses

Quick Answer: **95**
Detailed Answer: **111**

23. Which of the following should be used to access a database site?

- ❑ A. LPR
- ❑ B. FTP
- ❑ C. LDAP
- ❑ D. Telnet

Quick Answer: **95**
Detailed Answer: **111**

Quick Check

24. What TCP/IP protocol can be used for directory access?
    - ❑ A. LDAP
    - ❑ B. FTP
    - ❑ C. TCP
    - ❑ D. NNTP

Quick Answer: **95**
Detailed Answer: **111**

25. What's the difference between FTP and TFTP?
    - ❑ A. FTP is less secure than TFTP.
    - ❑ B. FTP is more secure than TFTP.
    - ❑ C. FTP is used for receiving email and TFTP is used for sending email.
    - ❑ D. FTP is used for sending email and TFTP is used for receiving email.

Quick Answer: **95**
Detailed Answer: **111**

26. What is the reason for not using TFTP to upload important files?
    - ❑ A. You might crash the system and lose your files while uploading them.
    - ❑ B. It takes too much time to upload files.
    - ❑ C. It doesn't provide any authentication checking—anyone on the site can download the files.
    - ❑ D. TFTP can only be used in an intranet.

Quick Answer: **95**
Detailed Answer: **111**

27. Which protocol is used by a news server to store messages and to allow messages to be sent for others to read?
    - ❑ A. NNTP
    - ❑ B. SMTP
    - ❑ C. LDAP
    - ❑ D. X.400

Quick Answer: **95**
Detailed Answer: **111**

28. To access Usenet News, what should be installed on the client?
    - ❑ A. HTTP
    - ❑ B. LPR
    - ❑ C. NNTP
    - ❑ D. FTP

Quick Answer: **95**
Detailed Answer: **111**

Quick Check

29. How does an NTP primary time server synchronize timekeeping on its network clients?

Quick Answer: 95
Detailed Answer: 111

- ❑ A. It generates the accurate time using an internal digital clock and passes the time information to clients by requests.
- ❑ B. It generates the accurate time using an internal digital clock and broadcasts the time information to clients.
- ❑ C. It is synchronized to an external radio clock and passes the time information to clients by requests.
- ❑ D. It sends electric pulses to synchronize clocks on clients.

30. Which of the following is used by IP to report datagram processing errors to the source host?

Quick Answer: 95
Detailed Answer: 111

- ❑ A. ICMP
- ❑ B. TFTP
- ❑ C. SMTP
- ❑ D. TCP

31. What is the RARP protocol designed to do?

Quick Answer: 95
Detailed Answer: 111

- ❑ A. Convert an IP address to its MAC address
- ❑ B. Convert an IP address to its Ethernet address
- ❑ C. Convert an IP address to its ARP address
- ❑ D. Convert a MAC address to its IP address

32. IGMP is designed to support ______.

Quick Answer: 95
Detailed Answer: 111

- ❑ A. IP-MAC address mapping
- ❑ B. multicasting
- ❑ C. instant message
- ❑ D. secure Internet commerce

Quick Check

Objectives 2.11 and 2.12: Define the Function of TCP/UDP Ports and Identify Well-Known Ports Associated with the Following Commonly Used Services and Protocols: FTP, SSH, Telnet, SMTP, DNS, TFTP, HTTP, POP3, NNTP, NTP, IMPA4, and HTTPS

1. After installing a new Proxy server system, users are unable to connect to another system using FTP. Your manager asks you to reconfigure the Proxy server to correct this. Which port on the Proxy server would you open to facilitate FTP connections?

   ❑ A. 80
   ❑ B. 23
   ❑ C. 21
   ❑ D. 110

Quick Answer: **96**
Detailed Answer: **111**

2. Which of the following protocols uses port 80 by default?

   ❑ A. SMTP
   ❑ B. HTTP
   ❑ C. NTP
   ❑ D. FTP

Quick Answer: **96**
Detailed Answer: **111**

3. What is the well-known port number for HTTP?

   ❑ A. 80
   ❑ B. 25
   ❑ C. 110
   ❑ D. 21

Quick Answer: **96**
Detailed Answer: **112**

4. When a system running the TCP/IP protocol receives a data packet, how does it determine what service to forward the packet to?

   ❑ A. Port number
   ❑ B. Packet ID number
   ❑ C. Data IP number
   ❑ D. IP protocol service type

Quick Answer: **96**
Detailed Answer: **112**

Quick Check

5. You have been called in to troubleshoot a problem with a newly installed email application. Internal users can communicate with each other, but neither incoming nor outgoing email is working. You suspect a problem with the port-blocking configuration of the firewall system that protects the Internet connection. Which two of the following ports would you open to fix the problems with the email?
   - ❑ A. 110
   - ❑ B. 25
   - ❑ C. 80
   - ❑ D. 25
   - ❑ E. 443

Quick Answer: **96**
Detailed Answer: **112**

6. Which TCP/IP port number is used by the Domain Name Service?
   - ❑ A. 110
   - ❑ B. 25
   - ❑ C. 21
   - ❑ D. 53

Quick Answer: **96**
Detailed Answer: **112**

7. What is the well-known port number for HTTP?
   - ❑ A. 80
   - ❑ B. 25
   - ❑ C. 110
   - ❑ D. 21

Quick Answer: **96**
Detailed Answer: **112**

8. You install a new router for your network and configure it for operation. Users on your network immediately start complaining that they cannot access web pages from their browsers. When you test the web connection, you find that you can access web pages using their IP addresses but not with their Fully Qualified Domain Names. What type of problem is indicated?
   - ❑ A. You forgot to open TCP port 110 through the router.
   - ❑ B. You forgot to open TCP port 80 through the router.
   - ❑ C. You forgot to open TCP port 25 through the router.
   - ❑ D. You forgot to open TCP port 53 when you configured the router.

Quick Answer: **96**
Detailed Answer: **112**

Quick Check

9. Which TCP/UDP port is designated for use with the IMAP protocol?
   - ❑ A. 123
   - ❑ B. 443
   - ❑ C. 119
   - ❑ D. 143

Quick Answer: **96**
Detailed Answer: **112**

10. Which TCP/UDP port is designated for use with the SSH protocol?
    - ❑ A. 53
    - ❑ B. 22
    - ❑ C. 119
    - ❑ D. 143

Quick Answer: **96**
Detailed Answer: **112**

11. Which TCP/UDP port is designated for use with the TFTP protocol?
    - ❑ A. 69
    - ❑ B. 22
    - ❑ C. 443
    - ❑ D. 123

Quick Answer: **96**
Detailed Answer: **112**

12. Which TCP/UDP port is designated for use with the NNTP protocol?
    - ❑ A. 443
    - ❑ B. 69
    - ❑ C. 123
    - ❑ D. 119

Quick Answer: **96**
Detailed Answer: **112**

13. Which TCP/UDP port is designated for use with the NTP protocol?
    - ❑ A. 443
    - ❑ B. 123
    - ❑ C. 53
    - ❑ D. 69

Quick Answer: **96**
Detailed Answer: **112**

14. Which TCP/UDP port is designated for use with the HTTPS protocol?
    - ❑ A. 123
    - ❑ B. 137
    - ❑ C. 443
    - ❑ D. 119

Quick Answer: **96**
Detailed Answer: **113**

Quick Check

15. Which TCP/IP port number is reserved for Telnet operations?
    - ❑ A. 25
    - ❑ B. 23
    - ❑ C. 21
    - ❑ D. 110

Quick Answer: **96**
Detailed Answer: **113**

16. What is the well-known port number for SMTP operations?
    - ❑ A. 21
    - ❑ B. 80
    - ❑ C. 25
    - ❑ D. 110

Quick Answer: **96**
Detailed Answer: **113**

17. What is the well-known port number for POP3?
    - ❑ A. 21
    - ❑ B. 25
    - ❑ C. 110
    - ❑ D. 80

Quick Answer: **96**
Detailed Answer: **113**

Objective 2.13: Identify the Purpose of the Following Network Services and Protocols: DHCP/BOOTP, DNS, NAT/ICS, WINS, SNMP, NFS, Zeroconfig, SMB, AFP, LDP, and Samba

1. Which of the following services provides name resolution services for FQDNs?
    - ❑ A. ARP
    - ❑ B. DHCP
    - ❑ C. WINS
    - ❑ D. DNS
    - ❑ E. NTP

Quick Answer: **96**
Detailed Answer: **113**

2. You are implementing Internet Connection Sharing (ICS). Which operating system platform are you working on?
    - ❑ A. Novell Netware
    - ❑ B. Linux
    - ❑ C. Windows 2000
    - ❑ D. Windows 95

Quick Answer: **96**
Detailed Answer: **113**

Quick Check

3. In SNMP, when an event occurs, what is the message sent by the agent called?
   - ❑ A. Trap
   - ❑ B. Event
   - ❑ C. Alert
   - ❑ D. Alarm

Quick Answer: 96
Detailed Answer: 113

4. Which of the following is representative of a host?
   - ❑ A. A host doesn't have a MAC address.
   - ❑ B. A host has an IP address.
   - ❑ C. A host is confined to NetBEUI networks.
   - ❑ D. All devices on a network are hosts.

Quick Answer: 96
Detailed Answer: 113

5. To translate Internet domain names, or host names, to IP addresses, which of the following is used?
   - ❑ A. NDS
   - ❑ B. DNS
   - ❑ C. ARP
   - ❑ D. CCP

Quick Answer: 96
Detailed Answer: 113

6. An email is to be sent from site.com to a site called offshore.com.uk. Which of the following is the correct DNS search order?
   - ❑ A. site.com, .com, .uk, .com.uk, offshore.com.uk
   - ❑ B. site.com.uk, offshore.com.uk
   - ❑ C. com, site.com, .uk, .com.uk, offshore.com.uk
   - ❑ D. site.com, offshore, offshore.com, offshore.com.uk

Quick Answer: 96
Detailed Answer: 113

7. If, on a network using all Windows clients, it's necessary to guarantee that NetBIOS names will be mapped to IP addresses, which of the following should be enabled?
   - ❑ A. NetBEUI
   - ❑ B. PPP
   - ❑ C. WINS
   - ❑ D. RAS

Quick Answer: 96
Detailed Answer: 114

8. What is the purpose of DHCP?
   - ❑ A. To assign static IP addresses to client workstations
   - ❑ B. To dynamically assign IP addresses to client workstations
   - ❑ C. To convert from a Windows computer name to an IP address
   - ❑ D. To convert from an Internet domain name to an IP address

Quick Answer: 96
Detailed Answer: 114

Quick Check

9. Which of the following statements best describes the purpose of name resolution?

Quick Answer: **96**
Detailed Answer: **114**

- ❑ A. It reconciles logical addresses and user-friendly host names or NetBIOS names.
- ❑ B. It converts Windows NT frames to Novell Netware frames.
- ❑ C. It must occur for a bridge to operate.
- ❑ D. It converts from one IEEE protocol to another IEEE protocol.

10. Which of the following pieces of information is not likely to be supplied via DHCP?

Quick Answer: **96**
Detailed Answer: **114**

- ❑ A. Default gateway
- ❑ B. IP address
- ❑ C. Subnet mask
- ❑ D. NetBIOS computer name

11. Which network service is used to reconcile IP addresses and domain names?

Quick Answer: **96**
Detailed Answer: **114**

- ❑ A. DNS
- ❑ B. DHCP
- ❑ C. WINS
- ❑ D. BootP

12. To boot a diskless router so that it can discover its IP address, which tool can be used?

Quick Answer: **96**
Detailed Answer: **114**

- ❑ A. PPTP
- ❑ B. ICA
- ❑ C. NAT
- ❑ D. BootP

13. What was the forerunner to DHCP that allowed diskless clients to boot from a remote server to determine its IP address?

Quick Answer: **96**
Detailed Answer: **114**

- ❑ A. RAS
- ❑ B. BootP
- ❑ C. SSL
- ❑ D. TCP/IP

14. Which network service allows IP addresses to be dynamically assigned to clients?

Quick Answer: **96**
Detailed Answer: **114**

- ❑ A. DNS
- ❑ B. DHCP
- ❑ C. WINS
- ❑ D. SNMP

Quick Check

15. Which of the following is used to automatically assign IP addresses to workstations?

Quick Answer: 96
Detailed Answer: 114

- ❑ A. WINS
- ❑ B. DHCP
- ❑ C. DNS
- ❑ D. NetBIOS

16. A small network uses NetBIOS names with computers. TCP/IP also runs on the network. To reconcile the NetBIOS names to IP addresses, which of the following needs to be enabled?

Quick Answer: 96
Detailed Answer: 114

- ❑ A. WINS
- ❑ B. PAP
- ❑ C. DHCP
- ❑ D. DNS

17. To connect to the server EAST1, and to a folder called DOCUMENT, which of the following is the correct format for UNC?

Quick Answer: 96
Detailed Answer: 114

- ❑ A. \\DOCUMENT\EAST1
- ❑ B. \EAST1\DOCUMENT
- ❑ C. \\EAST1\DOCUMENT
- ❑ D. \DOCUMENT\\EAST1

18. If it is necessary to guarantee that NetBIOS names will be mapped to IP addresses on a network using all Windows clients, which of the following should be enabled?

Quick Answer: 96
Detailed Answer: 115

- ❑ A. PPP
- ❑ B. WINS
- ❑ C. NetBEUI
- ❑ D. RAS

19. What service is responsible for reconciling Microsoft NetBIOS names to IP addresses?

Quick Answer: 96
Detailed Answer: 115

- ❑ A. SNMP
- ❑ B. DNS
- ❑ C. DHCP
- ❑ D. WINS

20. Which of the following is an example of Universal Naming Convention (UNC)?

Quick Answer: 96
Detailed Answer: 115

- ❑ A. user@network.org
- ❑ B. www.computer.com
- ❑ C. 10.56.23.1
- ❑ D. \\Servername\sharename

Quick Check

21. What tool may be used to provide network management functions?
    - ❑ A. SLIP
    - ❑ B. SNMP
    - ❑ C. PPP
    - ❑ D. NAT

Quick Answer: **96**
Detailed Answer: **115**

22. What solution would be best used to resolve a lack of public IP addresses?
    - ❑ A. PPP
    - ❑ B. NAT
    - ❑ C. WINS
    - ❑ D. SNMP

Quick Answer: **96**
Detailed Answer: **115**

23. Which protocol employs the IP protocol for error reporting?
    - ❑ A. SNMP
    - ❑ B. ICMP
    - ❑ C. NAT
    - ❑ D. WINS

Quick Answer: **96**
Detailed Answer: **115**

24. Which of the following network protocols developed by Sun Microsystems provides transparent remote file access?
    - ❑ A. NFS
    - ❑ B. TFTP
    - ❑ C. SFTP
    - ❑ D. AFP

Quick Answer: **96**
Detailed Answer: **115**

25. What are the advantages to implement NFS as the remote file access protocol on your system? (Select two correct answers.)
    - ❑ A. NFS can be used across different operating systems.
    - ❑ B. NFS can be used across different network topologies.
    - ❑ C. An NFS client machine can access any machine on the system for shared files.
    - ❑ D. NFS locates and copies the desired file to the client machine.

Quick Answer: **96**
Detailed Answer: **115**

26. Which of the following file sharing protocols is used in an AppleTalk network?
    - ❑ A. NFS
    - ❑ B. FTP
    - ❑ C. SFTP
    - ❑ D. AFP

Quick Answer: **96**
Detailed Answer: **115**

Quick Check

27. What is a major concern when implementing AFP on your system?

Quick Answer: **96**
Detailed Answer: **115**

- ❑ A. Information disclosure vulnerability
- ❑ B. Redundancy of data
- ❑ C. Available for Apple systems only
- ❑ D. Lack of compression capability

28. Which of the following network protocols defines the communications between a server machine and its clients?

Quick Answer: **96**
Detailed Answer: **115**

- ❑ A. NAT
- ❑ B. SNMP
- ❑ C. SMB
- ❑ D. WINS

29. What are the two security levels implemented in the SMB model?

Quick Answer: **96**
Detailed Answer: **116**

- ❑ A. Server
- ❑ B. Share
- ❑ C. User
- ❑ D. Administrator

30. Which of the following is the software used by the print server to manage file printing services?

Quick Answer: **96**
Detailed Answer: **116**

- ❑ A. AFP
- ❑ B. SMB
- ❑ C. SNMP
- ❑ D. LPD

31. What enables a UNIX server to communicate with a Windows PC network?

Quick Answer: **96**
Detailed Answer: **116**

- ❑ A. SMB
- ❑ B. Samba
- ❑ C. NFS
- ❑ D. ICS

32. What is the purpose of applying Zeroconf on an IP network?

Quick Answer: **96**
Detailed Answer: **116**

- ❑ A. To connect nodes in the IP network without configuration
- ❑ B. To configure a client in the IP network as a server
- ❑ C. To troubleshoot the IP network
- ❑ D. To configure a client in the IP network remotely through a server

Quick Check

33. Which of the following are not used in a Zeroconf IP network?
    - ❑ A. Print server
    - ❑ B. DHCP server
    - ❑ C. DNS server
    - ❑ D. RADIUS server

Quick Answer: **96**
Detailed Answer: **116**

Objective 2.14: Identify the Basic Characteristics (For Example, Speed, Capacity, Media) of the Following WAN Technologies: Packet Switching, Circuit Switching, ISDN, FDDI, T1/E1/J1, T3/E3/J3, OC-x, and X.25

1. On an ISDN BRI, how many channels are used to carry data?
    - ❑ A. 16
    - ❑ B. 4
    - ❑ C. 2
    - ❑ D. 23

Quick Answer: **97**
Detailed Answer: **116**

2. Which of the following is an end-to-end digital communication path?
    - ❑ A. POTS
    - ❑ B. PSTN
    - ❑ C. ISDN
    - ❑ D. PPTP

Quick Answer: **97**
Detailed Answer: **116**

3. What is an advantage of ISDN over the plain old telephone system (POTS)?
    - ❑ A. No specialized equipment is needed.
    - ❑ B. It requires an analog modem.
    - ❑ C. It's faster.
    - ❑ D. It's less expensive.

Quick Answer: **97**
Detailed Answer: **116**

4. What kind of network is built with no guarantee of a path between the two devices trying to communicate?
    - ❑ A. Time Division Multiple
    - ❑ B. Connection-oriented
    - ❑ C. Virtual Circuit
    - ❑ D. Connectionless

Quick Answer: **97**
Detailed Answer: **116**

Quick Check

5. What kind of multiplexing technique has the full channel bandwidth available to each user for specific time periods?
   - ❑ A. FDMA
   - ❑ B. TDMA
   - ❑ C. Connectionless
   - ❑ D. Virtual Circuit

Quick Answer: **97**
Detailed Answer: **116**

6. Which of the following is a multiplexing technique with the channel bandwidth divided into discrete units that are permanently made available to all users?
   - ❑ A. FDMA
   - ❑ B. TDMA
   - ❑ C. Connection-oriented
   - ❑ D. Connectionless

Quick Answer: **97**
Detailed Answer: **117**

7. Which two of the following is connection-oriented?
   - ❑ A. RGP
   - ❑ B. Circuit switching
   - ❑ C. HTTP
   - ❑ D. TCP

Quick Answer: **97**
Detailed Answer: **117**

8. TCP is an example of a(n) ____ protocol.
   - ❑ A. access
   - ❑ B. connection-oriented
   - ❑ C. connectionless
   - ❑ D. physical

Quick Answer: **97**
Detailed Answer: **117**

9. How many channels is a circuit-switching network capable of carrying?
   - ❑ A. 4
   - ❑ B. 2
   - ❑ C. 1
   - ❑ D. 16

Quick Answer: **97**
Detailed Answer: **117**

10. What is the maximum length of an FDDI packet?
   - ❑ A. 36,000 bits
   - ❑ B. 20,000 bits
   - ❑ C. 40,000 bits
   - ❑ D. 24,000 bits

Quick Answer: **97**
Detailed Answer: **117**

Quick Check

11. How many voice channels does a T1 facility multiplex?
  - ❑ A. 16
  - ❑ B. 8
  - ❑ C. 24
  - ❑ D. 32

Quick Answer: 97
Detailed Answer: 117

12. What is the maximum channel capacity of a T3 Carrier line?
  - ❑ A. 1 channel
  - ❑ B. 48 channels
  - ❑ C. 24 channels
  - ❑ D. 672 channels

Quick Answer: 97
Detailed Answer: 117

13. What is the line speed of a T1 Carrier line?
  - ❑ A. 1.544Mbps
  - ❑ B. 89.472Mbps
  - ❑ C. 44.736Mbps
  - ❑ D. 3.152Mbps

Quick Answer: 97
Detailed Answer: 117

14. What is the data rate of a T4 Carrier line?
  - ❑ A. 44.736Mbps
  - ❑ B. 274.176Mbps
  - ❑ C. 3.152Mbps
  - ❑ D. 1.544Mbps

Quick Answer: 97
Detailed Answer: 117

15. What is the line rate in a DSL pulse?
  - ❑ A. 5Mbps
  - ❑ B. 1.544Mbps
  - ❑ C. 1.44Mbps
  - ❑ D. 64kbps

Quick Answer: 97
Detailed Answer: 117

16. What piece of equipment is required to connect older style equipment to an ISDN line?
  - ❑ A. NT1
  - ❑ B. TE2
  - ❑ C. TE1
  - ❑ D. TA

Quick Answer: 97
Detailed Answer: 117

17. What is the data unit length of the ISDN layer protocol?
  - ❑ A. 240 bits
  - ❑ B. 6480 bits
  - ❑ C. 1024 bits
  - ❑ D. 128 bits

Quick Answer: 97
Detailed Answer: 117

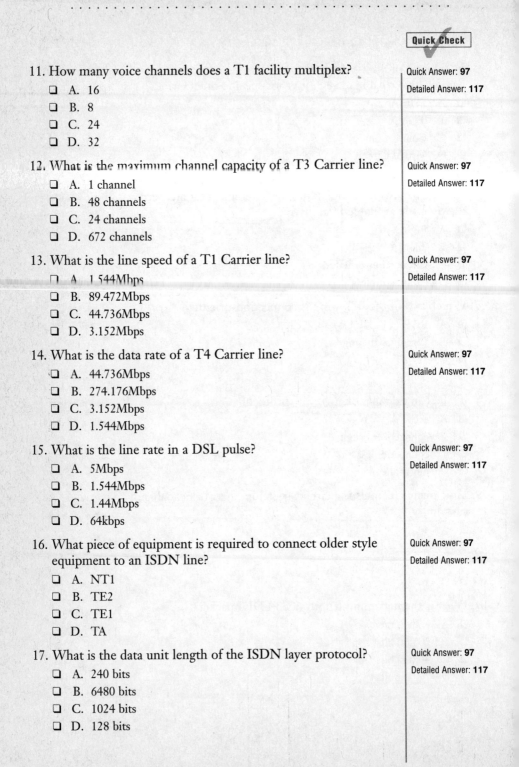

Quick Check

18. Which of the following uses packet switching to transfer data?
    - ❑ A. ISDN
    - ❑ B. X.25
    - ❑ C. DSL
    - ❑ D. ATM

Quick Answer: 97
Detailed Answer: 118

19. What is the size of an X.25 frame?
    - ❑ A. 1500 bytes
    - ❑ B. Variable
    - ❑ C. 192 bits
    - ❑ D. 54 bytes

Quick Answer: 97
Detailed Answer: 118

Objective 2.15: Identify the Basic Characteristics of the Following Internet Access Technologies: xDSL, Broadband Cable, POTS/PSTN, Satellite, and Wireless

1. A client complains that his Internet isn't working. When you go to his office, you note that he's using DSL as his method of accessing the Internet. The user mentions that the Ethernet cable that plugs into the DSL modem does not plug properly into the computer's 56k modem, and that he had to force the Ethernet cable into the modem to get it to fit properly. What should you do to solve the problem?
    - ❑ A. Change the modem settings using the Control Panel Wizards to enable DSL.
    - ❑ B. Replace the Ethernet cable with a phone line.
    - ❑ C. Plug the DSL modem into a workstation via a network interface card.
    - ❑ D. Add a DSL line filter to the phone outlet that the DSL modem plugs into.

Quick Answer: 97
Detailed Answer: 118

Quick Check

2. Your company moves to a new location. Because your company is very small, you use a DSL connection to connect all users to the Internet. When setting up the network, you connect the DSL modem using an RJ-11 connector to the phone outlet, connect the DSL modem to a router using a CAT5 cable, and plug the DSL modem into a power source. You connect all the workstations to the router using CAT5 cable, and put line filters on all phone lines and the phone line used for the DSL modem. When testing the system, none of the users can connect to the Internet. However, after you unplug the DSL modem and remove all the line filters, the phone line is still operational. What is the most likely solution to this situation?

Quick Answer: **97**
Detailed Answer: **118**

- ❑ A. Replace the DSL modem.
- ❑ B. Remove the line filter for the phone line for the DSL modem.
- ❑ C. Connect the DSL modem using an RJ-45 connector to the phone outlet instead.
- ❑ D. Replace the CAT5 cable with coaxial cable.

3. The CIO of your company asks you for technical assistance in choosing an Internet service provider for your company. Because of cost cutting, she is interested in choosing a satellite Internet access solution, but is unfamiliar with how uplinked versus downlinked satellites operate. Which of the following statements is correct regarding satellite Internet access?

Quick Answer: **97**
Detailed Answer: **118**

- ❑ A. Data is uplinked when received by a satellite dish from a satellite in orbit.
- ❑ B. Satellite downlink operation means that a satellite in orbit receives television signals from a satellite transceiver dish.
- ❑ C. Satellite downlink has a maximum download speed of 1.5Mbps.
- ❑ D. In most satellite Internet access systems, the satellite dish uses a transceiver to uplink data to the Web.

Quick Check

4. You install a new wireless network for a client. However, your client has been reading about network security, and asks you to increase the security of the network while maintaining the wireless nature of the network. What do you suggest to accomplish this?

   ❑ A. Connect all workstations to the Wireless Access Point using CAT5.

   ❑ B. Turn on Wired Equivalent Privacy.

   ❑ C. Install more Wireless Access Points throughout the network.

   ❑ D. Change Encryption from 40-bit keys to 16-bit keys.

Quick Answer: 97
Detailed Answer: 118

5. In networking terms, a hot spot is ______.

   ❑ A. a communication zone where wireless connectivity can be established

   ❑ B. an electrically active zone where wireless transmissions can experience interference

   ❑ C. an electrically active zone where wireless connectivity is excellent

   ❑ D. a wireless network access zone set up by businesses to enable portable wireless units to access the Internet

Quick Answer: 97
Detailed Answer: 118

6. Select the answer that correctly describes a feature of the Bluetooth wireless specification.

   ❑ A. The Bluetooth specification has four power levels defined for a variety of operating environments.

   ❑ B. The Bluetooth radio interface operates in the 2.4GHz ISM band and employs Frequency Hopped Spread Spectrum (FHSS) modulation.

   ❑ C. The Bluetooth radio interface operates in the 5.2MHz ISM band and employs Direct Sequence Spread Spectrum (DSSS) modulation.

   ❑ D. The Bluetooth specification has six power levels defined for a variety of operating environments.

Quick Answer: 97
Detailed Answer: 118

Objective 2.16: Define the Function of the Following Remote Access Protocols and Services: RAS, PPP, SLIP, PPPoE, PPTP, VPN and RDP

1. To ensure that access to a remote server is secure, which of the following is the best choice?

   ❑ A. PPTP

   ❑ B. SLIP

   ❑ C. PPP

   ❑ D. FTP

Quick Answer: 97
Detailed Answer: 118

Quick Check

2. Which of the following serial protocols can encapsulate only TCP/IP packets?
   - ❑ A. PPP
   - ❑ B. SLIP
   - ❑ C. PPTP
   - ❑ D. ISDN

Quick Answer: 97
Detailed Answer: 119

3. Which of the following represents an appropriate condition for using PPTP?
   - ❑ A. When a client computer in a LAN connects to a server through a hub
   - ❑ B. When a fiber optic line connects a client and server
   - ❑ C. When a client requires database access
   - ❑ D. When the Internet is used as the communication medium

Quick Answer: 97
Detailed Answer: 119

4. To connect a client who works at home to a corporate server, which of the following is required?
   - ❑ A. RAS
   - ❑ B. L2F
   - ❑ C. Ipv6
   - ❑ D. NetBEUI

Quick Answer: 97
Detailed Answer: 119

5. To configure a remote client so that dial-up RAS access can use multiple Network layer protocols, which of the following should be used?
   - ❑ A. ICA
   - ❑ B. PPP
   - ❑ C. SLIP
   - ❑ D. SPX

Quick Answer: 97
Detailed Answer: 119

6. In the Point-to-Point protocol, what is the protocol responsible for setting up, configuring, maintaining, and terminating the connection?
   - ❑ A. Point-to-Point Tunneling Protocol
   - ❑ B. Password Authentication Protocol
   - ❑ C. Link Control Protocol
   - ❑ D. Network Control Protocol

Quick Answer: 97
Detailed Answer: 119

7. What is *not* a layer protocol of PPP?
   - ❑ A. PPP Link Control Protocol
   - ❑ B. PPP Link Layer Protocol
   - ❑ C. PPP Transport Control Protocol
   - ❑ D. PPP Network Control Protocol

Quick Answer: 97
Detailed Answer: 119

Quick Check

8. To securely transport PPP over the Internet, which of the following should be used?
   - ❑ A. FTP
   - ❑ B. HTTPS
   - ❑ C. PPTP
   - ❑ D. TFTP

Quick Answer: **97**
Detailed Answer: **119**

9. Which of the following protocols is associated with PPTP?
   - ❑ A. RIP
   - ❑ B. TCP/IP
   - ❑ C. NetBEUI
   - ❑ D. IPX

Quick Answer: **97**
Detailed Answer: **119**

10. For secure file transfers to a Windows NT server connected to the Internet, which one of the following protocols should be used?
    - ❑ A. PPTP
    - ❑ B. SLIP
    - ❑ C. NDS
    - ❑ D. PPP

Quick Answer: **97**
Detailed Answer: **119**

11. What is an advantage that PPTP has over PPP when it comes to security?
    - ❑ A. PPTP uses 1024-bit key encryption.
    - ❑ B. There is no advantage.
    - ❑ C. PPP is more secure.
    - ❑ D. PPTP requires that data be encrypted using either PAP or CHAP.

Quick Answer: **97**
Detailed Answer: **119**

12. What protocol was the forerunner to PPP?
    - ❑ A. SLIP
    - ❑ B. PPTP
    - ❑ C. LT2P
    - ❑ D. TCP/IP

Quick Answer: **97**
Detailed Answer: **119**

13. __________ should be used to allow applications to be run from a remote server and appear on a client screen as if actually running on the client.
    - ❑ A. ICA
    - ❑ B. L2F
    - ❑ C. POP3
    - ❑ D. PPTP

Quick Answer: **97**
Detailed Answer: **119**

Quick Check

14. Which of the following protocols is associated with an encrypted VPN connection? (Select all that apply.)
    - ❑ A. SSL
    - ❑ B. PPTP
    - ❑ C. SLIP
    - ❑ D. L2TP

Quick Answer: **97**
Detailed Answer: **119**

15. Which protocol is used to establish dial-up networking connections?
    - ❑ A. PPTP
    - ❑ B. PPP
    - ❑ C. L2TP
    - ❑ D. CHAP

Quick Answer: **97**
Detailed Answer: **120**

16. What is the minimum requirement for a remote user to authenticate to a dial-up connection?
    - ❑ A. An IP address and username
    - ❑ B. A password and username
    - ❑ C. An IP address and password
    - ❑ D. A privately encrypted key

Quick Answer: **97**
Detailed Answer: **120**

17. What information is required to log onto an RAS Server connection?
    - ❑ A. Username, password and domain name
    - ❑ B. Username and password
    - ❑ C. IP address and gateway address
    - ❑ D. Publicly encrypted key

Quick Answer: **97**
Detailed Answer: **120**

18. Which of the following remote access protocols specifies how users on an Ethernet LAN connect to the Internet through a broadband medium?
    - ❑ A. PPPoE
    - ❑ B. RDP
    - ❑ C. PPTP
    - ❑ D. RAS

Quick Answer: **97**
Detailed Answer: **120**

19. Which of the following authentication and security protocols does PPPoE support? (Select two correct answers.)
    - ❑ A. WPA
    - ❑ B. SSL
    - ❑ C. Kerberos
    - ❑ D. PAP

Quick Answer: **97**
Detailed Answer: **120**

Quick Check

20. Which of the following provides remote display and input capabilities over network connections to Windows systems?
    - ❑ A. WPA
    - ❑ B. RDP
    - ❑ C. SLIP
    - ❑ D. PPTP

Quick Answer: **97**
Detailed Answer: **120**

21. Which of the following Windows operating systems support RDP to manage the server remotely? (Select two correct answers.)
    - ❑ A. Windows 95
    - ❑ B. Windows 98SE
    - ❑ C. Windows 2000 Server
    - ❑ D. Windows XP Professional

Quick Answer: **97**
Detailed Answer: **120**

Objective 2.17: Identify the Following Security Protocols and Describe Their Purpose and Function: IPsec, L2TP, SSL, WEP, WPA, and 802.1x

1. Which encryption system can be used on Windows 2000 to ensure that the communication between systems is secured?
    - ❑ A. L2TP
    - ❑ B. SSL
    - ❑ C. IPsec
    - ❑ D. SMB
    - ❑ E. Kerberos

Quick Answer: **98**
Detailed Answer: **120**

2. Which of the following authentication systems uses tickets as part of the authentication process?
    - ❑ A. HTTPS
    - ❑ B. POP3
    - ❑ C. Kerberos
    - ❑ D. SSL

Quick Answer: **98**
Detailed Answer: **120**

3. Which layer of the 7-layer OSI model is the L2F protocol associated with?
    - ❑ A. Layer 3
    - ❑ B. Layer 2
    - ❑ C. Layer 4
    - ❑ D. Layer 5

Quick Answer: **98**
Detailed Answer: **120**

Quick Check

4. What is the purpose of L2TP?

Quick Answer: 98
Detailed Answer: 120

- ❑ A. It encrypts email messages.
- ❑ B. It enables protocols other than IP to be run over a dial-up connection.
- ❑ C. It is used to open the socket between client and server.
- ❑ D. It is a port for downloading audio files.

5. What protocol uses PPP to provide dial-up authentication access?

Quick Answer: 98
Detailed Answer: 121

- ❑ A. PPTP
- ❑ B. IPsec
- ❑ C. LT2P
- ❑ D. L2F

6. What is the purpose of IPsec?

Quick Answer: 98
Detailed Answer: 121

- ❑ A. It provides static addresses for client computers.
- ❑ B. It enables dial-up access to Web servers.
- ❑ C. It offers efficient downloads from Web servers.
- ❑ D. It provides authentication and encryption for Ipv4.

7. Which of the following is a common data encryption technique provided by IPsec?

Quick Answer: 98
Detailed Answer: 121

- ❑ A. Public Key
- ❑ B. ARP
- ❑ C. Parity
- ❑ D. CRC

8. What is not a common feature of IPsec?

Quick Answer: 98
Detailed Answer: 121

- ❑ A. IPsec uses SSL for added data protection.
- ❑ B. IPsec is used only on IP-based networks, not IPX- or NetBEUI-based networks.
- ❑ C. IPsec incorporates the authentication and encryption features of Ipv6 for use over Ipv4 networks.
- ❑ D. IPsec is used only on authentication and encryption at the TCP and IP header.

9. What layer of the 7-layer OSI model is the IPsec protocol?

Quick Answer: 98
Detailed Answer: 121

- ❑ A. Layer 4
- ❑ B. Layer 2
- ❑ C. Layer 3
- ❑ D. Layer 5

Quick Check

10. What is the purpose of SSL?
    - ❑ A. It enables clients to connect to multiple Web servers.
    - ❑ B. It authenticates e-commerce servers or users on the Internet.
    - ❑ C. It enables SLIP to run on PPP connections.
    - ❑ D. It enables users to pay e-commerce sites using any currency.

Quick Answer: **98**
Detailed Answer: **121**

11. What protocol is used to encrypt and decrypt messages using public key encryption?
    - ❑ A. L2TP
    - ❑ B. PPP
    - ❑ C. SSL
    - ❑ D. TCP/IP

Quick Answer: **98**
Detailed Answer: **121**

12. SSL encrypts data between the ______ and Internet server.
    - ❑ A. POP3 server
    - ❑ B. Internet gateway
    - ❑ C. DNS server
    - ❑ D. Internet browser

Quick Answer: **98**
Detailed Answer: **121**

13. _____ is an extension to the PPP protocol that enables Internet Service Providers to provide Virtual Private Networks.
    - ❑ A. PPTP
    - ❑ B. L2TP
    - ❑ C. SFT
    - ❑ D. MSCHAP

Quick Answer: **98**
Detailed Answer: **121**

Objective 2.18: Identify Authentication Protocols (For Example: CHAP, MS-CHAP, PAP, RADIUS, Kerberos, and EAP)

1. What is the purpose of Kerberos?
    - ❑ A. It transports IPX files over the Internet.
    - ❑ B. It allows UDP to replace IP.
    - ❑ C. It monitors usage on websites.
    - ❑ D. It's an authentication tool that employs private key encryption.

Quick Answer: **98**
Detailed Answer: **121**

Quick Check

2. Which of the following authentication systems uses keys as part of the authentication process?

Quick Answer: **98**
Detailed Answer: **122**

- ❑ A. POP3
- ❑ B. Kerberos
- ❑ C. HTTPS
- ❑ D. SSL

3. What is a major feature of Kerberos?
- ❑ A. It uses a private key for encryption.
- ❑ B. It is purely hardware.
- ❑ C. It uses a hash key for encryption.
- ❑ D. It uses a public key for encryption.

4. Which protocol is used to establish mutual authentication for dial-up connections?

Quick Answer: **98**
Detailed Answer: **122**

- ❑ A. Kerberos
- ❑ B. PAP
- ❑ C. PPP
- ❑ D. CHAP

5. Which authentication protocol is used to support the RADIUS protocol?

Quick Answer: **98**
Detailed Answer: **122**

- ❑ A. EAP
- ❑ B. PPP
- ❑ C. SSL
- ❑ D. TLS

6. Your network administrator wants to make certain that the connections to the Remote Access server are mutually authenticated. What protocol should you implement to ensure this?

Quick Answer: **98**
Detailed Answer: **122**

- ❑ A. SSL
- ❑ B. TLS
- ❑ C. HTTPS
- ❑ D. MS-CHAP

7. Which authentication protocol does the Mac OSX mail service use by default?

Quick Answer: **98**
Detailed Answer: **122**

- ❑ A. CHAP
- ❑ B. MS-CHAP
- ❑ C. PAP
- ❑ D. RADIUS

Quick Check

8. Which of the following is an authentication scheme used with PPP?
   - ❑ A. EAP
   - ❑ B. ICA
   - ❑ C. Kerberos
   - ❑ D. CHAP

Quick Answer: 98
Detailed Answer: 122

9. What is CHAP?
   - ❑ A. A means of communicating in real-time on the Internet
   - ❑ B. A means of sending multiple messages to a Web server
   - ❑ C. An authentication protocol used with PPP
   - ❑ D. A routing protocol used with PPP

Quick Answer: 98
Detailed Answer: 122

10. Which of the following protocols is used for encrypted authentication over a PPP connection?
    - ❑ A. ARP
    - ❑ B. PAP
    - ❑ C. CHAP
    - ❑ D. LDAP

Quick Answer: 98
Detailed Answer: 122

11. Which of the following protocols enables a RAS server to use smart cards?
    - ❑ A. PAP
    - ❑ B. CHAP
    - ❑ C. PPP
    - ❑ D. EAP

Quick Answer: 98
Detailed Answer: 123

12. EAP was designed to supplement ______ for higher security.
    - ❑ A. PPP
    - ❑ B. CHAP
    - ❑ C. MS-CHAP
    - ❑ D. PAP

Quick Answer: 98
Detailed Answer: 123

13. Which of the following is a disadvantage of implementing the PAP protocol on your network system?
    - ❑ A. PAP is used for LAN only.
    - ❑ B. It is less secure than other protocols.
    - ❑ C. There are more components involved in PAP than other similar protocols.
    - ❑ D. PAP is harder to manage than other protocols.

Quick Answer: 98
Detailed Answer: 123

Quick Check

14. Which of the following authentication protocols transmits the username and password over a network in the form of plain text?

    - ❑ A. EAP
    - ❑ B. MS-CHAP
    - ❑ C. CHAP
    - ❑ D. PAP

Quick Answer: 98
Detailed Answer: 123

15. Which of the following authentication methods can only be implemented on a Windows system?

    - ❑ A. EAP
    - ❑ B. MS-CHAP
    - ❑ C. CHAP
    - ❑ D. PAP

Quick Answer: 98
Detailed Answer: 123

16. What is the difference between version 1 and version 2 of MS-CHAP?

    - ❑ A. MS-CHAP v1 supports mutual authentication and MS-CHAP v2 provides one-way authentication.
    - ❑ B. MS-CHAP v1 supports encrypted authentication and MS-CHAP v2 provides plain-text authentication.
    - ❑ C. MS-CHAP v1 supports one-way authentication and MS-CHAP v2 provides mutual authentication.
    - ❑ D. MS-CHAP v1 supports plain-text authentication and MS-CHAP v2 provides encrypted authentication.

Quick Answer: 98
Detailed Answer: 123

Quick Check Answer Key

Objective 2.1: Given an Example, Identify a Media Access Control (MAC) Address

1. A
2. A
3. C
4. A
5. A
6. D

Objective 2.2: Identify the Seven Layers of the OSI Model and Their Functions

1. B
2. A
3. A
4. C
5. A
6. D
7. B
8. B
9. D
10. A
11. D
12. B
13. C
14. B
15. A
16. A
17. B
18. B
19. D
20. A
21. C
22. C
23. C
24. B
25. D
26. C
27. A
28. A
29. B
30. B
31. B
32. C
33. C

Objective 2.3: Identify the OSI Layers at Which the Following Network Devices Operate: Hubs, Switches, Bridges, Routers, NICs, and WAPs

1. A
2. D
3. B
4. A
5. A
6. A
7. C
8. B
9. C
10. D

Quick Check Answer Key

Objective 2.4: Differentiate Between the Network Protocols in Terms of Routing, Addressing Schemes, Interoperability, and Naming Conventions for IPX/SPX, NetBEUI, AppleTalk, and TCP/IP

1. A, B, C
2. C, D
3. B
4. B
5. D
6. C
7. B
8. A
9. A, D
10. C
11. B
12. D
13. C
14. A
15. A
16. B
17. D
18. A
19. A
20. D

Objective 2.5: Identify the Components and Structure of IP Addresses (Ipv4, Ipv6) and Required Settings for Connections Across the Internet

1. C
2. B
3. D

Objective 2.6: Identify Classful IP Address Ranges and Their Default Subnet Masks

1. B
2. D
3. A
4. C
5. C
6. D

Objective 2.7: Identify the Purpose of Subnetting

1. B
2. C
3. C
4. A
5. A
6. B
7. B

Quick Check Answer Key

Objective 2.8: Identify the Differences Between Public Versus Private Network Addressing Schemes

1. D
2. B
3. A
4. D
5. D
6. A

Objective 2.9: Identify and Differentiate Between the Following IP Addressing Methods: Static, Dynamic, and Self-Assigned (APIPA)

1. C
2. D
3. D

Objective 2.10: Define the Purpose, Function, and Use of the Following Protocols Within the TCP/IP Suite: TCP, UDP, FTP, SFTP, TFTP, SMTP, HTTP, HTTPS, POP3/IMAP4, Telnet, SSH, ICMP, ARP, NTP, NNTP, SCP, LDAP, IGMP, and LPR

1. A
2. A
3. B
4. C
5. D
6. A, D
7. B
8. C
9. B
10. A, B, D
11. B, C, D
12. D
13. A, B, D
14. A
15. B
16. A
17. B
18. A
19. A
20. D
21. B
22. A
23. C
24. A
25. B
26. C
27. A
28. C
29. C
30. A
31. D
32. B

Quick Check Answer Key

Objectives 2.11 and 2.12: Define the Function of TCP/UDP Ports and Identify Well-Known Ports Associated with the Following Commonly Used Services and Protocols: FTP, SSH, Telnet, SMTP, DNS, TFTP, HTTP, POP3, NNTP, NTP, IMPA4, and HTTPS

1. C

2. B

3. A

4. A

5. A, D

6. D

7. A

8. D

9. D

10. B

11. A

12. D

13. B

14. C

15. B

16. C

17. C

Objective 2.13: Identify the Purpose of the Following Network Services and Protocols: DHCP/BOOTP, DNS, NAT/ICS, WINS, SNMP, NFS, Zeroconf, SMB, AFP, LDP, and Samba

1. D

2. C

3. A

4. B

5. D

6. A

7. A

8. B

9. A

10. D

11. A

12. D

13. B

14. B

15. B

16. A

17. C

18. B

19. D

20. D

21. B

22. B

23. A

24. A

25. A, B

26. D

27. A

28. C

29. B, C

30. D

31. B

32. A

33. B, C

Quick Check Answer Key

Objective 2.14: Identify the Basic Characteristics (For Example, Speed, Capacity, Media) of the Following WAN Technologies: Packet Switching, Circuit Switching, ISDN, FDDI, T1/E1/J1, T3/E3/J3, OC-x, and X.25

1. C
2. C
3. C
4. D
5. B
6. A
7. A, C
8. B
9. C
10. A, C
11. C
12. D
13. A
14. B
15. B
16. D
17. A
18. B
19. B

Objective 2.15: Identify the Basic Characteristics of the Following Internet Access Technologies: xDSL, Broadband Cable, POTS/PSTN, Satellite, and Wireless

1. C
2. A
3. C
4. B
5. D
6. B

Objective 2.16: Define the Function of the Following Remote Access Protocols and Services: RAS, PPP, SLIP, PPPoE, PPTP, VPN and RDP

1. A
2. B
3. D
4. A
5. B
6. C
7. C
8. C
9. B
10. A
11. D
12. A
13. A
14. B, D
15. B
16. B
17. B
18. A
19. B, C
20. B
21. C, D

Quick Check Answer Key

Objective 2.17: Identify the Following Security Protocols and Describe Their Purpose and Function: IPsec, L2TP, SSL, WEP, WPA, and 802.1x

1. C
2. C
3. B
4. B
5. C
6. D
7. A
8. A
9. C
10. B
11. C
12. D
13. B

Objective 2.18: Identify Authentication Protocols (For Example: CHAP, MS-CHAP, PAP, RADIUS, Kerberos, and EAP)

1. D
2. B
3. A
4. D
5. A
6. D
7. C
8. D
9. C
10. C
11. D
12. A
13. B
14. D
15. B
16. C

Answers and Explanations

Objective 2.1

1. **Answer: A.** 00-D0-59-09-07-51 is a valid MAC address. MAC addresses are represented in six parts, not five. 199.221.34.10 is an example of an IP address. MAC addresses are hexadecimal and can therefore only be comprised of the letters A through F and numbers.

2. **Answer: A.** A six-byte MAC address is unique for each device on a network. MAC addresses are programmed into NIC cards in workstations, so that if the workstation is moved, the MAC addresses are moved with it.

3. **Answer: C.** Ethernet addresses are commonly called "MAC addresses" or "physical addresses." This is used to differentiate them from logical addresses assigned at the Network layer (in Network layer software). Because a MAC address is hard-wired into the circuitry of a node, it must go wherever the node goes. Typically, MAC addresses are displayed in the hexadecimal numbering system. Hexadecimal are base-16 numbers, rather than the base-10 numbers you are accustomed to use when counting. Be able to recognize a valid MAC address.

4. **Answer: A.** You can easily determine a workstation's physical MAC address, IP address, and subnet mask by using the ipconfig utility.

5. **Answer: A.** At each router hop, the router will compare its list of MAC addresses to the destination IP address. If they aren't the same, it will reframe the data and pass it on.

6. **Answer: D.** The first three byte of a MAC address are typically vendor specific because vendors reserve blocks of addresses for their products. This enables the manufacturer to create unique Ethernet addresses for each NIC card.

Objective 2.2

1. **Answer: B.** The Presentation layer is responsible for, among other things, encryption and decryption of datA. The Network layer protocols are responsible for route discovery and network addressing tasks. The Session layer protocols are responsible for establishing, maintaining, and breaking communication sessions between applications. The Physical layer defines the physical characteristics of the network connection.

2. **Answer: A.** The Session layer protocols are responsible for establishing, maintaining, and breaking communication sessions between applications. Application layer protocols allow network functionality to be used by applications and user programs. The Presentation layer functions include encryption, compression, and data format translation. The Network layer protocols are responsible for route discovery and network addressing tasks.

3. **Answer: A.** The Session layer is responsible for setting up and maintaining the dialog between communicating nodes. The Presentation layer is responsible for determining the correct way to present data or user screens. The Application layer is responsible for providing the interface to the network applications, such as FTP or email. The Physical layer is responsible for actual data flow on the network media.

4. **Answer: C.** Network reliability lies with the Transport layer, usually through the use of acknowledgements. The Session layer is responsible for end-to-end node dialog. The Network layer is responsible for routing data. The Data Link layer is responsible for frame formatting and error control.

5. **Answer: A.** The Network layer uses IP addressing to locate a remote node.

6. **Answer: D.** The Network layer needs a logical address so that packets can be routed from network to network.

7. **Answer: B.** The Presentation layer is involved in syntax and the appearance of data as it appears on a monitor screen.

8. **Answer: B.** The Physical layer of the OSI seven layer model is responsible for placing the signal on the network media. The Data Link layer is responsible for physical addressing and media access. The MAC and LLC are sublayers of the Data Link layer.

9. **Answer: D.** The Transmission Control Protocol (TCP) operates at the Transport layer of the OSI model. TCP does not operate at the network, session, or presentation layer.

10. **Answer: A.** Both email and FTP work at the Application layer of the OSI model. They are neither Session layer protocols nor Presentation layer protocols. "User" is not a layer of the OSI model.

11. **Answer: D.** The RS-232 protocol is a hardware protocol that operates asynchronously at the Physical layer of the OSI model.

12. **Answer: B.** The Ethernet protocol operates at the Data Link layer of the OSI model.

13. **Answer: C.** The Application layer provides support to those functions that are necessary to initiate the application.

14. **Answer: B.** Simple Network Management Protocol (SNMP) is used at the Application layer.

15. **Answer: A.** The purpose of the Session layer is to set up a communication dialog that allows two devices to exchange data over a network.

16. **Answer: A.** Another example of a Session layer service involves server message blocks (SMB). Windows operating systems use SMB to maintain connections between devices (computers and servers, or computers and printers, for example) on a network.

17. **Answer: B.** The server will respond with a redirector. A redirector is a software object that receives the request and sends the request to the originating computer. In other words, the redirector will send the file to the computer.

18. **Answer: B.** HTTP is the application used on the World Wide Web portion of the Internet. HTTP is specified at the Application layer, a Web browser is defined in the Presentation layer, and the actual channel is set up between workstation and server at the Session layer.

19. **Answer: D.** A server redirector is handled at the Session layer of the OSI model. The server will respond with a redirector. A redirector is a software object that receives the request and sends the request to the originating computer. In other words, the redirector will send the file to the computer.

20. **Answer: A.** These functions are called classes of service, and they allow data to be sent over a network with varying degrees of quality. They are, strictly speaking, Transport layer functions.

21. **Answer: C.** Examples of Transport layer protocols are TCP, Transmission Control Protocol (used to establish a reliable connection between client and server); and UDP, User Datagram Protocol (simple TCP implementation, without the reliability).

22. **Answer: C.** The Network layer needs a logical address so that packets can be routed from network to network.

23. **Answer: C.** The Network layer determines the actual route the data will take across the network. Routing to the correct network node occurs at the Network layer.

24. **Answer: B.** Because this layer is responsible for forwarding packets onto other stations, it includes a logical addressing scheme. The most common one is called Internet Protocol (IP), which consists of a logical address that may be assigned to a node or to an entire network. The address is logical, meaning that the location of a node with an assigned IP can be moved anywhere, or transferred to another node as needed. This frequently occurs with Internet service providers when they assign so-called "dynamic" IPs to their subscribers. Each time you log on to the Internet (logons occur at the Transport layer), you're assigned a different IP, although your physical address remains unchanged.

25. **Answer: D.** The Logical Link Control sublayer describes conventions to be followed by the sender and the receiver to ensure that the link's communication is reliable and the data flow is orderly.

26. **Answer: C.** The Data Link layer contains two major subdivisions: the Media Access Control (MAC) protocols and the Logical Link Control (LLC) protocols.

27. **Answer: A.** The purpose of the Physical layer is the actual transmission of data. It includes the physical connection of stations to the network, and the parameters of electrical signals, such as the amplitude and polarity of data bits. The OSI Physical layer is quite detailed in its description of the acceptable mechanical and electrical parameters. Unfortunately, the protocol hasn't been widely accepted in the United States.

28. **Answer: A.** The purpose of the Physical layer is the actual transmission of data. It includes the physical connection of stations to the network, and the parameters of electrical signals such as the amplitude and polarity of data bits.

29. **Answer: B.** The OSI Reference Model is a blueprint for data communications. It competes for acceptance with IBM's System Network Architecture (SNA), and Digital Equipment Corporation's Digital Network Architecture (DNA).

30. **Answer: B.** A connectionless protocol doesn't track the sequence of frames or packets of frames. A connectionless service, at the Data Link layer, is Type I LLC. Connectionless frames may also be referred to as Datagrams, a carryover from IBM. A connectionless protocol does not send acknowledgements. There is no way to be certain that a packet has been received with connectionless protocols.

31. **Answer: B.** Although the Ping utility is actually an Application layer program, it uses ICMP to pass datagrams. These datagrams are used to establish that a device is responsive to a query. Because the ICMP protocol functions at the Network layer, the Ping utility by extension operates at this layer.

32. **Answer: C.** The Presentation layer is responsible for code conversion and formatting in addition to compression, encryption, and decryption of data.

33. **Answer: C.** The Presentation layer is responsible for, among other things, encryption and decryption of data. Network layer protocols are responsible for route discovery and logical network addressing tasks. The Session layer protocols are responsible for establishing, maintaining, and breaking communication sessions between applications. The Physical layer defines the physical characteristics of the network connection.

Objective 2.3

1. **Answer: A.** A router makes its forwarding decisions based on the software-configured network address. These addresses are used by protocols that reside at the Network layer of the OSI model. Therefore, a router is said to be a Network layer device. A repeater does not perform any action on the data it receives. Instead, it just regenerates the signal so that it can be transmitted over a longer

distance. A repeater is a Physical Layer device. A hub, like a repeater, does not perform any action on the data apart from, in the case of an active hub, regenerating the signal. A hub is said to be a Physical layer device. A switch makes its forwarding decisions based on the unique hardware configured MAC address, which is burned into each network interface. The MAC address is defined in the MAC sublayer of the Data Link layer of the OSI model, so a switch is defined as a Data Link Layer device.

2. **Answer: D.** A bridge transfers data frames between different network types, independent of the Network layer protocol. A router transfers data packets between different networks. A brouter may operate at either the Network or Data Link layer. A hub passes the data packets without translating the Network layer protocols.

3. **Answer: B.** A brouter contains the functions of a router and a bridge. A bridge operates at the Data Link layer, and a router operates at the Network layer. A gateway performs protocol conversions on all layers of a data communications model.

4. **Answer: A.** A network hub operates at the Physical layer of the OSI model. A router operates at the Network layer of the OSI model. A bridge operates at the Data Link layer of the OSI model. A network interface card (NIC) operates at the Data Link layer of the OSI model.

5. **Answer: A.** For a NIC that can't be configured with PnP, you must manually configure the card. There are two ways to do so. The first is accomplished using a software configuration. The second method requires you to manually position jumper or DIP switches.

6. **Answer: A.** Common hardware associated with the Data Link layer includes NIC cards, adapters, hubs, switches, and bridges (and the bridge portion of brouters).

7. **Answer: C.** Common hardware associated with the Physical layer includes connectors such as RJ-45, SC, and RJ-11; and cabling such as UTP, fiber optic, or coaxial.

8. **Answer: B.** Routers process information at the Network layer (Layer 3) of the OSI model.

9. **Answer: C.** The NIC receives all the packets passing along the network media and reads them to determine whether they are intended for that node. This is determined by examining the MAC address in the header of the packet to see whether it matches that of the card.

10. **Answer: D.** Routers process information at the Network layer (Layer 3) of the OSI model.

Objective 2.4

1. **Answers: A, B, C.** The Dynamic Host Configuration Protocol (DHCP), the Transmission Control Protocol (TCP), and the Hypertext Transfer Protocol (HTTP) are all part of the TCP/IP protocol suite. The Sequenced Packet Exchange (SPX) protocol is a connection-oriented transport protocol that is part of the IPX/SPX protocol suite. The Netware Link State Protocol (NLSP) is a link state routing protocol used on IPX-based networks.
2. **Answers: C, D.** Because there are multiple segments, a routable protocol is required. Both NetWare and Windows 2000 support the routable TCP/IP and IPX. The Point-to-Point protocol (PPP) is used for dial-up connections, not as a network transport protocol. NetBEUI is not a routable protocol, nor is it supported by NetWare. Therefore, it is not a suitable protocol for the given configuration.
3. **Answer: B.** NetBIOS computer names can be up to 15 characters in length and can contain spaces. ADE4:DC34:0800:4C32:B003 is an example of an IPX address, not a NetBIOS computer name. 00-0C-D1-E4-C3-F4 is an example of a MAC address, not a NetBIOS computer name.
4. **Answer: B.** IPX is a routable protocol because it includes appropriate addressing fields in the header. NetBEUI isn't routable because it relies on NetBIOS computer names for routing. IPX is a proprietary Network layer protocol of Novell. NetWare client software must be installed for IPX. IPX is based on IEEE 802.3 Ethernet, so collisions will be a normal part of the network operation.
5. **Answer: D.** IPX is the proprietary protocol of Novell NetWare. Questions like this can be tricky. In some situations, IPX may be found with any of the network operating systems listed.
6. **Answer: C.** With NetBEUI, an IP or IPX address isn't needed because computer names are used as addresses. An IP or an IPX address is required with TCP/IP, NetWare, or UNIX.
7. **Answer: B.** NetBEUI doesn't include enough addressing information to guarantee routing. UDP, IP, and TCP are all incorrect because each of them uses the logical addressing schemes of IP.
8. **Answer: A.** Routable protocols contain a field for logical addresses that include a network and host number. Nonroutable protocols don't have this field.
9. **Answers: A, D.** IP and IPX are responsible for network addressing. SPX and TCP are Transport layer protocols and so are not responsible for network addressing.

10. **Answer**: **C.** The AppleTalk Address Resolution Protocol (AARP) is used to map the AppleTalk addresses to both Ethernet and token ring physical addresses. The distance vector routing protocol used on AppleTalk networks is RMTP. AARP resolves AppleTalk addresses to MAC addresses, not the other way around. AARP is not a link state routing protocol.

11. **Answer**: **B.** With NetBEUI, an IP or IPX address isn't needed because computer names are used as addresses. An IP or an IPX address is required with TCP/IP, NetWare, or UNIX.

12. **Answer**: **D.** Because that system of addressing does not guarantee a unique address for every machine (a computer name can be duplicated from one network to the next), NetBEUI isn't routable. For example, you can't use it to send a message across the Internet to a distant network. (IP or IPX must be used.)

13. **Answer**: **C.** IPX, which stands for Internetworking Packet Exchange, is a proprietary networking protocol used by Novell. It's the default network protocol for all NetWare networks.

14. **Answer**: **A.** IPX is a routable protocol, meaning it can be used to send packets of data between different networks. IPX includes a proprietary Novell addressing scheme that can be routed among many, but not all, types of networks. That is, the addressing used with IPX is nonstandard, so machines that aren't running Novell software don't accept the data contained in the addressed packet.

15. **Answer**: **A.** Because the addressing scheme is very simple, NetBEUI is a fast network protocol. It's typically used in smaller networks that aren't connected to other networks. Windows 9x operating systems include NetBEUI as does Windows NT. It requires little in the way of setup and maintenance on network computers.

16. **Answer**: **B.** Select the IP Address tab in the TCP/IP Properties dialog box. Click on Specify an IP address field. In the IP Address field, enter the assigned IP address for the workstation. In the Subnet Mask field, enter the subnet mask for the network (if one is used). Click OK and restart the computer.

17. **Answer**: **D.** LMHOSTS, also available on Windows 9x and later workstations, performs computer-name-to-IP-address resolution as well.

18. **Answer**: **A.** A connectionless service doesn't guarantee delivery. UDP is an example of a connectionless protocol, and TCP is an example of a connection-oriented protocol.

19. **Answer**: **A.** For the Internet, the TCP/IP protocol stack is frequently used to design, build, or describe an internetworking system.

20. **Answer: D.** The minimum requirements for establishing a TCP/IP connection to the Internet include an IP address, a subnet mask, and a default gateway setting.

Objective 2.5

1. **Answer: C.** Ipv6 addresses are expressed in hexadecimal format with the letters A through F and numbers, and each octet is separated by colons. A typical example of an Ipv6 address is 1080:BA56:1234:5678:8ABC:DEF1:74A2:89C1.

2. **Answer: B.** IMAP4 (Internet Message Access Protocol v.4) is a client/server protocol used to store, retrieve, and manipulate email messages. Unlike POP3, you can search through email messages stored on a mail server for a keyword with IMAP4, and use the result to determine which messages you want to download from the server.

3. **Answer: D.** IMAP4 enables multiple simultaneous accesses to a single mailbox. If the mail server supports this feature, several client machines can read messages from the same inbox at the same time by utilizing IMAP4.

Objective 2.6

1. **Answer: B.** The subnet mask defines what portion of the IP address refers to the network portion and what part refers to the node. In this question, the subnet mask of 255.255.0.0 means that the network address is 212.16. For 212.16.175 to be correct, the subnet mask would have to be 255.255.255.0. 212.16.24 is incorrect because it shows the third octet as 24 when in fact it is 175. 212.16.175.24 actually gives the entire IP address.

2. **Answer: D.** Class C addresses range from 192 to 223. The maximum value of an octet is 255. Therefore, 211.261.145.16 is not a valid IP address. 191.23.145.16 is a Class B address. 12.17.221.6 is a Class A address.

3. **Answer: A.** The first three decimal numbers of a Class C IP address fall in the range of 192 through 223.

4. **Answer: C.** It's the only Class B address listed. 192.168.22.1 is a Class C address. 10.15.13.1 is a Class A address. 127.0.0.1 is a Class C address.

5. **Answer: C.** A Class A address can accommodate 224 –2 = 16,777,214 hosts, with 24 bits in the host field. The reason 2 is subtracted is that 0.0.0.0 is reserved for the default network, and 127.0.0.10 is reserved for a loopback test. Datagrams can be sent to 27 – 2 = 126 destination networks. At this time, all Class A addresses have been assigned.

6. **Answer: D.** The first two bytes of a Class B address are the network address, along with the 2-bit class identifier, and the last two bytes are the host number.

Objective 2.7

1. **Answer: B.** The term *subnetting* is used to refer to the process of using parts of the node address range for network addressing purposes. Supernetting refers to the process of borrowing parts of the network address portion of an assigned address to be used for node addressing. Subnet masking is the term used to describe the process of applying a subnet mask to an address. Super routing is not a valid term.

2. **Answer: C.** The best method of testing a server in line with the network is to create a test network to keep it from interfering with other units on the operational network. In the other scenarios, the server could be running services such as DHCP that could interfere with the production servers and services.

3. **Answer: C.** 255.255.0.0 includes the only subnet mask for a Class B address. 255.0.0.0 is the subnet mask for a Class A address. 255.255.255.0 is the default subnet mask for a Class C address. 255.255.255.224 represents a subnet mask for a subnetted Class C address.

4. **Answer: A.** 255.255.0.0 includes the only subnet mask for a Class B address. 255.0.0.0 is the subnet mask for a Class A address. 255.255.255.0 is the default subnet mask for a Class C address. 255.255.255.224 is a subnetted subnet mask.

5. **Answer: A.** A Class A IP address with the first byte reserved for network addresses has a default subnet mask of 255.0.0.0.

6. **Answer: B.** The natural mask for a Class A address is 255.0.0.0, and 255.255.0.0 for a Class B address.

7. **Answer: B.** An IP subnet *mask* is used in a TCP/IP network to isolate the network portion from the host portion of an IP address. This is done because NIC cards need to determine whether a packet will be going to another station on the local network, or to a station on an entirely different network.

Objective 2.8

1. **Answer: D.** Encryption masks the actual meaning of the data. This is important for financial transactions as well as those who work from their home and connect to a corporate server or intranet.

2. **Answer: B.** There are private address ranges designed for use on private networks. The commonly used ranges are 192.168.0.0 – 192.168.255.255, 10.0.0.0 – 10.255.255.255, and 172.16.0.0 – 172.31.255.255.

3. **Answer: A.** The most promising technology to date for reining in data and telecommunications costs is a virtual local area network (VLAN). A virtual private network (VPN) is a popular type of VLAN that uses special security and encryption techniques to provide secure and private connections across a public network such as the Internet.

4. **Answer: D.** Internet Assigned Numbers Authority (IANA) is responsible for assigning IP addresses for systems on public networks, specifically the Internet. Domain names are administered by domain registry organizations. You don't need to apply for a network address for use on a private network.

5. **Answer: D.** 172.x.x.x is a range of addresses set aside for private IP addresses.

6. **Answer: A.** 127.x.x.x is a range of reserved addresses and includes specific addresses for network testing.

Objective 2.9

1. **Answer: C.** When a DHCP-enabled client first starts up, it sends a message to the DHCP server requesting an IP address and subnet mask. When the client receives and accepts the IP address offer, the IP address is leased to that client for a specified period of time.

2. **Answer: D.** ISPs and other network outsiders cannot access private IP addresses. This is the point of a private IP address.

3. **Answer: D.** When a DHCP server is not available, APIPA enables a workstation to configure itself with an APIPA address (between 169.254.0.1 and 169.254.255.254), which is a good indication of a DHCP server failure.

Objective 2.10

1. **Answer: A.** The Transmission Control Protocol (TCP) offers a connection-oriented transport protocol with advanced error correction and recovery capabilities. Internetwork Packet Exchange (IPX) is a connectionless, best-effort delivery protocol used by the IPX/SPX protocol suite. The Address Resolution Protocol (ARP) resolves IP addresses to MAC addresses and is not used as a transport protocol. The Internet Protocol (IP) is a connectionless, best-effort delivery protocol used by the TCP/IP protocol suite.

2. **Answer: A.** The Network Time Protocol (NTP) is used to communicate time synchronization information between servers. It is commonly used on the Internet, but it can also be used on private networks.

3. **Answer: B.** UDP is a connectionless transport protocol and therefore operates at the Transport layer of the OSI model. Session layer protocols are responsible for setup, maintenance, and tear-down of sessions between applications. Network layer protocols deal with functions such as route discovery and addressing. There is no such thing as the Connection layer.

4. **Answer: C.** FTP software allows files to be uploaded and downloaded to a remote system. Telnet is terminal emulation software. Samba is a product that can be installed on a Linux system that provides file and print service capabili-

ties to Windows-based clients. Squid is a product that provides caching proxy server functionality.

5. **Answer: D.** The Simple Mail Transfer Protocol (SMTP) is used to send email. The Internet Message Access Protocol (IMAP) is used for retrieving email, not sending it. The Post Office Protocol (POP) is used for retrieving email, not sending it. The Network Time Protocol (NTP) is used for communicating time information between systems.
6. **Answers: A, D.** The File Transfer Protocol (FTP) and the HyperText Transfer Protocol (HTTP) use a connection-oriented transport protocol, TCP. The Trivial File Transfer Protocol (TFTP) uses a connectionless transport protocol (UDP). There is no such protocol as RGP.
7. **Answer: B.** Connection-oriented is synonymous with reliability in networking. TCP ensures a reliable connection, typically by sending acknowledgements to the sending node from the receiving node. TCP will be bundled with a Network layer protocol, such as IP. TCP is a reliable protocol, as opposed to UDP, which is connectionless, or unreliable.
8. **Answer: C.** UDP, User Datagram Protocol, doesn't include acknowledgements in the packet header. Both TCP and IPX use acknowledgements because they are connection-oriented protocols. NetBEUI is a Network layer protocol and not a Transport layer protocol.
9. **Answer: B.** The FTP protocol can be used to transfer files between Windows and UNIX systems. FTP is part of the TCP/IP protocol suite and is platform independent. The Telnet utility is used to open a virtual terminal session on a remote host. The Point-to-Point Protocol (PPP) is used to establish communications over a serial link. The Point-to-Point Tunneling Protocol (PPTP) is used to establish a secure link over a public network such as the Internet.
10. **Answers: A, B, D.** The File Transfer Protocol (FTP), the Dynamic Host Configuration Protocol (DHCP), and the HyperText Transfer Protocol (HTTP) are all protocols in the TCP/IP protocol suite. AFP is the AppleTalk Filing Protocol and part of the AppleTalk protocol suite.
11. **Answers: B, C, D.** The User Datagram Protocol (UDP), the Internetwork Packet Exchange (IPX), and the Internet Protocol (IP) are all connectionless protocols. The Sequenced Packet Exchange (SPX) protocol is a connection-oriented protocol.
12. **Answer: D.** The Simple Mail Transfer Protocol (SMTP) is used for sending email. NMP is not a valid answer. POP3 is an email retrieval protocol, not a protocol for sending email. IMAP is an email retrieval protocol, not a protocol for sending email.

13. **Answers: A, B, D.** The File Transfer Protocol (FTP), the Dynamic Host Configuration Protocol (DHCP), and the Hypertext Transfer Protocol (HTTP) are all protocols in the TCP/IP protocol suite. AFP is the AppleTalk Filing Protocol and part of the AppleTalk protocol suite. The NetWare Core Protocol (NCP) is part of the IPX/SPX protocol suite.

14. **Answer: A.** UDP, User Datagram Protocol, doesn't include acknowledgements in the packet header. Both TCP and IPX use acknowledgements because they are connection-oriented protocols. NetBEUI is a Network layer protocol and not a Transport layer protocol.

15. **Answer: B.** The FTP protocol can be used to transfer files between Windows and UNIX systems. FTP is part of the TCP/IP protocol suite and is platform independent.

16. **Answer: A.** Before you can send or receive email, you must have access to a server running the SMTP protocol. The client workstation connected to the mail server must have access to the email server that runs SMTP. The protocol that defines email is called the Simple Mail Transport Protocol, or SMTP.

17. **Answer: B.** SMTP is the Application layer protocol for sending email.

18. **Answer: A.** POP3 mimics the SMTP end of an email dialogue and stores the received message until you ask to retrieve it. POP3 is a client-side protocol that must be installed on the workstation in order for email to be downloaded to the client. That way, your email is automatic and continues to be received when you're not around to handle it yourself, or when you're not connected to the Internet.

19. **Answer: A.** POP3 mimics the SMTP end of an email dialogue and stores the received message until you ask to retrieve it. POP3 is a client-side protocol that must be installed on the workstation in order for email to be downloaded to the client. That way, your email is automatic and continues to be received when you're not around to handle it yourself, or when you're not connected to the Internet.

20. **Answer: D.** HTTP, or HyperText Transfer Protocol, is a client-server protocol used to send and receive files on the Internet. Most Internet applications on the World Wide Web (WWW) use HTTP.

21. **Answer: B.** Telnet includes a command-line interface similar to a DOS-based system. Most Web browsers do not include a client for Telnet access. Most operating systems include a utility that allows you to launch Telnet from a DOS shell (for Windows) by entering telnet at the command prompt. For other operating systems, a terminal emulator may be needed along with a telnet client. A terminal emulator is a software package that allows a terminal to mimic another terminal type.

22. **Answer: A.** SSH (Secure Shell) provides a secure client/server connection and is primarily used to protect Web commerce for encrypted remote connectivity.
23. **Answer: C.** Lightweight Directory Access Protocol (LDAP) is a client-server protocol that allows users to access remote database servers. LDAP uses TCP/IP as the Transport layer protocol, which allows any client running TCP/IP to access an LDAP server.
24. **Answer: A.** A directory server uses the LDAP (Lightweight Directory Access Protocol) protocol to access and search information that's distributed in a directory.
25. **Answer: B.** TFTP is a simplified version of FTP. TFTP provides no security in the form of password prompts. Essentially, it's even less secure than FTP.
26. **Answer: C.** TFTP does not provide any authentication before allowing downloads.
27. **Answer: A.** A news server uses the Network News Transport Protocol (NNTP) to store messages and to allow messages to be sent for others to read.
28. **Answer: C.** News is an Internet service that includes Usenet News. NNTP is the protocol that allows a client to read the Usenet articles from a server running the NNTP protocol.
29. **Answer: C.** The primary NTP time server acquires accurate timekeeping information from national standards through an external radio clock and passes this information to other secondary time servers or clients. It also crosschecks system clocks and corrects error due to equipment or propagation failures.
30. **Answer: A.** In a system of interconnected networks utilizing the Internet Protocol (IP) for host-to-host service, an error might be found in processing packets. The Internet Control Message Protocol (ICMP) is used by the gateway or the destination host to report these datagram processing errors to the source host machine.
31. **Answer: D.** Some network hosts only know their network interface addresses, but not their protocol addresses. They rely on the RARP server to resolve their IP addresses to communicate with other network hosts.
32. **Answer: B.** IGMP (Internet Group Management Protocol) is designed to support IP multicasting in the Internet. When a multicast datagram is delivered to a single IP address for a host group, all members in that group receive the datagram.

Objectives 2.11 and 2.12

1. **Answer: C.** FTP uses TCP/IP port 21 for its communications. Telnet uses Port 23. HTTP uses Port 80 and POP3 uses Port 110.

2. **Answer: B.** Port 80 is the default port number of the HTTP protocol. SMTP uses port 25 by default. NTP uses port 123 by default. FTP uses port 21 by default.
3. **Answer: A.** HTTP always launches at port 80. Port 25 is for SMTP. Port 110 is for POP3. Port 21 is for FTP.
4. **Answer: A.** The service to which a data packet is destined is determined by the port number, not the packet ID number, data IP number, or IP protocol service type, to which it is sent.
5. **Answers: A, D.** TCP/IP port 25 is used by the SMTP protocol. TCP/IP port 110 is used by the Post Office protocol (POP3). Because SMTP is used to send mail and POP3 is used to retrieve mail these are the two ports that would need to be allowed for incoming and outgoing mail. TCP/IP port 21 is used by FTP. TCP/IP port 80 is used by HTTP. TCP/IP port 443 is used by HTTPS.
6. **Answer: D.** The Domain Name System (DNS) uses TCP port 53. Port 21 is used by FTP. Port 25 is used by SMTP. Port 110 is used by POP3.
7. **Answer: A.** HTTP is always launched at port 80. Port 25 is for SMTP. Port 110 is for POP3. Port 21 is for FTP.
8. **Answer: D.** Port 53 is used to convert URLs into IP addresses. It is part of RFC 1034 and 1035. In this example, port 53 operation is blocked preventing this conversion function from working (preventing the request from being forwarded to the DNS server). The IP address simply passes through the firewall without the need to be converted.
9. **Answer: D.** IMAP uses port 143 by default. Port 123 is used for the Network Time protocol. Port 443 is for HTTPS. Port 119 is used by the NNTP protocol.
10. **Answer: B.** SSH is always launched at port 22. Port 53 is used by the DNS service. Port 119 is used by the NNTP protocol. The IMAP protocol uses port 143.
11. **Answer: A.** TFTP is always launched at port 69. Port 22 is for SSH operations. Port 443 is for HTTPS. Port 123 is used for the Network Time function.
12. **Answer: D.** The NNTP protocol employs port 119. Port 443 is for HTTPS. Port 69 is used with the TFTP protocol. Port 123 is used for the Network Time function.
13. **Answer: B.** The Network Time function uses port 123. Port 443 is for HTTPS. Port 53 is used by the DNS service. Port 69 is used with the TFTP protocol.

14. **Answer: C.** Secure HTTP (HTTPS) has been designated as using port 443. Port 123 is used for the Network Time protocol. Port 137 is for NetBIOS Name Service. Port 119 is used by the NNTP protocol.

15. **Answer: B.** The TCP/IP port number 23 is used by the Telnet service.

16. **Answer: C.** The well-known port number for SMTP is 25.

17. **Answer: C.** The well-known port number for POP3 is 110.

Objective 2.13

1. **Answer: D.** The Domain Name System (DNS) resolves Fully Qualified Domain Names (FQDNs) to IP addresses. The Dynamic Host Configuration Protocol (DHCP) provides automatic IP address assignment. The Windows Internet Naming Service (WINS) provides NetBIOS computer names to IP address resolution. The Address Resolution Protocol (ARP) resolves IP addresses to MAC addresses. The Network Time Protocol (NTP) facilitates the communication of time information between systems.

2. **Answer: C.** Internet Connection Sharing (ICS) is a feature of certain Windows operating systems, including Windows 2000. ICS is not a feature of Linux or Novell NetWare, although it can be used for Internet access. ICS was not included with Windows 95.

3. **Answer: A.** SNMP messages sent by agents when a threshold is exceeded or an event occurs are called trap messages. Event, Alert, and Alarm are not correct terms.

4. **Answer: B.** Only a node with an IP address is a host. This is a narrow definition but the only correct one for this exam. A network with NetBEUI running doesn't use IP addressing. In any network, all nodes have a MAC address. Not all network devices (such as simple hubs) require an IP address.

5. **Answer: D.** Domain Name System is used to reconcile Internet domain names to IP addresses. ARP is used to reconcile MAC to IP addresses. NDS refers to the Novell NetWare directory service. WINS is used to reconcile NetBIOS computer names to IP addresses.

6. **Answer: A.** A DNS search begins with the local DNS server, which is site.com. Assuming the local DNS server can't locate the remote site, the search is escalated to a root server. Root servers in North America can be identified by the suffix in an Internet domain name, .com in the question. Assuming the remote site still can't be found, the search will move to a root server in the United Kingdom. Outside North America, root servers are identified by a country code, or uk in the question. The search percolates down through the sub-DNS servers until an exact match is found.

7. **Answer: A.** WINS, or Windows Internet Naming Service, is used to convert NetBIOS computer names to IP addresses.

8. **Answer: B.** DHCP assigns IP addresses to clients on an as-needed basis.

9. **Answer: A.** Name resolution doesn't perform protocol conversions. A bridge can't route logical addresses.

10. **Answer: D.** A DHCP server does not supply the NetBIOS computer name to client systems. The IP address is one of the pieces of information provided by the DHCP server. The subnet mask is also one of the pieces of information provided by DHCP. The default gateway is another one of the pieces of information supplied by DHCP.

11. **Answer: A.** Domain Name System is used to reconcile Internet domain names to IP addresses. ARP is used to reconcile MAC to IP addresses. NDS refers to the Novell NetWare directory service. WINS is used to reconcile NetBIOS computer names to IP addresses.

12. **Answer: D.** BootP (Boot Protocol) allows a diskless client to boot from a remote server in order to determine its IP address.

13. **Answer: B.** A diskless client means that the client may not have the standard hard drive featured in computers. Instead, the client, such as a router, switch, or sophisticated hub, has nonvolatile RAM (random access memory) that is used to load a file that will boot the client. BootP uses a command-line interface and is best suited to UNIX environments. With the preponderance of NetWare and Windows, an opportunity was presented to make the interface easier while expanding the options of BootP. The resulting improvement is called DHCP.

14. **Answer: B.** BootP has been the most common method used to assign IP addresses to remote clients. It alleviated increasing the complexity of client hardware for assigning a static IP. Essentially, then, BootP is a method for dynamically assigning IP addresses.

15. **Answer: B.** Dynamic Host Configuration Protocol, or DHCP, is the protocol used for dynamically assigning IP addresses to remote clients. It's used on many local networks, and used almost exclusively by ISPs when assigning IP addresses to computers connecting to the Internet.

16. **Answer: A.** Windows Internet Naming Service, WINS, is responsible for reconciling Microsoft NetBIOS names to IP addresses.

17. **Answer: C.** \\EAST1\DOCUMENT is the standard Universal Naming Convention (UNC) method for connecting to a file named DOCUMENT located on a network server named EAST1. Note that the syntax begins with

two forward slashes, followed by the computer name, a single forward slash, then the name of a file, directory, etc.

18. **Answer: B.** WINS, or Windows Internet Naming Service, is used to convert NetBIOS computer names to IP addresses.

19. **Answer: D.** Windows Internet Naming Service, WINS, is responsible for reconciling Microsoft NetBIOS names to IP addresses.

20. **Answer: D.** The standard format for specifying a connection according to the Universal Naming Convention (UNC) is \\servername\sharename(folder name). Note that the syntax begins with two forward slashes, followed by the computer name, a single forward slash, then the name of a file, directory, etc.

21. **Answer: B.** SNMP, or Simple Network Management Protocol, is used to manage networks.

22. **Answer: B.** The purpose of NAT is to conserve Ipv4 address assignments by encouraging the use of private IP addresses on a LAN, while still allowing the LAN nodes Internet access. To access the Internet, the private IP address used by the LAN nodes must be replaced with a public IP address. NAT is the protocol used to make the switch in IP addresses.

23. **Answer: A.** The Simple Network Management Protocol (SNMP) is a network management protocol that provides many services, one of which is using IP to report errors.

24. **Answer: A.** Developed by Sun Microsystems and designated as a file server standard, NFS (Network File System) is a client/server application that enables a user to access files on a remote NFS server from a NFS client as though they were on the user's own computer.

25. **Answers: A, B.** NFS can be used across different operating systems, network topologies, and transport protocols.

26. **Answer: D.** AFP (AppleTalk File Protocol) is the file sharing protocol used in an AppleTalk network. It is designed to provide file sharing service over TCP/IP.

27. **Answer: A.** AFP (AppleTalk File Protocol) allows unencrypted login information to be sent over an unsecure connection. Local attackers can gain privileges on an Apple Mac OS X machine using the exposed administrative password.

28. **Answer: C.** SMB (Server Message Block) is a network protocol that defines communications between a server and a client. It is used to share files, printers, serial ports, and communications abstractions, such as named pipes and mail slots between computers over a network.

29. **Answers: B, C.** The SMB model defines two levels of security: share level and user level. Each share on a server is protected using a password. Individual files in each share are protected based on user access rights. Users can access network resources only after logging into the server and being authenticated by the server.

30. **Answer: D.** A Line Printer Daemon (LPD) stored in the printer or print server prints a file at the request of an LPR (line printer remote) client over a network. If the printer is not available, the LPD queues the file and prints it when the printer becomes available.

31. **Answer: B.** Samba is a suite of UNIX applications supporting the SMB (Server Message Block) protocol that is also used by Windows to achieve the server/client networking function. Therefore, a UNIX server with Samba installed on it can serve a Windows network system efficiently, and make it possible for UNIX and Windows clients to coexist in a network.

32. **Answer: A.** Zeroconf, short for zero configuration networking, is a method used to establish an IP network without requiring any manual configuration.

33. **Answers: B, C.** Zeroconf allocates link-local addresses automatically without a DHCP server. It also enables each node to manage its own domain name-to-IP address mapping without a DNS server.

Objective 2.14

1. **Answer**: **C.** ISDN BRI uses two channels to carry the data and one D channel to carry the signaling information.

2. **Answer**: **C.** PSTN and POTS concern the analog dial-up network. PPTP is a serial protocol that will transport over digital or analog connections. Only ISDN is an end-to-end digital implementation.

3. **Answer**: **C.** Integrated Services Digital Network (ISDN) is a set of digital services that are available over telephone lines. ISDN is a complete digital solution from end-user to end-user. Because the connection is all digital, data rates can be much higher than on an analog telephone connection, as high as 128 kbps.

4. **Answer**: **D.** A connectionless network is one in which there is no guarantee of a path between two end-devices, or that the bandwidth will be available for the two devices to communicate. This type of connection is often called "best-effort."

5. **Answer**: **B.** Time Division Multiple Access (TDMA) is a multiplexing technique in which the full channel bandwidth is available to each user for specific time periods. All of the bandwidth technology types described in this section use TDMA.

6. **Answer: A.** Frequency Division Multiple Access (FDMA) is a multiplexing technique in which the channel bandwidth is divided into discrete units that are permanently made available to all users. Broadcast AM, FM, and television are examples of FDMA.

7. **Answer: A, C.** Connectionless protocols such as UDP (User Datagram Protocol) and HTTP (Hypertext Transfer Protocol) use a best-effort strategy for sending data packets.

8. **Answer: B.** A connection-oriented network, when applied to wide area networks (WANs), refers to the guarantee of a transmission path or bandwidth. A virtual circuit is an example of a connection-oriented network. The most common connection-oriented protocol is TCP.

9. **Answer: C.** The capacity of circuit switching carries only one channel.

10. **Answer: A, C.** A FDDI packet has a maximum length of 36,000 bits.

11. **Answer: C.** The most common T-Carrier group is the T1. A T1 facility multiplexes 24 voice channels. Each channel is transmitted at 64 kbps for a total T1 data rate of 1.544Mbps.

12. **Answer: D.** Seven T2 facilities are multiplexed at the T3 facility to produce the 672-channel DS-3 signal. Six T3 groups are multiplexed to form the 274.176Mbps T4 carrier. The T4 facility produces 4032 voice channels.

13. **Answer: A.** The most common T-Carrier group is the T1. A T1 facility multiplexes 24 voice channels. Each channel is transmitted at 64 kbps for a total T1 data rate of 1.544Mbps.

14. **Answer: B.** Six T3 groups are multiplexed to form the 274.176Mbps T4 carriers. The T4 facility produces 4,032 voice channels.

15. **Answer: B.** A DS1 pulse has positive amplitude of 3.0 volts and a line rate of 1.544Mbps.

16. **Answer: D.** A terminal adapter is needed only to connect older style equipment to an ISDN line. The analog telephone is shown with a TA because it's not ISDN-ready. TAs are sometimes, incorrectly, called ISDN modems. A TA may be either a standalone device, or a printed circuit board inside the TE2 device.

17. **Answer: A.** The data unit length of an ISDN is 240 bits. At the U interface, ISDN frames are combined into a single unit that contains five 48-bit frames. This gives a total length of 240 bits. This is the size of the frame that's sent from the ISDN switch to the NT1 at the subscriber side. Bit times on an ISDN line are 6.25 μs, for a total bandwidth of 160 kbps.

18. **Answer: B.** X.25 packet switching is an older transport protocol used in WANs, and is modeled after the public telephone system. X.25 is an interface standard that describes the connection of data-terminal equipment and data-communication equipment to public switching networks.

19. **Answer: B.** X.25 uses a variable-size packet to communicate between two devices.

Objective 2.15

1. **Answer: C.** DSL modems plug into a workstation via a network interface card, which uses an RJ-45 connector. A 56k modem connects directly into a phone line, and does not interact with a DSL modem in any fashion.

2. **Answer: A.** If a filter is put on the DSL connection, the Internet connection might not work correctly.

3. **Answer: C.** Signals are uplinked to a satellite in orbit around the Earth and then downlinked to satellite receiver dishes. In most systems, the satellite dish has no uplink capabilities, so to retrieve information from the Web, they send data through the telephone connection. Download speeds are very good (up to 1.5Mbps) but upload speeds are limited to the 56Kbps speed of the dial-up modem.

4. **Answer: B.** To minimize the risk of security compromise on a wireless LAN, the IEEE-802.11b standard provides a security feature called Wired Equivalent Privacy (WEP). WEP provides a method for encrypting data transmissions and authenticating each computer on the network.

5. **Answer: D.** Notebook computers are natural selections for use as wireless networking clients. Because they are portable, they can be used anywhere within any wireless access point's hot spot. Many enterprises are creating hot spots to enable traveling computer users to access the Internet through their access point for a fee.

6. **Answer: B.** The Bluetooth radio interface operates in the 2.4GHz ISM band and employs Frequency Hopped Spread Spectrum (FHSS) modulation.

Objective 2.16

1. **Answer: A.** PPTP includes authentication methods when a workstation attempts to connect to a remote server. PPP is incorrect because security is an option rather than a requirement. SLIP is incorrect because it also provides optional security. FTP has no security features.

2. **Answer: B.** SLIP is an older serial protocol that works as well as PPP as long as TCP/IP is the only routed protocol that will be used in the remote connection. Both PPP and PPTP support other protocols, such as Novell IXP. ISDN isn't a serial protocol.
3. **Answer: D.** Using the Internet infrastructure as a communication channel between client and remote server is one of the applications of PPTP. The use of a fiber-optic channel between remote client and server has no bearing on PPTP. The client may very well be using the remote access account for database work, but this has no bearing on the decision to use PPTP. Local LANs do not use PPTP.
4. **Answer: A.** Remote Access Service (RAS) refers to the techniques and practices employed in connecting a client computer to the services of a remote server.
5. **Answer: B.** Remote access protocols refer to the protocols used to set up, maintain, and transfer data across the remote connection. The most common RAS protocols that handle these tasks are PPP, PPTP, and SLIP.
6. **Answer: C.** The Link Control Protocol is responsible for setting up, configuring, maintaining, and terminating the connection.
7. **Answer: C.** Beyond the physical characteristics of the protocol, PPP specifies three components that comprise the protocol: the PPP Link Layer Protocol, the PPP Link Control Protocol, and the PPP Network Control Protocol.
8. **Answer: C.** Point-to-Point Tunneling Protocol (PPTP) is a protocol used to securely transport PPP packets over a TCP/IP network such as the Internet.
9. **Answer: B.** Point-to-Point Tunneling Protocol (PPTP) is a protocol used to securely transport PPP packets over a TCP/IP network such as the Internet.
10. **Answer: A.** Point-to-Point Tunneling Protocol (PPTP) is a protocol used to securely transport PPP packets over a TCP/IP network such as the Internet.
11. **Answer: D.** PPTP offers a distinct advantage over PPP. It requires that data be encrypted (with PPP, encryption is an option) using either PAP or CHAP.
12. **Answer: A.** Serial Line Internet Protocol (SLIP) is the forerunner to PPP.
13. **Answer: A.** ICA, or Independent Computer Architecture, is a server-based technology that allows applications to be run from a remote server and appear on a client screen as if actually running on the screen.
14. **Answers: B, D.** Both the PPTP and L2TP protocols can be used to provide encrypted connections to set up a VPN. Both protocols provide encryption at Level 2, as do all the authentication protocols.

15. **Answer: B.** The PPP protocol is the standard for authentication in dial-up connections.

16. **Answer: B.** Passwords and usernames are the only authentication tools required to log in to a dial-up connection.

17. **Answer: B.** The minimum requirements for logging on to an RAS server are a username and a password.

18. **Answer: A.** Point to Point Protocol over Ethernet (PPPoE) provides the capability to connect hosts on an Ethernet LAN to an ISP through a broadband connection, such as DSL, wireless, and cable modems.

19. **Answers: B, C.** PPPoE supports the Secure Sockets Layer (SSL) security protocol and the Kerberos authentication protocol.

20. **Answer: B.** The Microsoft Remote Desktop Protocol (RDP) manages Windows-based applications running on a server remotely with the encryption and compression capabilities.

21. **Answers: C, D.** RDP (Remote Desktop Protocol) was first introduced with special editions of Windows NT.4.0. It is native to Windows 2000 Server, Windows XP Professional, and Windows 2003 Server.

Objective 2.17

1. **Answer: C.** Windows 2000 uses IPsec, a protocol that allows TCP/IP communications to be encrypted and thus secured. Secure Sockets Layer (SSL) is a technology associated with securely accessing web pages. The Layer 2 Tunneling Protocol (L2TP) is a transport mechanism used on serial connections. The Server Message Block Protocol (SMB) is used for accessing Windows-based file systems. Although Kerberos is a security related protocol, it is used for securing authentication, not data transfer.

2. **Answer: C.** The Kerberos authentication system uses tickets as part of the authentication process. HTTPS is an implementation of the Secure Sockets Layer. It does not use tickets. POP3 is an email retrieval protocol. SSL does not use tickets.

3. **Answer: B.** L2F is a Layer 2 protocol, so it can carry network protocols other than IP such as IPX or NetBEUI.

4. **Answer: B.** L2TP can carry packets from non-IP networks. The tunneling mechanism used with L2TP is based on the multiple-connection tunnel used with L2F. However, a tunnel protocol is being defined for technologies other than IP-based networks (such as the Internet) that includes X.25, Frame Relay, and ATM.

5. **Answer: C.** The L2TP protocol uses PPP to provide dial-up authentication access.
6. **Answer: D.** IP security (IPsec) was developed in conjunction with the next version of IP, IP version 6. Because Ipv6 is compatible with Ipv4, it's being used to provide authentication and encryption for Ipv4-based networks.
7. **Answer: A.** Because the source and destination IP addresses are drawn from a pool of addresses, the source of the packet is protected from intruders on the Internet. IPsec provides for numerous encryption schemes. The list at this time is as follows:
   - Private Key, DES, Triple DES
   - Public Key, RSA
   - Hash Key message digests
   - Digital Certificates
8. **Answer: A.** IP security (IPsec) was developed in conjunction with the next version of IP, IP version 6. Because Ipv6 is compatible with Ipv4, it's being used to provide authentication and encryption for Ipv4-based networks. It incorporates the authentication and encryption features of Ipv6 for use over Ipv4 networks. It is used only on IP-based networks—not IPX or NetBEUI networks. It is used on authentication and encryption at either the TCP or IP header, or both.
9. **Answer: C.** IPsec is a Layer 3 protocol. It can only be used with IP packets; consequently, it won't carry IPX or NetBEUI packets.
10. **Answer: B.** The Secure Socket Layer (SSL) protocol is used to authenticate users or e-commerce servers on the Internet, and to encrypt/ decrypt messages (particularly credit card purchases) using public key encryption.
11. **Answer: C.** The Secure Socket Layer (SSL) protocol is used to authenticate users or e-commerce servers on the Internet, and to encrypt/ decrypt messages (particularly credit card purchases) using public key encryption.
12. **Answer: D.** SSL encrypts data between the Internet browser and Internet server. The protocol consists of a digital certificate that the e-commerce site must possess before a Web browser will be able to authenticate the site.
13. **Answer: B.** PPTP is an extension of the PPP protocol. It provides the encryption mechanisms that are necessary to create the secure tunnel that establishes the VPN connection. It creates a secure session for authentication.

Objective 2.18

1. **Answer: D.** Kerberos authenticates the parties by embedding a key (assigned to each of the parties) in the messages that are exchanged. When a message is sent, the key in the message is compared to the key assigned to the sender. If the two match, the receiving party will know that a trusted party sent the message. Because both parties use the same key, and both parties know the key, the key is a private key.

2. **Answer: B.** Kerberos is an authentication scheme used to identify parties engaged in electronic communication.

3. **Answer: A.** Kerberos is an authentication tool and uses a private key for encryption.

4. **Answer: D.** By applying CHAP, a server sends a random string of bits to a client. The client encrypts the string with a predetermined cipher key and sends it back to the host. The host uses the same key to decrypt the string. If it matches the original random string sent to the client, the connection is opened.

5. **Answer: A.** The Extensible Authentication Protocol (EAP) is one of the authentication protocols that support RADIUS. The other options listed as possible answers do not perform this function.

6. **Answer: D.** MS-CHAP is one of the protocols that can be used to provide mutual authentication for Remote Access connections.

7. **Answer: C.** The Mac OS X operating system offers PAP as the default authentication protocol. However, it also offers the MD-5 Challenge-Response protocol, Kerberos 4 or 5, and Kerberized POP (KPOP).

8. **Answer: D.** Challenge Handshake Authentication Protocol (CHAP). The server generates a random string of bits and sends them, along with its hostname, to the client. The client uses the hostname to look up a cipher key, encrypts the random string, and sends it back to the host. The host uses the same key to decrypt the random string. If it matches the original random string sent to the client, the connection is opened.

9. **Answer: C.** The Challenge Handshake Authentication Protocol (CHAP) is used to authenticate the request of a PPP connection.

10. **Answer: C.** Challenge Handshake Authentication Protocol (CHAP) is used for authentication over a PPP connection. By applying CHAP, a server sends a random string of bits to a client. The client encrypts the string with a predetermined cipher key and sends it back to the host. The host uses the same key to decrypt the string. If it matches the original random string sent to the client, the connection is opened.

11. **Answer: D.** Extensible Authentication Protocol (EAP) enables a RAS server to implement multiple authentication methods, such as token cards, Kerberos, one-time passwords, smart cards, and so on.

12. **Answer: A.** Extensible Authentication Protocol (EAP) was designed to supplement PPP for higher security beyond simply the username and password requirement.

13. **Answer: B.** Password Authentication Protocol (PAP) is a basic form of authentication, which transmits the unencrypted username and password over a network for the authentication purpose.

14. **Answer: D.** Password Authentication Protocol (PAP) is a basic form of authentication, which transmits the unencrypted username and password over a network for the authentication purpose.

15. **Answer: B.** MS-CHAP is Microsoft's proprietary version of CHAP. MS-CHAP encrypts the username and passwords in the authentication process and enables you to encrypt data sent on PPP or PPTP connections.

16. **Answer: C.** MS-CHAP v1 supports one-way authentication (only the RAS server can determine the authenticity of a client), and MS-CHAP v2 provides mutual authentication (both the RAS server and client can identify each other).

Network Implementation

Quick Check

Domain 3.0: Network Implementation

Objective 3.1: Identify the Basic Capabilities (Client Support, Interoperability, Authentication, File and Print Services, Application Support, and Security) of the Following Server Operating Systems: UNIX/Linux, NetWare, Windows, and Appleshare IP (Internet Protocol)

1. You have been given the task of installing Samba on a Linux server. Which services does the product provide?

   ❑ A. File and print services
   ❑ B. Thin client services
   ❑ C. Web server services
   ❑ D. Proxy server services

Quick Answer: **159**
Detailed Answer: **163**

2. Which of the following is an advantage to formatting a Windows NT server drive as NTFS rather than FAT?

   ❑ A. NTFS permits the server to be used as a workstation.
   ❑ B. With NTFS, tape backups aren't needed.
   ❑ C. NTFS offers a higher degree of security.
   ❑ D. NTFS eliminates the need for multiple hard drives.

Quick Answer: **159**
Detailed Answer: **163**

3. NDS is proprietary to which of the following?

   ❑ A. NetWare
   ❑ B. Windows NT
   ❑ C. Windows 9x
   ❑ D. UNIX

Quick Answer: **159**
Detailed Answer: **163**

Quick Check

4. Which one of the following is the directory structure used with Novell NetWare?

❑ A. NTFS
❑ B. FAT
❑ C. NDS
❑ D. Root

Quick Answer: 159
Detailed Answer: 163

5. Which of the following network protocols can be run on a NetWare network?

❑ A. IPX
❑ B. NetBEUI
❑ C. AppleTalk
❑ D. MS-DOS

Quick Answer: 159
Detailed Answer: 163

6. Which of the following is an advantage to formatting a Windows NT server drive as NTFS rather than FAT?

❑ A. With NTFS, tape backups aren't needed.
❑ B. NTFS offers a higher degree of security.
❑ C. NTFS permits the server to be used as a workstation.
❑ D. NTFS eliminates the need for multiple hard drives.

Quick Answer: 159
Detailed Answer: 163

7. Which of the following is an advantage of NTFS over FAT?

❑ A. It permits the server to be used as both server and workstation.
❑ B. It alleviates the need for data backups.
❑ C. It utilizes the disk space far more efficiently than FAT.
❑ D. It directly accesses the system hardware.

Quick Answer: 159
Detailed Answer: 163

8. Which of the following is used to manage file systems on a NetWare server?

❑ A. NDS
❑ B. NFS
❑ C. DHCP
❑ D. WINS

Quick Answer: 159
Detailed Answer: 163

9. Which two of the following client operating systems are supported by Windows and NetWare?

❑ A. UNIX workstations
❑ B. Novell CAFS Client
❑ C. Windows NT Workstation
❑ D. MAC OS X

Quick Answer: 159
Detailed Answer: 164

Quick Check

10. The NetWare directory structure begins with ______.

Quick Answer: **159**
Detailed Answer: **164**

- ❑ A. Directory
- ❑ B. Leaf
- ❑ C. Domain
- ❑ D. Root

11. Which of the following network operating systems is associated with NDS?

Quick Answer: **159**
Detailed Answer: **164**

- ❑ A. NetWare
- ❑ B. Windows NT
- ❑ C. Windows 9x
- ❑ D. UNIX

12. What is the basis of Novell NetWare?

Quick Answer: **159**
Detailed Answer: **164**

- ❑ A. X.25
- ❑ B. X.500
- ❑ C. V.34
- ❑ D. X.400

13. Which of the following is an advantage of UNIX that's not offered by other network operating systems?

Quick Answer: **159**
Detailed Answer: **164**

- ❑ A. Only UNIX supports TCP/IP.
- ❑ B. It's portable among different machine types.
- ❑ C. It's the only NOS that supports routable protocols.
- ❑ D. It doesn't require client addressing.

14. What is the default network protocol on a UNIX server?

Quick Answer: **159**
Detailed Answer: **164**

- ❑ A. IPX/SPX
- ❑ B. IPX
- ❑ C. TCP/IP
- ❑ D. NetBIOS

15. Which network protocol is shipped with commercial versions of UNIX?

Quick Answer: **159**
Detailed Answer: **164**

- ❑ A. TCP/IP
- ❑ B. IPX/SPX
- ❑ C. BGRP
- ❑ D. NWLink

16. ______ supports 64-bit applications.

Quick Answer: **159**
Detailed Answer: **164**

- ❑ A. AppleTalk
- ❑ B. Windows NT
- ❑ C. NetWare
- ❑ D. UNIX

Quick Check

17. Which protocol is used with the Internet and UNIX?

Quick Answer: **159**
Detailed Answer: **164**

- ❑ A. WINS
- ❑ B. NetBEUI
- ❑ C. IEEE 802.5
- ❑ D. TCP/IP

18. Which of the following networking protocols does Linux use?

Quick Answer: **159**
Detailed Answer: **164**

- ❑ A. TCP/IP
- ❑ B. AppleTalk
- ❑ C. IPX
- ❑ D. NWLink

19. Three servers are scheduled for an upgrade. What do you do first?

Quick Answer: **159**
Detailed Answer: **164**

- ❑ A. Install the upgrade on all three servers.
- ❑ B. Install the upgrade on a test server.
- ❑ C. Install the upgrade on one server and observe the effects on users.
- ❑ D. Don't perform the upgrade.

20. In what type of network environment do individual computers maintain a list of user accounts describing passwords and access rights?

Quick Answer: **159**
Detailed Answer: **165**

- ❑ A. Domain
- ❑ B. Standalone
- ❑ C. Workgroup
- ❑ D. Active Directory

21. What type of network is share-level security often associated with?

Quick Answer: **159**
Detailed Answer: **165**

- ❑ A. Peer-to-peer
- ❑ B. Server based
- ❑ C. WANs
- ❑ D. Centralized server

22. Which of the following best describes the difference between user and share-level security?

Quick Answer: **159**
Detailed Answer: **165**

- ❑ A. Share-level security is more restrictive.
- ❑ B. User-level security is more restrictive.
- ❑ C. There is no difference.
- ❑ D. User-level security can be set up in group accounts.

Quick Check

23. Which of the following best describes folder replication?
   - ❑ A. Attaching a tape unit to the hard drives of a server
   - ❑ B. Copying the contents of a hard drive to another hard drive
   - ❑ C. Copying a folder to another server or workstation
   - ❑ D. Configuring a workstation for temporary use as a server

Quick Answer: **159**
Detailed Answer: **165**

24. The method used to back up server data is to copy the server files to another server. Which one of the following best describes this type of backup method?
   - ❑ A. Differential
   - ❑ B. Folder replication
   - ❑ C. Tape backup
   - ❑ D. Incremental

Quick Answer: **159**
Detailed Answer: **165**

25. You are adding a Windows XP workstation to a network hosted by UNIX servers. There is also an Apple MAC workstation on the network. Which protocols must be loaded in the system to enable communications between all the computers in the network? (Select all that apply.)
   - ❑ A. NWLINK
   - ❑ B. AppleTalk
   - ❑ C. TCP/IP
   - ❑ D. NetBEUI

Quick Answer: **159**
Detailed Answer: **165**

26. You are setting up a Windows 2000 Professional computer in a network that contains Novell NetWare 4.11 servers. What client software do you need to install in the Windows machine to communicate with these servers?
   - ❑ A. TCP/IP
   - ❑ B. CSNW
   - ❑ C. Netlink
   - ❑ D. NWCT

Quick Answer: **159**
Detailed Answer: **165**

27. What items are required for a UNIX client to connect to an entirely UNIX-based network environment's network share using the host name?
   - ❑ A. IP, Subnet Mask, WINS
   - ❑ B. IP, Subnet Mask, LMHOSTS
   - ❑ C. IP, Subnet Mask, HOSTS
   - ❑ D. IP, DNS, WINS

Quick Answer: **159**
Detailed Answer: **165**

Quick Check

28. Which server stores information about resources in a Windows Server 2003 domain running Active Directory?
    - ❑ A. Domain Master
    - ❑ B. Domain Tree
    - ❑ C. Domain Controller
    - ❑ D. Domain Configurator

Quick Answer: 159
Detailed Answer: 165

29. Identify the hierarchical directory service.
    - ❑ A. Windows NT domains
    - ❑ B. Active Directory
    - ❑ C. Linux Password files
    - ❑ D. The NetWare Bindery

Quick Answer: 159
Detailed Answer: 165

30. A user cannot modify her username and password in Open Directory for Mac OS X server. Which of the following actions will best resolve this issue?
    - ❑ A. Convert the user to give master configurator rights.
    - ❑ B. Change the password from "Crypt" to "Open Directory."
    - ❑ C. Establish Turbo Shell as the login shell.
    - ❑ D. Modify the login to use "Key Chain" access rather than the login window.

Quick Answer: 159
Detailed Answer: 165

31. You have a Windows 2000 server-based domain with an Apple MAC client that is unable to see the server on the network. What items need to be installed to enable the client to communicate with the server?
    - ❑ A. 802.11A
    - ❑ B. NetBEUI
    - ❑ C. Token Ring
    - ❑ D. Appleshare

Quick Answer: 159
Detailed Answer: 166

32. When a user in a Linux environment wishes to authenticate using Kerberos, the request is processed and granted by a____.
    - ❑ A. Kerberos Key Distribution Center
    - ❑ B. Kerberos Password Distributor
    - ❑ C. Secure Layer Protocol Server
    - ❑ D. Kerberos Authentication Server

Quick Answer: 159
Detailed Answer: 166

33. Which Windows groups can share folders by default?
    - ❑ A. Admin group only
    - ❑ B. Admin and Power Users groups
    - ❑ C. Admin and Share Users groups
    - ❑ D. Admin and Guest groups

Quick Answer: 159
Detailed Answer: 166

Quick Check

34. Which of the following are true concerning NDS?

Quick Answer: 159
Detailed Answer: 166

- ❑ A. Remote users cannot access network connections via dial-up connections.
- ❑ B. Mobile users do not require changing the NDS name context.
- ❑ C. Mobile users do not require a special object entry.
- ❑ D. There is no difference between mobile and remote users.

Objective 3.2: Identify the Basic Capabilities Needed for Client Workstations to Connect to and Use Network Resources (For Example: Media, Network Protocols, and Peer and Server Services)

1. A workstation is being added to an Ethernet LAN. The NIC card has been installed, IRQ assigned along with an I/O range with no conflicts. What else must be done before the workstation can access the network resources?

Quick Answer: 159
Detailed Answer: 166

- ❑ A. Convert the workstation to a server by installing server software.
- ❑ B. Install the client software.
- ❑ C. Connect the workstation to a router.
- ❑ D. Install the client software and add a cable to the NIC card.

2. A user has been approved for an increase in the size of their home directory on the server. Which of the following must be changed?

Quick Answer: 159
Detailed Answer: 166

- ❑ A. Permission
- ❑ B. Profile
- ❑ C. Right
- ❑ D. Password

3. Before a client can receive a dynamic IP address from a server ______.

Quick Answer: 159
Detailed Answer: 166

- ❑ A. DHCP must be running on the server
- ❑ B. DNS must be running on the server
- ❑ C. WINS must be running on the server
- ❑ D. a gateway must be installed on the server

Quick Check

4. A network administrator is trying to decide whether to implement user-level or share-level security on a network. Which will be more time intensive?

Quick Answer: 159
Detailed Answer: 166

- ❑ A. User level
- ❑ B. Share level
- ❑ C. Security levels are dictated by the NOS and not the administrator.
- ❑ D. There's no difference in the amount of administrative time.

5. Which of the following best describes share-level access?

Quick Answer: 159
Detailed Answer: 166

- ❑ A. Used to specify users or groups of users that have access to a network resource.
- ❑ B. Used to specify the depth of a security model.
- ❑ C. Used to specify password protection for each resource.
- ❑ D. Used to employ a public-key encryption scheme.

6. Which of the following best describes user-level access?

Quick Answer: 159
Detailed Answer: 166

- ❑ A. Used to specify the depth of a security model.
- ❑ B. Used to specify users or groups of users that have access to a network resource.
- ❑ C. Used to specify password protection for each resource.
- ❑ D. Used to employ a public-key encryption scheme.

7. A network administrator assigns users to groups, all of which have similar levels of access. What type of security is being employed?

Quick Answer: 159
Detailed Answer: 166

- ❑ A. User level
- ❑ B. Logon Account
- ❑ C. Server Level
- ❑ D. Group level

8. When accessing a network share, you attempt to modify its contents, but you're unable to do so. What is the most likely reason for this?

Quick Answer: 159
Detailed Answer: 167

- ❑ A. GPOs are typically pulled from cache memory.
- ❑ B. The files are in Read-Only mode because another user is using them.
- ❑ C. The files are being pulled from a backup resource.
- ❑ D. You only have Read, Write and Change permissions to the files.

Quick Check

9. By interpreting baselines, you determine that the volume of network traffic on your network is reaching unacceptable levels. The network is a 10BASE-T system with hubs. Which of the following upgrade paths are you most likely to recommend?

Quick Answer: 159
Detailed Answer: 167

- ❑ A. Implement switches in place of the hubs.
- ❑ B. Implement 100BASE-T by replacing all the network cards and hubs with 100Mbps devices.
- ❑ C. Install a router to divide the network into two segments, thereby reducing the overall amount of network traffic.
- ❑ D. Implement a bridge.

10. You have a workstation that is 153 meters from the server, there is no repeater, and it is using 10BASE-T wiring. You cannot connect to the network.

Quick Answer: 159
Detailed Answer: 167

Required Objective: Connect to the server

Optional Objectives: Faster connection, easier access for users

Proposed Solution: Replace the old NIC with a 100BASE-FX NIC

- ❑ A. This meets only the required objective.
- ❑ B. This meets the optional objectives.
- ❑ C. This meets the required and one of the optional objectives.
- ❑ D. This does not meet the required or optional objectives.

11. You are the network administrator for a token ring network. A NIC in a system fails and you replace it with a new one. However, the system is unable to connect to the network. What is the most likely cause of the problem?

Quick Answer: 159
Detailed Answer: 167

- ❑ A. The card is a 100Mbps card, and the ring is configured for only 10Mbps.
- ❑ B. The card is set to the wrong ring speed.
- ❑ C. The card is set to full duplex operation and the ring is running at only half-duplex.
- ❑ D. The card is faulty.

Quick Check

12. As network administrator, you are given the task of integrating the existing network with a new network that will be located in another building. In total, there will be three network segments. The systems on the network are Windows 2000 and Novell NetWare servers and Windows 2000 workstations. You want to confine the network to a single protocol. Which two of the following network protocols might you consider using for the entire network?

 - ❑ A. IPX/SPX
 - ❑ B. TCP/IP
 - ❑ C. PPP
 - ❑ D. NetBEUI

Quick Answer: 159
Detailed Answer: 167

Objective 3.3: Identify the Appropriate Tool for a Given Wiring Task (Wire Crimper, Media Tester/Certifier, Punch Down Tool or Tone Generator)

1. You are experiencing problems with network connectivity and suspect that there is a break in the cable that connects two floors. The cable is a Category 5 twisted-pair cable. Which of the following tools can you use to locate the break in the cable?

 - ❑ A. Wire tap
 - ❑ B. Voltmeter
 - ❑ C. Tone generator and locator
 - ❑ D. Time domain reflectometer (TDR)

Quick Answer: 160
Detailed Answer: 167

2. What devices are sometimes referred to as "fox and hound" detectors?

 - ❑ A. Tone generator and locator
 - ❑ B. A time domain reflectometer (TDR)
 - ❑ C. A voltmeter
 - ❑ D. A cable chaser
 - ❑ E. A wire tap

Quick Answer: 160
Detailed Answer: 167

3. Which of the following tools is used to interface a token ring adapter card to category 3 or category 5 UTP cable?

 - ❑ A. A UDP adapter
 - ❑ B. A crossover cable
 - ❑ C. A token-ring media filter
 - ❑ D. A NIC adapter

Quick Answer: 160
Detailed Answer: 167

Quick Check

4. A wire in a UTP cable is suspected of having a break. Which of the following would confirm connectivity of each wire in the cable?

   ❑ A. Link light
   ❑ B. Crossover cable
   ❑ C. Cable tester
   ❑ D. Network adapter card

Quick Answer: **160**
Detailed Answer: **168**

5. In a hardware loop back plug, which two wire numbers are connected?

   ❑ A. 2 and 6
   ❑ B. 1 and 2
   ❑ C. 1 and3
   ❑ D. 3 and 4
   ❑ E. 3 and 5

Quick Answer: **160**
Detailed Answer: **168**

6. What type of device is required to connect a workstation to a hub port labeled MDI?

   ❑ A. A fox and hound
   ❑ B. A crossover cable
   ❑ C. A hardware loopback cable
   ❑ D. A straight-through cable
   ❑ E. A wire tap

Quick Answer: **160**
Detailed Answer: **168**

7. Which of the following Windows NT tools will display many of the attributes of an IP packet?

   ❑ A. Network Monitor Audit
   ❑ B. WINS
   ❑ C. DHCP
   ❑ D. Network Monitor

Quick Answer: **160**
Detailed Answer: **168**

8. Your company is getting a new DSL connection and you have been asked to install the new connection equipment in the communication closet of your office building. What type of tool do you need to make these connections?

   ❑ A. A wirepuller
   ❑ B. A drill
   ❑ C. A punch down tool
   ❑ D. A line extender tool

Quick Answer: **160**
Detailed Answer: **168**

Quick Check

9. What type of network troubleshooting tool do you use to actually put test signal on the copper wire of a network connection?

   - ❑ A. An OTDR
   - ❑ B. A TDR
   - ❑ C. A Line Tester
   - ❑ D. A Multimeter

Quick Answer: **160**
Detailed Answer: **168**

Objective 3.4: Given a Remote Connectivity Scenario Comprised of a Protocol, an Authentication Scheme, and Physical Connectivity, Configure the Connection for UNIX/Linux/MAC OS X Server, NetWare, Windows, and Appleshare IP

1. A server has two NIC cards installed. The first one uses IRQ 10 and I/O range of B800-B81F. The second uses IRQ 10 and I/O range of D700-D80A. What action, if any, should be taken?

   - ❑ A. No action is required.
   - ❑ B. Locate any available IRQ to resolve the IRQ conflict that is present.
   - ❑ C. Locate any available I/O range to resolve the I/O conflict.
   - ❑ D. Change the I/O of the second NIC to B800-B81F.

Quick Answer: **160**
Detailed Answer: **168**

2. A server has two NIC cards installed. The first one uses IRQ10 and I/O range of B800–B81F. The second uses IRQ5 and I/O range of D700–D80A. What action, if any, should be taken?

   - ❑ A. Locate any available IRQ to resolve the IRQ conflict that is present.
   - ❑ B. No action is required.
   - ❑ C. Locate any available I/O range to resolve the I/O conflict.
   - ❑ D. Change the I/O of the second NIC to B800–B81F.

Quick Answer: **160**
Detailed Answer: **168**

Quick Check

3. While installing and configuring a new modem, you receive an error message that indicates there is a resource conflict. You are installing the modem on COM2. What is the most likely source of the conflict?

Quick Answer: 160
Detailed Answer: 168

- ❑ A. IRQ2
- ❑ B. IRQ3
- ❑ C. IRQ5
- ❑ D. 3FD

4. Which of the following system resources should be configured in a modem installation?

Quick Answer: 160
Detailed Answer: 169

- ❑ A. FTP number, DMA channel, IRQ channel
- ❑ B. MAC address, I/O Address, DMA Channel
- ❑ C. COM port, Interrupt request channel, IP address
- ❑ D. COM port, I/O Address, Interrupt request channel

5. When an ISP elects to use DHCP, which one of the following must the subscriber set up?

Quick Answer: 160
Detailed Answer: 169

- ❑ A. PPP
- ❑ B. SMB
- ❑ C. IPX
- ❑ D. SLIP

6. What is the correct procedure for configuring RAS in a Windows 2000 server?

Quick Answer: 160
Detailed Answer: 169

- ❑ A. Start, Settings, Control Panel, Network
- ❑ B. Start, Programs, Administrative Tools, Routing, and Remote Access
- ❑ C. System, Services, Networking, Dial In
- ❑ D. Control Panel, Network, Dial In, Remote Services

7. A remote user calls your help desk and complains that she is unable to access internal corporate network resources from her home. The user states she can access the Internet. How can the user restore her connection to the corporate network?

Quick Answer: 160
Detailed Answer: 169

- ❑ A. Disconnect from the Internet
- ❑ B. Re-establish the VPN connection
- ❑ C. Re-establish the Dial-up Networking (DUN) connection
- ❑ D. Change the VPN connection to use IPsec instead of MS-CHAP

Quick Check

8. The Open Directory Authentication in Mac OS X can authenticate non-Kerberized services using _______.
   - ❑ A. Cleartext passwords
   - ❑ B. SSH authentication
   - ❑ C. SASL
   - ❑ D. NTP authentication

Quick Answer: **160**
Detailed Answer: **169**

Objective 3.5: Identify the Purpose, Benefits, and Characteristics of Using a Firewall

1. Your manager has given you the task of setting up a shared Internet connection for all the users on the network. She is concerned about security and has asked you to recommend a solution that will protect the internal network. What kind of server are you likely to install to address her security concern?
   - ❑ A. Install a Linux server
   - ❑ B. Install a firewall server
   - ❑ C. Install a secure browser on each workstation that will have Internet access
   - ❑ D. Install a Proxy server

Quick Answer: **160**
Detailed Answer: **169**

2. On a network, where is a system 'acting as a firewall' typically located?
   - ❑ A. Between the internal network and the Internet access point
   - ❑ B. Between two internal networks
   - ❑ C. Between the Internet access point and the Internet
   - ❑ D. Between the client systems and the servers

Quick Answer: **160**
Detailed Answer: **169**

3. Consider the following situation, and then select the best security practice from the list that follows: A network consisting of 500 users is to be modified so that all users will be able to access the Internet. All IP addresses are assigned from a list maintained in NT servers. The list of IP addresses is well known outside the network.
   - ❑ A. All messages intended for the Internet are encrypted.
   - ❑ B. All users are assigned a unique password for accessing the Internet.
   - ❑ C. The share-level security model is selectively applied to each user.
   - ❑ D. A firewall is installed at the Internet ports.

Quick Answer: **160**
Detailed Answer: **169**

Quick Check

4. What is the basic purpose of a firewall system?
   - ❑ A. It protects one network from another by acting as an intermediary system.
   - ❑ B. It caches commonly used Web pages, thereby reducing the bandwidth demands on an Internet connection.
   - ❑ C. It allows hostnames to be resolved to IP addresses.
   - ❑ D. It provides a single point of access to the Internet.

Quick Answer: **160**
Detailed Answer: **169**

5. While reviewing the security logs for your server, you notice that a user on the Internet has attempted to access your internal mail server. Although it appears that the user's attempts were unsuccessful, you are still very concerned about the possibility that your systems may be compromised. Which of the following solutions are you most likely to implement?
   - ❑ A. A firewall system at the connection point to the Internet
   - ❑ B. A more secure password policy
   - ❑ C. File-level encryption
   - ❑ D. Kerberos authentication

Quick Answer: **160**
Detailed Answer: **170**

6. Which of the following is not a commonly implemented feature of a firewall system?
   - ❑ A. Packet filtering
   - ❑ B. NAS
   - ❑ C. Proxy
   - ❑ D. NAT

Quick Answer: **160**
Detailed Answer: **170**

7. Which of the following best describes the purpose of a firewall?
   - ❑ A. To prevent external intruders from accessing a network
   - ❑ B. To prevent network users from accessing the Internet
   - ❑ C. To prevent network users from virus attack
   - ❑ D. To detect protocol conflicts

Quick Answer: **160**
Detailed Answer: **170**

8. A packet filtering firewall performs at which levels of the OSI model?
   - ❑ A. Network and Data
   - ❑ B. Network and Transport
   - ❑ C. Transport and Session
   - ❑ D. Physical and Data

Quick Answer: **160**
Detailed Answer: **170**

Quick Check

Objective 3.6: Identify the Purpose, Benefits, and Characteristics of Using a Proxy Server

1. Your manager has given you the task of installing a caching Proxy server. Which three of the following are the benefits of using a Proxy server system?

   Quick Answer: 160
   Detailed Answer: 170

   - ❑ A. It provides faster page retrieval for commonly used Web pages.
   - ❑ B. It provides centralized Internet access.
   - ❑ C. It provides automatic assignment of IP addresses to workstations.
   - ❑ D. It provides protection of the internal network from attack by outside sources.

2. Your manager has given you the task of installing a caching Proxy server. Which two of the following are the benefits of using a Proxy server system?

   Quick Answer: 160
   Detailed Answer: 170

   - ❑ A. Increasing demands on Internet connection bandwidth
   - ❑ B. Centralizing Internet access
   - ❑ C. Preventing network workstation IP addresses from being advertised on the Internet
   - ❑ D. Automatically assigning IP addresses to workstations

3. A network consisting of 500 users is to be modified so that all users will be able to access the Internet. All IP addresses are assigned from a list maintained in NT servers. The list of IP addresses is well known outside the network. Which of the following is the best security practice for this network?

   Quick Answer: 160
   Detailed Answer: 170

   - ❑ A. All messages intended for the Internet are encrypted.
   - ❑ B. All users are assigned a unique password for accessing the Internet.
   - ❑ C. The share-level security model is selectively applied to each user.
   - ❑ D. A firewall is installed at the Internet ports.

4. What is the purpose of using a proxy IP?

   Quick Answer: 160
   Detailed Answer: 170

   - ❑ A. To provide all workstations with the same IP address
   - ❑ B. To eliminate the need for TCP/IP
   - ❑ C. To secure actual workstation IP addresses from intruders
   - ❑ D. To map IP addresses to MAC addresses

Quick Check

5. Computer users are reporting slow Internet access. Which of the following actions could be taken to improve their browsing?

Quick Answer: 160
Detailed Answer: 170

- ❑ A. Install a Proxy server
- ❑ B. Install a Web server
- ❑ C. Set up a subnet
- ❑ D. Install a Terminal server

6. You are in charge of installing your company's new network structure. You have asked one of your assistants to install a proxy server for the new environment. They ask you if the proxy server is the same as a firewall. What should you tell them?

Quick Answer: 160
Detailed Answer: 171

- ❑ A. A proxy server is used to protect one network from another by preventing IP addresses from passing between the networks.
- ❑ B. A Proxy server resolves hostnames to IP addresses and replaces workstation IP addresses with a proxy IP address.
- ❑ C. A proxy server is used to provide a single point of access to the LAN by filtering the IP addresses presented to the network.
- ❑ D. A proxy server holds the Security Access List for the network and prevents unauthorized users from gaining access to the network resources.

7. A Proxy server operates at which OSI level?

Quick Answer: 160
Detailed Answer: 171

- ❑ A. Application
- ❑ B. Network
- ❑ C. Transport
- ❑ D. Session

Quick Check

Objective 3.7: Given a Connectivity Scenario, Predict the Impact of a Particular Security Implementation on Network Functionality (Blocking Port Numbers, Authentication, Encryption, and so on)

1. You are designing a password policy for your company. Which of the following measures are you least likely to recommend?
   - ❑ A. Include passwords in system documentation
   - ❑ B. Ensure that passwords are not reused
   - ❑ C. Make sure that users use only "strong" passwords that are a certain length
   - ❑ D. Change passwords on a periodic basis

Quick Answer: 161
Detailed Answer: 171

2. Which of the following represents the most secure password?
   - ❑ A. PASSWORD1
   - ❑ B. password
   - ❑ C. PaSsWoRd1
   - ❑ D. PASSWORD

Quick Answer: 161
Detailed Answer: 171

3. A peer-to-peer network is to be upgraded to a server-based network. Before performing the upgrade, which one of the following should be done first?
   - ❑ A. Configure a default gateway
   - ❑ B. Commit to an administrator password
   - ❑ C. Install the NOS
   - ❑ D. Assign IP addresses to all workstations

Quick Answer: 161
Detailed Answer: 171

4. You have been told to set up a firewall for the company network that will filter TCP ports 100–200. What network services will this action affect?
   - ❑ A. POP3 incoming mail service
   - ❑ B. FTP service
   - ❑ C. SMTP outgoing mail service
   - ❑ D. World Wide Web (WWW) access

Quick Answer: 161
Detailed Answer: 171

Quick Check

5. After several passwords have been compromised in your organization, you have been asked to implement a network-wide password policy. Which of the following represents the most practical and secure password policy?
   - ❑ A. Daily password changes
   - ❑ B. Weekly password changes
   - ❑ C. Monthly password changes
   - ❑ D. Password changes only after an account has been compromised

Quick Answer: **161**
Detailed Answer: **171**

6. What directory system does a UNIX server use to resolve names?
   - ❑ A. NDS
   - ❑ B. DNS
   - ❑ C. HOSTS
   - ❑ D. DHCP

Quick Answer: **161**
Detailed Answer: **171**

7. Your manager has asked you to implement security on your peer-to-peer network. Which of the following security models offers the highest level of security?
   - ❑ A. Share level
   - ❑ B. User level
   - ❑ C. Password level
   - ❑ D. Layered

Quick Answer: **161**
Detailed Answer: **171**

8. You are working on a Linux system and are having problems trying to ping a remote system by its hostname. DNS resolution is not configured for the system. What file might you examine to begin troubleshooting the resolution problem?
   - ❑ A. hosts
   - ❑ B. staticdns
   - ❑ C. passwd
   - ❑ D. resolv

Quick Answer: **161**
Detailed Answer: **172**

9. Which of the following is not a valid file permission on a Linux system?
   - ❑ A. Execute
   - ❑ B. Read
   - ❑ C. Attribute
   - ❑ D. Write

Quick Answer: **161**
Detailed Answer: **172**

Quick Check

10. How often should passwords be changed?

Quick Answer: 161
Detailed Answer: 172

- ❑ A. No less than monthly
- ❑ B. No less than weekly
- ❑ C. No less than annually
- ❑ D. No less than biannually

11. What does a secure password policy require?

Quick Answer: 161
Detailed Answer: 172

- ❑ A. Passwords must be changed on a random basis.
- ❑ B. Passwords must be changed at a scheduled time-interval.
- ❑ C. A random length for passwords.
- ❑ D. A prescribed length to passwords.

12. The network administrator sends email to all users explaining that passwords must be changed on a monthly basis. This is a departure from the current system of passwords never changing. Which of the following must be changed?

Quick Answer: 161
Detailed Answer: 172

- ❑ A. Groups
- ❑ B. Profiles
- ❑ C. Rights
- ❑ D. Policy

13. After creating a new secure page for your Web site, external users complain that they cannot access it, but they can access other areas of the site. When you try to access it from a workstation internally, everything seems fine. What is the most likely explanation of the problem?

Quick Answer: 161
Detailed Answer: 172

- ❑ A. Your firewall is blocking all traffic.
- ❑ B. Your firewall is blocking port 80.
- ❑ C. Your firewall is blocking port 110.
- ❑ D. Your firewall is blocking port 443.

14. You have just set up a filter on your network router and SMTP operations have stopped responding. What is the likely cause of this problem?

Quick Answer: 161
Detailed Answer: 173

- ❑ A. Port 25 is closed.
- ❑ B. Port 110 is closed.
- ❑ C. Port 80 is closed.
- ❑ D. Port 443 is closed.

Quick Check

15. You have installed a new firewall in your network and users are complaining that now they can't access the Web. What action should you take to restore their Web access?
    - ❑ A. Reconfigure DNS
    - ❑ B. Configure DHCP for the firewall
    - ❑ C. Open port 80
    - ❑ D. Configure the router to work with the firewall

Quick Answer: 161
Detailed Answer: 173

16. Choose the most secure password from the following list.
    - ❑ A. Db3Tu$L
    - ❑ B. klsrmoa
    - ❑ C. NeW UseR
    - ❑ D. harold

Quick Answer: 161
Detailed Answer: 173

Objective 3.8: Identify the Main Characteristics of VLANs

1. Which properties can be used to define a VLAN?
    - ❑ A. IP addresses
    - ❑ B. Port assignments
    - ❑ C. Computer names
    - ❑ D. MAC addresses

Quick Answer: 161
Detailed Answer: 173

2. Which of the following technologies can be implemented on a switch to create multiple separate networks?
    - ❑ A. Subnet masking
    - ❑ B. VLAN
    - ❑ C. NAS
    - ❑ D. Proxy

Quick Answer: 161
Detailed Answer: 173

3. Which three of the following properties can be used to define a VLAN?
    - ❑ A. IP addresses
    - ❑ B. Computer names
    - ❑ C. MAC addresses
    - ❑ D. Port assignments

Quick Answer: 161
Detailed Answer: 173

Quick Check

4. Your company has two offices in different locations. You need to establish a secure link between the two. You want to use the Internet as a communication mechanism to keep the costs down. Which of the following technologies might you consider using?

Quick Answer: 161
Detailed Answer: 173

- ❑ A. VLAN
- ❑ B. 802.11b
- ❑ C. VPN
- ❑ D. TDR

5. A VLAN can be used to:

Quick Answer: 161
Detailed Answer: 173

- ❑ A. Create a network without using any cables
- ❑ B. Create a network at the cost of using more bandwidth
- ❑ C. Separate networks into smaller logical networks
- ❑ D. Re-use IP addresses

6. Your company has recently merged with another company and each has its own VLAN. Users on both VLANs need to communicate with each other. What needs to be installed to make this possible?

Quick Answer: 161
Detailed Answer: 173

- ❑ A. A router
- ❑ B. A switch
- ❑ C. Matching protocols
- ❑ D. A bridge

7. You have several remote salespeople who routinely connect to your office via a VPN. However, today they can no longer connect, and are unable to access the login. However, they are still able to access the Internet. What action should be taken to determine the scope of this problem?

Quick Answer: 161
Detailed Answer: 174

- ❑ A. Reconfigure the VPN setup
- ❑ B. Re-enter their usernames and passwords
- ❑ C. Call your broadband service provider
- ❑ D. Ping the VPN host

Quick Check

Objective 3.9: Identify the Main Characteristics and Purpose of Extranets and Intranets

1. A company producing medicine is sharing production data with another company that outsources shipping via a VPN. In return, the shipping company is sharing some of its real-time updated logistics schedules with the medical company, also using a VPN. What type of networking arrangement is involved?

   ❑ A. A token ring network

   ❑ B. An intranet

   ❑ C. An extranet

   ❑ D. A local area network (LAN)

Quick Answer: **161**
Detailed Answer: **174**

2. Which of the following best describes an intranet?

   ❑ A. A global public network that uses an infrastructure consisting of network access points, a commercial backbone and service providers

   ❑ B. A private network that supports Internet applications and that doesn't use the public telecommunications system to connect users

   ❑ C. A private network that supports Internet applications, uses the public telecommunications system, and has limited access to the public

   ❑ D. A network in which data packets sent over the public Internet and are encapsulated in a protocol that provides for data encapsulation as well as encryption of the user data

Quick Answer: **161**
Detailed Answer: **174**

3. Which of the following provides the best protection against network intruders?

   ❑ A. The Internet

   ❑ B. An intranet

   ❑ C. An extranet

   ❑ D. A VPN

Quick Answer: **161**
Detailed Answer: **174**

4. Which of the following types of network can a company use to allow data sharing internally only, without the use of the public telephone system?

   ❑ A. Internet

   ❑ B. Intranet

   ❑ C. Extranet

   ❑ D. VPN

Quick Answer: **161**
Detailed Answer: **174**

Quick Check

5. An intranet is ______, typically established by an organization for the purpose of running an exclusive site not open to the public.
    - ❑ A. A local area network (LAN)
    - ❑ B. An internal extranet network
    - ❑ C. A wide area network (WAN)
    - ❑ D. A Web-based network

Quick Answer: 161
Detailed Answer: 174

6. A ______ is used to block unauthorized outside users from accessing an intranet site.
    - ❑ A. Hub
    - ❑ B. Router
    - ❑ C. Gateway
    - ❑ D. Firewall

Quick Answer: 161
Detailed Answer: 174

7. Which one of the following characteristics of an intranet is incorrect?
    - ❑ A. An intranet can be a part of a Local Area Network (LAN).
    - ❑ B. An intranet is designed to be publicly available.
    - ❑ C. An intranet can work with Wide Area Networks (WAN).
    - ❑ D. An intranet may be restricted to a community of users.

Quick Answer: 161
Detailed Answer: 174

8. Which of the following best describes an extranet?
    - ❑ A. A global public network that uses an infrastructure consisting of network access points, a commercial backbone and service providers
    - ❑ B. A private network that supports Internet applications and that doesn't use the public telecommunications system to connect users
    - ❑ C. A private network that supports Internet applications, uses the public telecommunications system, and has limited access to the public
    - ❑ D. A network in which data packets are sent over the public Internet and are encapsulated in a protocol that provides for data encapsulation as well as encryption of the user data

Quick Answer: 161
Detailed Answer: 174

9. Your company is set up to use the Internet to do business with your business partners who are scattered across the country; this is an example of ______.
    - ❑ A. Intranet
    - ❑ B. Extranet
    - ❑ C. Internet
    - ❑ D. Virtual Private Network (VPN)

Quick Answer: 161
Detailed Answer: 174

Quick Check

10. To set up a secure network that will enable your customers to view your current production schedule, you would set up ______.

Quick Answer: **161**
Detailed Answer: **174**

- ❑ A. An intranet
- ❑ B. A wide area network
- ❑ C. An extranet
- ❑ D. A Virtual Private Network

11. Your company wants to make its internal product information accessible to selected customers from anywhere in the world. Which type of network environment should you create for this scenario?

Quick Answer: **161**
Detailed Answer: **175**

- ❑ A. An extranet
- ❑ B. An intranet
- ❑ C. A WAN
- ❑ D. A VPN

Objective 3.10: Identify the Purpose, Benefits, and Characteristics of Using Antivirus Software

1. From what items do antivirus software packages protect computers?

Quick Answer: **161**
Detailed Answer: **175**

- ❑ A. Trojans
- ❑ B. SPAM
- ❑ C. Pop-up ads
- ❑ D. Spyware

2. What is an unwanted software program that can multiply from one system to another?

Quick Answer: **161**
Detailed Answer: **175**

- ❑ A. Virus
- ❑ B. Spam
- ❑ C. Spyware
- ❑ D. Cookies

3. Which of the following should always be installed on an email server?

Quick Answer: **161**
Detailed Answer: **175**

- ❑ A. Antivirus software
- ❑ B. Popup blocker
- ❑ C. Spyware blocker
- ❑ D. The SSL protocol

Quick Check

4. How can proxy servers provide an opening for viruses to enter a network?

Quick Answer: 161
Detailed Answer: 175

- ❑ A. The proxy server uses the IP address of the remote server.
- ❑ B. The proxy receives HTTP responses that might contain viruses.
- ❑ C. The proxy server receives telnet data that might have viruses.
- ❑ D. The proxy receives IP acknowledgements that might have viruses.

5. What action should always be taken before installing new application software?

Quick Answer: 161
Detailed Answer: 175

- ❑ A. Check the system for viruses
- ❑ B. Deactivate the antivirus software
- ❑ C. Verify that all the system's virus protection is active
- ❑ D. Check the application installation media for viruses

6. Why should all email originating from the Internet be scanned for viruses?

Quick Answer: 161
Detailed Answer: 175

- ❑ A. Because Windows operating systems are known for viruses.
- ❑ B. Because the Internet is the largest source of viruses.
- ❑ C. Because email floods can cripple a server.
- ❑ D. Because not all email is encrypted.

7. A client that has FTP access should also have ______.

Quick Answer: 161
Detailed Answer: 175

- ❑ A. a port 21 firewall block
- ❑ B. an encrypted link to the FTP server
- ❑ C. email access
- ❑ D. antivirus software installed

8. Normally, antivirus software needs to be updated on a(n) ______ basis.

Quick Answer: 161
Detailed Answer: 175

- ❑ A. quarterly
- ❑ B. bi-annual
- ❑ C. monthly
- ❑ D. annual

9. What needs to be done before using a file obtained from a third party?

Quick Answer: 161
Detailed Answer: 175

- ❑ A. Scan the file for pop-ups
- ❑ B. Scan the file for worms
- ❑ C. Scan the file for spyware
- ❑ D. Scan the file for viruses

Quick Check

Objective 3.11: Identify the Purpose and Characteristics of Fault Tolerance

1. After a hard disk failure that took a number of hours from which to recover, your manager has instructed you to implement a fault-tolerant solution to reduce the amount of downtime if the same thing happens again. After researching the various options available to you, you decide to use disk striping with parity. What is the minimum number of disks required to implement this solution?

   ❑ A. 3
   ❑ B. 2
   ❑ C. 1
   ❑ D. 4

Quick Answer: **162**
Detailed Answer: **176**

2. To combine hard drive fault tolerance with good read/write performance, which of the following should be used?

   ❑ A. Striping without parity
   ❑ B. Tape backup
   ❑ C. Mirroring
   ❑ D. Striping with parity

Quick Answer: **162**
Detailed Answer: **176**

3. Each hard drive in a server has a dedicated disk controller. What is this practice called?

   ❑ A. Striping
   ❑ B. Duplexing
   ❑ C. Parity
   ❑ D. SNMP

Quick Answer: **162**
Detailed Answer: **176**

4. Your manager has given you the task of implementing a RAID solution on the server. You have two hard disk controllers and two hard disks. Which three of the following RAID levels could you implement?

   ❑ A. Disk mirroring
   ❑ B. Disk striping with parity
   ❑ C. Disk striping
   ❑ D. Disk duplexing
   ❑ E. Disk shadowing

Quick Answer: **162**
Detailed Answer: **176**

Quick Check

5. To provide true, continuous power to a server, which of the following should be used?

Quick Answer: 162
Detailed Answer: 176

- ❑ A. BNC
- ❑ B. UPS
- ❑ C. SPS
- ❑ D. Generator

6. You have been asked to implement a RAID solution on one of your company's servers. You have two hard disks and two hard disk controllers. Which three of the following RAID levels could you implement?

Quick Answer: 162
Detailed Answer: 176

- ❑ A. RAID 0
- ❑ B. RAID 1
- ❑ C. Disk duplexing
- ❑ D. RAID 10
- ❑ E. RAID 5

7. Which of the following statements best describes RAID 5?

Quick Answer: 162
Detailed Answer: 177

- ❑ A. A RAID 5 array consists of at least three drives and distributes parity information across all the drives in the array.
- ❑ B. A RAID 5 array consists of at least two drives. Parity information is written across both drives to provide fault tolerance.
- ❑ C. A RAID 5 array consists of at least three drives and stores the parity information on a single drive.
- ❑ D. A RAID 5 array consists of at least four drives. The first and last drives in the array are used to store parity information.

8. What is the purpose of implementing fault tolerance?

Quick Answer: 162
Detailed Answer: 177

- ❑ A. It protects data from accidental deletion.
- ❑ B. It eliminates the amount of time the administrator spends performing backups.
- ❑ C. It allows systems to be bought back online more quickly.
- ❑ D. It promotes data availability by eliminating a single point of failure.

9. Writing data in blocks across multiple hard drives is called ______.

Quick Answer: 162
Detailed Answer: 177

- ❑ A. Striping
- ❑ B. RAID 0
- ❑ C. Mirroring
- ❑ D. Parity

Quick Check

10. Which RAID level does not incorporate fault tolerance?
    - ❑ A. RAID 1
    - ❑ B. RAID 0
    - ❑ C. RAID 5
    - ❑ D. RAID 3

Quick Answer: **162**
Detailed Answer: **177**

11. Each hard drive in a server has a dedicated disk controller. What is this practice called?
    - ❑ A. SNMP
    - ❑ B. Striping
    - ❑ C. Parity
    - ❑ D. Duplexing

Quick Answer: **162**
Detailed Answer: **177**

12. Which RAID level relies on mirroring for fault tolerance?
    - ❑ A. RAID 0
    - ❑ B. RAID 3
    - ❑ C. RAID 5
    - ❑ D. RAID 1

Quick Answer: **162**
Detailed Answer: **177**

13. Which of the following represent fault tolerance measures? (Select all that apply.)
    - ❑ A. Installing a UPS
    - ❑ B. Installing a RAID system
    - ❑ C. Installing a mirror server
    - ❑ D. Performing a daily backup

Quick Answer: **162**
Detailed Answer: **177**

14. Which of the following techniques improves the fault tolerance of a RAID 1 arrangement so that the system can remain functional if the disk controller fails?
    - ❑ A. Duplex the RAID 1 subsystem by adding a second controller
    - ❑ B. Mirroring the RAID 1 subsystem by adding an additional drive and controller
    - ❑ C. Striping the RAID 1 system using an additional drive for parity
    - ❑ D. Add a tape backup system to the drive subsystem

Quick Answer: **162**
Detailed Answer: **177**

15. Which of the following provides fault tolerance and the best read/write performance?
    - ❑ A. Duplexing
    - ❑ B. Striping with parity
    - ❑ C. RAID 0
    - ❑ D. Striping without parity

Quick Answer: **162**
Detailed Answer: **177**

Quick Check

16. One of your servers is configured for RAID 1 operation with duplexing. If it loses one of its RAID controllers, what will happen to the disk data and performance?

Quick Answer: 162
Detailed Answer: 178

- ❑ A. The data will be lost but the drive subsystem performance will not be affected.
- ❑ B. The data will be safe, but the drive subsystem performance will be decreased.
- ❑ C. Half of the data will be lost, but the drive subsystem performance will not be affected.
- ❑ D. The data and the performance level will remain unchanged.

17. You have a 3-drive RAID system where one drive is used for the operating system and the other two drives are used for data in a stripe set. The drives are hot swappable. One of the data drives fails. What needs to be done to correct the failure?

Quick Answer: 162
Detailed Answer: 178

- ❑ A. Replace the drive and restore the contents from backup.
- ❑ B. Hot swap the drive with the system active, and it will automatically rebuild the contents of the drive.
- ❑ C. Shut down the system, replace the drive, restart the system, and let it rebuild the missing drive.
- ❑ D. Use a warm spare to replace the drive. It already contains the data and will make it available when the drive is activated.

18. Which RAID type offers best fault tolerance with the least overhead for a system that has one controller and six drives?

Quick Answer: 162
Detailed Answer: 178

- ❑ A. Duplexing
- ❑ B. Striping
- ❑ C. Mirroring
- ❑ D. Striping with Parity

19. What fault tolerant system requires the least amount of overhead?

Quick Answer: 162
Detailed Answer: 178

- ❑ A. RAID 0
- ❑ B. RAID 1
- ❑ C. Mirroring
- ❑ D. RAID 5

20. A NetWare server uses four hard drives. Which of the following technologies divides the hard drives so that it provides the most data storage space?

Quick Answer: 162
Detailed Answer: 178

- ❑ A. Duplexing
- ❑ B. Striping
- ❑ C. Volume
- ❑ D. Partition

Quick Check

Objective 3.12: Identify the Purpose and Characteristics of Disaster Recovery

1. Which two of the following backup methods clear the archive bit from files that have been backed up?

Quick Answer: **162**
Detailed Answer: **178**

- ❑ A. Incremental
- ❑ B. Full
- ❑ C. Differential
- ❑ D. Periodic

2. In a GFS rotation, what does the GFS refer to?

Quick Answer: **162**
Detailed Answer: **178**

- ❑ A. Weekly, monthly, and yearly backups
- ❑ B. The frequency of RAID rebuilds
- ❑ C. Daily, weekly, and monthly backups
- ❑ D. The replacement of tapes with new ones in a backup cycle

3. Which of the following occurs during a normal server backup?

Quick Answer: **162**
Detailed Answer: **178**

- ❑ A. All workstation files are backed up
- ❑ B. Only files that have changed since the last backup are backed up
- ❑ C. Only those files that have changed since the last differential backup are backed up
- ❑ D. All files are backed up

4. What type of backup is being performed on a server when only files that have changed are backed up?

Quick Answer: **162**
Detailed Answer: **178**

- ❑ A. Full
- ❑ B. Incremental
- ❑ C. Differential
- ❑ D. Tape

5. Which of the following backup types use the fewest number of tapes?

Quick Answer: **162**
Detailed Answer: **179**

- ❑ A. Weekly normal-daily incremental
- ❑ B. Daily normal
- ❑ C. Weekly normal-daily differential
- ❑ D. Weekly differential-daily incremental

6. How often should a full backup of server data be scheduled?

Quick Answer: **162**
Detailed Answer: **179**

- ❑ A. Every three months
- ❑ B. Once a week
- ❑ C. Once a month
- ❑ D. Once a year

Quick Check

7. A server uses a backup strategy in which backups occur three times a week. The first backup is a full backup. The second backup copies files that have changed since the first backup, and the third backup copies all files that were changed since the first backup. What type of strategy does this describe?
   - ❑ A. Differential
   - ❑ B. Normal
   - ❑ C. Incremental
   - ❑ D. Full

Quick Answer: **162**
Detailed Answer: **179**

8. A server is backed up each day using a normal backup. Backup times using this method have become too long and an alternative plan that allows a full backup on weekends but a short backup during the weekdays is needed. Which of the following represents the best plan?
   - ❑ A. Weekly normal backup and daily differential backups
   - ❑ B. Weekly normal backups and daily incremental backups
   - ❑ C. Weekly incremental backups
   - ❑ D. Daily full backup

Quick Answer: **162**
Detailed Answer: **179**

9. Why should a backup strategy include provisions for off-site storage of data tapes?
   - ❑ A. So the server can be moved to the off-site location
   - ❑ B. So users won't be able to access server data
   - ❑ C. So all server data can be copied to a backup server
   - ❑ D. So the server data will be protected from environmental disasters

Quick Answer: **162**
Detailed Answer: **179**

10. Which two of the following backup methods clears the archive bit?
    - ❑ A. Full
    - ❑ B. Incremental
    - ❑ C. Differential
    - ❑ D. Sequential

Quick Answer: **162**
Detailed Answer: **179**

11. Which of the following backup types takes the longest time to operate?
    - ❑ A. Incremental
    - ❑ B. Normal
    - ❑ C. Differential
    - ❑ D. Sequential

Quick Answer: **162**
Detailed Answer: **179**

Quick Check

12. Which of the following backup methods will back up the files regardless of the state of the archive bit?
    - ❑ A. Incremental
    - ❑ B. Differential
    - ❑ C. Full
    - ❑ D. Sequential

Quick Answer: 162
Detailed Answer: 179

13. During a normal server backup _______.
    - ❑ A. only those files that have changed since the last differential backup are backed up
    - ❑ B. only files that have changed since the last backup are backed up
    - ❑ C. all files are backed up
    - ❑ D. all workstation files are backed up

Quick Answer: 162
Detailed Answer: 179

14. What is the most common backup method used with servers?
    - ❑ A. Tape
    - ❑ B. Floppy disk
    - ❑ C. Removable media
    - ❑ D. Windows Backup

Quick Answer: 162
Detailed Answer: 179

15. The backup of a server is set to perform daily backups of all files that have changed since the last complete backup of the server, regardless of whether they have changed since the backup on the previous day. What type of backup is being used?
    - ❑ A. Tape
    - ❑ B. Incremental
    - ❑ C. Full
    - ❑ D. Differential

Quick Answer: 162
Detailed Answer: 179

16. A backup strategy in which only files that have changed since the last full or incremental backup is called a _______.
    - ❑ A. Differential
    - ❑ B. Incremental
    - ❑ C. Full
    - ❑ D. Normal

Quick Answer: 162
Detailed Answer: 179

Quick Check

17. What is the standard method of verifying that a backup copy is valid?

Quick Answer: 162
Detailed Answer: 180

- ❑ A. Verify the archive bit status
- ❑ B. Check the backup tape integrity
- ❑ C. Restore the backup to a machine
- ❑ D. Run the system state data backup test

Quick Check Answer Key

Objective 3.1: Identify the Basic Capabilities (Client Support, Interoperability, Authentication, File and Print Services, Application Support, and Security) of the Following Server Operating Systems: UNIX/Linux, NetWare, Windows, and Appleshare IP (Internet Protocol)

1. A

2. C

3. A

4. C

5. A

6. B

7. C

8. B

9. A, C

10. D

11. A

12. B

13. B

14. C

15. A

16. D

17. D

18. A

19. B

20. C

21. A

22. D

23. C

24. B

25. B, C

26. B

27. C

28. C

29. B

30. D

31. D

32. A

33. B

34. D

Objective 3.2: Identify the Basic Capabilities Needed for Client Workstations to Connect to and Use Network Resources (For Example: Media, Network Protocols and Peer and Server Services)

1. D

2. B

3. A

4. B

5. C

6. B

7. A

8. B

9. A

10. D

11. B

12. A, B

Quick Check Answer Key

Objective 3.3: Identify the Appropriate Tool for a Given Wiring Task (Wire Crimper, Media Tester/Certifier, Punch Down Tool or Tone Generator)

1. D
2. A
3. C
4. C
5. A, C
6. B
7. D
8. C
9. B, C

Objective 3.4: Given a Remote Connectivity Scenario Comprised of a Protocol, an Authentication Scheme, and Physical Connectivity, Configure the Connection for UNIX/Linux/MAC OS X Server, NetWare, Windows, and Appleshare IP

1. B
2. B
3. B
4. D
5. A
6. B
7. B
8. C

Objective 3.5: Identify the Purpose, Benefits, and Characteristics of Using a Firewall

1. B
2. A
3. D
4. A
5. A
6. B
7. A
8. B

Objective 3.6: Identify the Purpose, Benefits, and Characteristics of Using a Proxy Server

1. A, B, D
2. C
3. D
4. C
5. A
6. C
7. A

Quick Check Answer Key

Objective 3.7: Given a Scenario, Predict the Impact of a Particular Security Implementation on Network Functionality (Blocking Port Numbers, Encryption, and so on)

1. A

2. C

3. B

4. A

5. C

6. C

7. B

8. A

9. C

10. A

11. A

12. D

13. D

14. A

15. C

16. A

Objective 3.8: Identify the Main Characteristics of VLANs

1. A, B, D

2. B

3. A, C, D

4. C

5. C

6. A

7. D

Objective 3.9: Identify the Main Characteristics and Purpose of Extranets and Intranets

1. C

2. B

3. B

4. B

5. D

6. D

7. B

8. C

9. B

10. C

11. A

Objective 3.10: Identify the Purpose, Benefits, and Characteristics of Using Antivirus Software

1. A

2. A

3. A

4. B

5. B

6. B

7. D

8. C

9. D

Quick Check Answer Key

Objective 3.11: Identify the Purpose and Characteristics of Fault Tolerance

1. A
2. D
3. B
4. A, C, D
5. B
6. A, B, C
7. A
8. D
9. A
10. B
11. D
12. D
13. A, B, C
14. A
15. B
16. B
17. A
18. D
19. D
20. C

Objective 3.12: Identify the Purpose and Characteristics of Disaster Recovery

1. A, B
2. C
3. D
4. B
5. B
6. B
7. A
8. B
9. D
10. A, B
11. B
12. C
13. D
14. A
15. D
16. B
17. C

Answers and Explanations

Objective 3.1

1. **Answer: A.** Samba is a product that provides file and print services to Windows-based clients. Samba does not offer thin client services, web server services or Proxy server services.

2. **Answer: C.** A Windows NT server hard drive may be formatted as NTFS and/or FAT. NTFS offers a wider range of services, including enhanced network security. The number of hard drives has nothing to do with the file structures NTFS or FAT; both can use multiple drives. Server backups are a normal and expected networking task no matter what type of file structure is used. Although the server can be used as a workstation (not recommended) NTFS does not provide this functionality.

3. **Answer: A.** NDS is the NetWare Directory Service and is proprietary to Novell, although it's based on the X.400 protocol. Windows NT and Windows 9x are Microsoft products. UNIX is nonproprietary.

4. **Answer: C.** The directory structure used with Novell NetWare is called NDS. FAT is a file system associated with DOS and NTFS is a file system associated with Windows NT. The root file structure is normally associated with UNIX/Linux.

5. **Answer: A.** IPX is a protocol associated with Novell NetWare. NetBEUI is associated with MS Windows and AppleTalk is associated with Mac OS networks. MS-DOS is not a network protocol.

6. **Answer: B.** A Windows NT server hard drive may be formatted as NTFS and/or FAT. NTFS offers a wider range of services, including enhanced network security. The number of hard drives has nothing to do with the file structures NTFS or FAT; both can use multiple drives. Server backups are a normal and expected networking task no matter what type of file structure is used. Although the server can be used as a workstation (not recommended) NTFS does not provide this functionality.

7. **Answer: C.** NTFS (New Technology File System) originated with the HPFS file system that Microsoft and IBM developed for the OS/2 operating system. It's the recommended choice for Windows NT. NTFS is recommended over FAT because NTFS is the more secure of the two, and NTFS is not limited by the 2GB partition limit of FAT. NTFS also utilizes the disk space far more efficiently than FAT.

8. **Answer: B.** Partitions and volumes are managed by two types of file services: Novell Storage Services (NSS), which first became available on version 5.0, and NetWare File System (NFS), which is the file service used on earlier versions of NetWare but is also available on version 5.0 and later.

9. **Answers: A, C.** Microsoft is noted for client operating systems. Virtually all the Microsoft operating systems run on a NetWare network as well as on an NT/2000/XP network. Both Microsoft and Novell support implementations of UNIX, generally with the TCP/IP protocol suite.

10. **Answer: D.** The Novell directory structure begins with a root. A root is the primary object from which the tree is built.

11. **Answer: A.** The basis of the Novell directory and file organization scheme is the Novell Directory Service, or NDS.

12. **Answer: B.** The basis of the Novell directory and file organization scheme is the Novell Directory Service, or NDS. NDS is based on the ITU (formerly known as CCITT) standard X.500.

13. **Answer: B.** The UNIX operating system is portable. It is adaptable to different situations, particularly machine types and file structures.

14. **Answer: C.** In contrast, NT and NetWare use some proprietary protocols that may not be compatible across networks. For example, UNIX uses the globally implemented TCP/IP as its networking protocol. In contrast, both NT and NetWare use proprietary networking protocols, NetBEUI and IPX, respectively, which poses some challenges for interconnectivity of networks.

15. **Answer: A.** Windows NT and NetWare include a proprietary set of TCP/IP utilities. However, all commercial versions of UNIX ship with a complete package of TCP/IP.

16. **Answer: D.** Windows NT and NetWare support only 32-bit applications. Because UNIX's 64-bit capability has far superior performance applications, such as graphics and mathematical computations, it is invariably preferred over either NT or NetWare for such applications.

17. **Answer: D.** In contrast, NT and NetWare use some proprietary protocols that may not be compatible across networks. For example, UNIX uses the globally implemented TCP/IP as its networking protocol. In contrast, both NT and NetWare use proprietary networking protocols, NetBEUI and IPX, respectively, which pose some challenges for interconnectivity of networks.

18. **Answer: A.** For networking, Linux includes a complete set of TCP/IP protocols.

19. **Answer: B.** In a server-based environment, up time is normally one of the primary objectives. Therefore, you should never test hop servers and workstations in a live environment if possible. You should install the upgrade on a test server for evaluation before loading it on a working network server.

20. **Answer: C.** A workgroup is a network of computers that can share access to each other's resources. Each computer in the workgroup maintains a list of user accounts describing passwords and access rights.
21. **Answer: A.** Share-level security involves password-protecting each shared resource on a workstation. It's typically associated with workgroup or peer-to-peer LANs, but can also be applied to server-based networks.
22. **Answer: D.** Once a group account has been set up, a user may be assigned to it. Essentially, groups are a tool that eases the management of user accounts. From an administrative perspective, they save time over setting security for each user (which is how it must be done with share-level access). The option to use group accounts is set at the workstation by specifying user-level access.
23. **Answer: C.** Folders are replicated from one server to another. The machine that copies the folder to another machine is referred to as the export server, while the machine that receives the copy is called the import server. Folder replication, in addition to copying a file, automatically updates the copy when changes are made to the original.
24. **Answer: B.** Folders are replicated from one server to another. The machine that copies the folder to another machine is referred to as the export server, while the machine that receives the copy is called the import server. Folder replication, in addition to copying a file, automatically updates the copy when changes are made to the original.
25. **Answer: B, C.** If the MAC is an older workstation, AppleTalk will need to be enabled. However, with newer MACs, TCP/IP will be sufficient for all the machines to communicate.
26. **Answer**: **B.** CSNW stands for Client Services for NetWare. It is used to connect NT clients to NetWare-based servers for access to file and print sharing.
27. **Answer: C.** A UNIX client would require an IP address, a correct subnet mask, and a HOSTS file. WINS is used to resolve Windows-based NetBIOS names, and the LMHOST file is used to map out IP addresses with their relevant NetBIOS-named computers.
28. **Answer: C.** The Domain Controller (DC) in a Windows Server 2003 environment is the server that clients log in to to receive their access rights to various resources throughout the domain. As a result, the Domain Controller has stored what resources are able to be accessed by what client.
29. **Answer: B.** The Active Directory is a hierarchical directory service.
30. **Answer: D.** Apple Keychain allows a user to store multiple logins and passwords on a single user login.

31. **Answer: D.** Appleshare is used to allow Mac clients to communicate with Windows-based servers using the Apple File protocol (AFP). 802.11A is a wireless protocol.

32. **Answer: A.** When a user in a Linux environment wants to authenticate using Kerberos, the request is processed and granted by a Kerberos Key Distribution Center.

33. **Answer: B.** Both Admin and Power users groups are able to share folders by default.

34. **Answer: D.** There is no difference between mobile users and remote users in the Novell environment.

Objective 3.2

1. **Answer: D.** If the card is PnP compatible you can configure the card using software configuration. You must connect using coaxial or UTP cabling with either a BNC or RJ-45 connector, respectively. You should connect the cable first before installing the client software.

2. **Answer: B.** When assigning individual user access, there are two terms to understand: rights and profiles. Rights refer to the authorized permission to perform specific actions on the network. Profiles are the configuration settings made for each user. For example, a profile may be created that places a user in a group. This group has been given certain rights to perform specific actions on the network.

3. **Answer: A.** DHCP must be running on the server before a client can receive a dynamic IP address from a server.

4. **Answer: B.** A share-level security model must be configured on each workstation in the network. Answer A, user-level security, is set up on a server. The administrator can manage all security accounts from a central location rather than visit each workstation each time a change must be made. The network operating system doesn't directly determine the security model used on a network.

5. **Answer: C.** Share-level access applies password protection to the folder level to control, read, and change access.

6. **Answer: B.** User-level access applies to permissions assigned to a single user account or group account with similar needs to network resources.

7. **Answer: A.** User-level security is more secure and requires a user to provide a login ID, usually a username and password combination to access network resources. Share-level security is not as secure as user-level security. Password level and Layered are not accepted terms for describing levels of security.

8. **Answer: B.** Data that is being accessed by another user is placed in Read-Only mode, so that subsequent users accessing the same data at the same time cannot overwrite simultaneously the work being done by the first user.

9. **Answer: A.** Replacing hubs with switches is a practical, economical, and very effective way to improve performance on twisted-pair networks. It is the accepted upgrade path in hub-based networks. Although implementing switches is a valid approach, the cost of doing so may be prohibitive, and it is not the best option of those given. Implementing a router is not the most likely approach and would require extensive reconfiguration of the network. Implementing a bridge is not the most likely approach.

10. **Answer: D.** A 100BASE-FX fiber-optic NIC will not work with 10BASE-T UTP copper cabling.

11. **Answer: B.** When a new card is installed on a token ring network, the speed of the card has to be set to match the speed used by the network. Token ring networks operate at either 4Mbps or 16Mbps. Full-duplex connections are not used on token ring networks. Although it is possible, it is not the most likely that the card is faulty.

12. **Answers: A, B.** Because there are multiple segments, a routable protocol is required. Both NetWare and Windows 2000 support the routable TCP/IP and IPX/SPX. The Point-to-Point protocol (PPP) is used for dial-up connections, not as a network transport protocol. NetBEUI is not a routable protocol, nor is it supported by NetWare. Therefore, it is not a suitable protocol for the given configuration.

Objective 3.3

1. **Answer: D.** A time domain reflectometer can be used to find the exact location of a break in the cable. A voltmeter can be used to see whether there is continuity of a cable, but it will not tell you where the break is, if one exists. A tone generator and locator can be used to find a cable that is faulty, but it will not help you find the location of the break. Wire taps are used for taking a signal off a line for the purpose of eavesdropping.

2. **Answer: A.** A tone generator and locator are two tools used for tracing cables. Collectively they are often referred to as the "fox and hound." A time domain reflectometer is a tool used to locate a break in the cable. A voltmeter is used to measure electrical connectivity and voltages. "Cable chaser" is not a commonly used term. Wire taps are used for taking a signal off a line for the purpose of eavesdropping.

3. **Answer: C.** A token-ring media filter is used to interface a token-ring adapter card to a UTP cable.

4. **Answer: C.** A cable tester may be equipped with LEDs that illuminate for each wire that isn't broken, or it may emit a tone to indicate connectivity across the length of the cable.

5. **Answers: A, C.** A hardware loopback plug connects the 2 and 6 wires and 1 and 3 wires to simulate a live network connection. The remaining possible answers are not correct for the cabling in a hardware loopback adapter.

6. **Answer: B.** A crossover cable is required for this connection. The MDI connection indicates that the hub does not perform the crossover function internally.

7. **Answer: D.** Network Monitor and Performance Monitor, both used with Windows NT, 2000, and 2003 operating systems, are examples. They have the advantage of displaying network-related information in both real-time (as it occurs) and in recorded-time (in a log file to be viewed at a later date).

8. **Answer: C.** A punch down tool will be required to make the connections in the company's wiring closet between the incoming line (or lines) and the fan out of cables into the building.

9. **Answers: B, C.** A TDR can be used to place active signals on a copper cable for testing. This device measures the amount of time between when the signal is placed on the wire and the time it is reflected back to source. It uses this timing to determine such things as the distance to breaks in the line. The line tester is a simpler device that places signals on the wires and detects them through a loopback process, made possible by a special attachment that must be installed at the end of the cable.

Objective 3.4

1. **Answer: B.** Because the same IRQ has been assigned to both NICs, locate any available IRQ to resolve the IRQ conflict. Changing the I/O of the second NIC to B800–B81F is incorrect because the I/O addresses must be unique. The IRQ 10 assigned to both NICs will create a hardware conflict. Locating any available I/O range to resolve the I/O conflict is incorrect because there is no I/O conflict.

2. **Answer: B.** There is no apparent resource conflict associated with these settings. However, there could be conflicts with other installed devices. So if actual errors occur with these settings, the resource settings of the other devices in the system should be checked.

3. **Answer: B.** Interrupt Request (IRQ) is a setting, assigned to each device in a computer, that's used to get the attention of the microprocessor. All devices must be assigned unique IRQs so the processor can tell which device it's servicing. IRQ3 is used on COM 2 or COM4.

4. **Answer: D.** The following resources should be configured up for a modem installation: COM port, I/O Address, and Interrupt request settings.
5. **Answer: A.** If you have a standalone modem connected to an ISP from your home, you connect to the ISP using the point-to-point (PPP) protocol.
6. **Answer: B.** The correct access path to configure RAS on a Windows 2000 Server is Start, Programs, Administrative Tools, Routing, and Remote Access.
7. **Answer: B.** If the user is able to access the Internet, then the problem isn't with the Internet settings. The first thing to do is to attempt a reconnection of the VPN, which is used to allow remote users to access internal corporate resources with the proper credentials.
8. **Answer: C.** SASL, or Simple Authentication and Security Layer, is what Apple servers use to determine what authentication protocol to use, if a service is not using Kerberos servers.

Objective 3.5

1. **Answer: B.** A firewall server acts to prevent users on external networks from accessing the internal network. You can use any of the popular operating systems as a base for running a firewall application. Browser security does not secure the network itself. A Proxy server system does not actually offer any security, although the proxy functionality is combined with firewall functionality in some products.
2. **Answer: A.** Firewall systems protect a network from attack by outside sources. They are placed at the edge of the private network, so they can control traffic from a single point. Although firewalls can be placed at any point on the network, they are not normally placed between two internal networks or between client systems and servers. Firewalls normally reside at the edge of the private network boundary, not outside it.
3. **Answer: D.** Because the IP addresses have been made public—or can be deduced from a company's public presence on the Internet—they are ready targets for intruders. The key point in the question is to determine a means of thwarting outsiders from accessing the network. From the selections, only a firewall filters those whose source IP can be authenticated.
4. **Answer: A.** The purpose of the firewall system is to protect one network from another. One of the most common places to see a firewall is to protect a private network from a public one such as the Internet. Although a firewall can provide a single point of access, this is not its primary purpose. A Proxy server allows hostnames to be resolved to IP addresses. A DNS server provides a single point of access to the Internet.

5. **Answer: A.** To prevent unauthorized access into a private network from the Internet, you can use a firewall server to restrict outside access. Implementing a more secure password policy may be a good idea, but it is not the best choice of those available. Implementing a file level encryption system may be a good idea, but it is not the best choice of those available. Kerberos is an authentication system, not a method to prevent unauthorized access to the system.

6. **Answer: B.** A firewall can provide several different services to the network, including Network Address Translation (NAT), proxy and packet filtering. NAS is Network Attached Storage and is not a function of a firewall server.

7. **Answer: A.** A firewall is software or hardware that's specifically used to prevent intruders from entering a network.

8. **Answer: B.** Packet filtering firewalls operate at the network and transport layers.

Objective 3.6

1. **Answers: A, B, D.** Using a caching Proxy server allows Internet access to be centralized. Caching Proxy servers reduce the demand on the Internet connection because commonly used Web pages are retrieved from the cache rather than being retrieved from the Internet directly. It is faster to retrieve commonly used Web pages from a cache than from the Internet directly. Automatic assignment of IP addresses to workstations is the function of a DHCP server. Protection of the internal network from attack by outside sources is a function of a firewall system.

2. **Answer: C.** A Proxy server is used to prevent network workstation IP addresses from being advertised on the Internet. The Proxy server performs all packet filtering. In addition, the proxy will replace a workstation IP address with a proxy IP address and may also authenticate users via a password for connecting to the Internet.

3. **Answer: D.** For traffic inbound from the Internet, the firewall may be configured to prevent any Internet application such as FTP uploads or email. In addition, the firewall may reject all packets that are broadcast to all workstations connected to the Internet. This prevents the network workstations from being a target or unwitting accomplice in attacks against the network.

4. **Answer: C.** The purpose of a proxy is to prevent an outsider from learning IP addresses of workstations and servers with the network. Because the outsider doesn't know the IP address of any device on the network, the physical location of the device can't be learned, either.

5. **Answer: A.** A proxy server caches web pages, so that pages that tend to be frequently accessed overtime will instead be handled by the proxy server, resulting

in fewer times that web pages have to be accessed over the Internet, resulting in less bandwidth requirements.

6. **Answer: C.** A Proxy server resolves hostnames to IP addresses and replaces workstation IP addresses with proxy IP addresses. The purpose of the firewall system is to protect one network from another. One of the most common places to see a firewall is to protect a private network from a public one such as the Internet. Although a firewall can provide a single point of access, this is not its primary purpose.

7. **Answer: A.** A proxy server operates at the application layer of the OSI model.

Objective 3.7

1. **Answer: A.** Passwords should not be included in documentation because doing so represents a security risk. Ensuring that passwords are not reused, making sure that users use only "strong" passwords that are a certain length, and changing passwords on a periodic basis are valid procedures that should be included in a password policy.

2. **Answer: C.** PaSsWoRd1 contains a mix of upper-and lowercase letters, as well as a number. All other answers contain limited choices that an intruder must attempt when guessing a password. Note that PASSWORD1 is less secure than PaSsWoRd1 because PASSWORD1 contains all uppercase letters.

3. **Answer: B.** It implies that a network must be planned before any implementation efforts are made. All other answers are incorrect because they involve activities that should occur after the planning stage.

4. **Answer: A.** POP3 operates on Port 110. While there are other services between ports 100 and 200, the other options listed are FTP = 20 and 21, SMTP = 25 and HTTP = 80.

5. **Answer: C.** Changing passwords too frequently is not practical and represents a security risk. Monthly password changes are typically adequate for most environments. Changing passwords too frequently can cause problems as users may have trouble remembering passwords and use passwords that are too similar. Although passwords should be changed if they are compromised, they should also be changed periodically.

6. **Answer: C.** UNIX/Linux uses the HOSTS file to resolve logical names with their corresponding IP addresses.

7. **Answer: B.** User-level security is more secure and requires a user to provide a login ID, usually a username and password combination to access network resources. Share-level security is not as secure as user-level security. Password level and Layered are not accepted terms for describing levels of security.

8. **Answer: A.** The HOSTS file is used to manually configure host name resolution and if there is a problem with host name resolution, entries in this file must be checked. Resolv and staticdns are not used on a Linux system. The passwd file is used to store user account information.

9. **Answer: C.** The Attribute file permission is not a valid Linux file permission. The rest of possible answers are all valid file permissions on a Linux system.

10. **Answer: A.** Users should be given the option of changing passwords whenever they want. If this isn't possible, establish a policy that forces them to do so at least once a month. Normally, a notice pops up when the monthly time limit approaches, say 10 to 15 days before. Users then have two weeks to make the change. If they don't, they'll be prohibited from logging on when the password expires. This is a good system because it incorporates randomness into password changes. If all users change passwords on the same day at the same time, it won't be too difficult for a hacker to be in the right place at that specific time to catch the new password. Randomness makes it far more difficult for this to happen.

11. **Answer: A.** Users should be given the option to change passwords whenever they want. If this isn't possible, establish a policy that forces them to do so at least once a month. Normally, a notice pops up when the monthly time limit approaches, say 10 to 15 days before. Users then have two weeks to make the change. If they don't, they'll be prohibited from logging on when the password expires. This is a good system because it incorporates randomness into password changes. If all users change passwords on the same day at the same time, it won't be too difficult for a hacker to be in the right place at that specific time to catch the new password. Randomness makes it far more difficult for this to happen.

12. **Answer: D.** Users should be given the option of changing passwords whenever they want. If this isn't possible, establish a policy that forces them to do so at least once a month. Normally, a notice pops up when the monthly time limit approaches, say 10 to 15 days before. Users then have two weeks to make the change. If they don't, they'll be prohibited from logging on when the password expires. This is a good system because it incorporates randomness into password changes.

13. **Answer: D.** Secure web pages are viewed using HTTPS. HTTPS uses port 443, which is different from a normal web page that uses HTTP over port 80. Therefore, in this scenario, the most likely explanation is that port 443 is being blocked by the firewall, preventing people from accessing any pages that use HTTPS. Standard web pages use HTTP, which uses port 80 by default. Because users can access other areas of the website, this is not the problem.

Port 110 is used by POP3, an email retrieval protocol, and is therefore unrelated to this problem. Because users still can access other areas of the website, it does not block all traffic.

14. **Answer: A.** SMTP operations reside on port 25. If the firewall has not been configured to allow data on that port, SMTP operations will be blocked, legitimate or not.

15. **Answer: C.** Accessing web pages qualifies as HTTP operations, which reside on port 80. If the firewall has not been configured to allow data on that port, all web page access will be blocked, legitimate or not.

16. **Answer: A.** A security policy should include keeping user names and passwords at or below eight characters so as to avoid errors when entering, and also to reduce the likelihood of the user forgetting them. Because most password encryption schemes are case-sensitive, the password should include a mix of upper- and lowercase letters as well as numerals and special characters.

Objective 3.8

1. **Answers: A, B, D.** VLANs can be created using the IP address, the switch port assignment, or the MAC address of the connected devices. Computer names are associated with NetBIOS and are not used to create VLANs.

2. **Answer: B.** VLANS are implemented on a switch to create multiple separate networks. A Proxy server is used to control access to the Internet. Subnet masking is not a valid method of creating separate networks. Network Attached Storage (NAS) describes storage devices that are attached directly to the network media.

3. **Answers: A, C, D.** VLANs can be created using the IP address, the switch port assignment, or the MAC address of the connected devices. Computer names are associated with NetBIOS and are not used to create VLANs.

4. **Answer: C.** Virtual Private Network (VPN) is a technology that allows a secure tunnel to be created across a network such as the Internet. VPNs can be used to secure a dial-up connection for a remote user or link two sites. 802.11b is an IEEE standard for wireless networking. Virtual LANs (VLANs) are a technology implemented in network switches that allow areas of the network to be segregated from each other using a variety of criteria. A time domain reflectometer (TDR) is a tool that allows you to locate a break in a length of cable.

5. **Answer: C.** A VLAN is able to separate a larger network into smaller logical networks. These smaller networks could potentially lower total bandwidth usage.

6. **Answer: A.** VLANs require the use of a router to communicate with each other.

7. **Answer: D.** Pinging the VPN host will allow you to determine if the VPN is operational or not. If it is not, bringing the VPN back to functionality will fix the problem.

Objective 3.9

1. **Answer: C.** The model of two companies working together to share data across the internet can be accomplished via an extranet. An extranet is a private network that supports Internet applications and uses the public telecommunications system to share company information with users, customers, and partners.

2. **Answer: B.** An intranet is a private network that supports Internet applications and doesn't use the public telecommunications system to connect users.

3. **Answer: B.** An intranet is a private network that supports Internet applications and doesn't use the public telecommunications system to connect users, which offers the best security.

4. **Answer: B.** An intranet is a private network that supports Internet applications (such as email and web browsing) but does not use the public telecommunications system to connect users. The web server in an intranet may be used only for an internal website that isn't accessible from the public Internet.

5. **Answer: D.** An intranet is a network built on the TCP/IP protocol that belongs to a single organization. It is, in essence, a private Internet. Like the Internet, intranets are designed to share information and services but they are accessible only to the organization's members with authorization. In an intranet system, a local web server provides Internet applications, such as email, FTP, and web browsing for the network without using the public telephone system.

6. **Answer: D.** A hardware or software firewall is typically employed to block unauthorized, outside users from accessing the intranet site.

7. **Answer: B.** The Internet, not an intranet, is designed to be publicly available.

8. **Answer: C.** An extranet is a private network that supports Internet applications and uses the public telecommunications system to share company information with users, customers, and partners.

9. **Answer: B.** An extranet is a private network that supports Internet applications and uses the public telecommunications system to share company information with users, customers, and partners. Essentially, an extranet extends an intranet to the public Internet. Parts of an extranet remain private and separate from the Internet, while other parts of it are accessible from the Internet.

10. **Answer: C.** An extranet is a private network that supports Internet applications and uses the public telecommunications system to share company information with users, customers, and partners.

11. **Answer: A.** An extranet is a private network that supports Internet applications and uses the public telecommunications system to share company information with users, customers, and partners. Essentially, an extranet extends an intranet to the public Internet. Parts of an extranet remain private and separate from the Internet, while other parts of it are accessible from the Internet.

Objective 3.10

1. **Answer: A.** Antivirus software can stop Trojan programs. However, other software would have to be installed to effectively deal with the problems posed by spam, pop-up ads, and spyware.
2. **Answer: A.** A computer virus is an unwanted software program that can attach itself to another program on a disk or hide in a computer's memory, and can multiply from one system to another.
3. **Answer: A.** All workstations should have antivirus software installed including an email server. Email received from the Internet is the most common source of viruses.
4. **Answer: B.** Proxy servers represent a potential hole through which intruders may enter a network. Since a proxy server receives all HTTP responses from web servers, it may also be a source for viruses. The best protection against web server viruses is to install antivirus software on all proxy servers along with all client workstations.
5. **Answer: B.** For an antivirus software package to be most effective across a network, one guideline to follow is before installing a new application, the user should deactivate the antivirus scanner.
6. **Answer: B.** All email attachments should be scanned before opening them because email is the most common carrier of viruses from the Internet.
7. **Answer: D.** For users that have an FTP client, you should ensure that FTP files are scanned for viruses when opened, before being saved to a disk, and before being executed.
8. **Answer: C.** You should update virus signatures on a monthly basis (at a minimum), and more often for recent virus attacks.
9. **Answer: D.** When receiving code from a third party, be sure to scan it for viruses before using it.

Objective 3.11

1. **Answer: A.** Disk striping with parity (RAID 5) uses a minimum of three disks. With two disks, the only fault-tolerant RAID level that can be implemented is RAID 1 (disk mirroring). There are no fault-tolerant configurations that only use a single disk. With four disks, it is possible to implement RAID 5, although only three disks are actually required.

2. **Answer: D.** Striping with parity means that data is written in stripes of bits, or bytes, usually across multiple hard drives. Parity refers to a section allotted on the drive that's used to regenerate lost data. Striping enhances drive performance; whereas parity provides for fault tolerance. Tape backup provides for fault tolerance only, but doesn't address performance. Mirroring provides for fault tolerance but doesn't necessarily boost performance because writes to the drive must be duplicated to the mirror drive (it typically improves reads from the drive, however). Striping without parity addresses performance but not fault tolerance.

3. **Answer: B.** Duplexing is used to provide a dedicated drive controller to each hard drive. This directly addresses fault tolerance and network reliability by providing redundancy. Parity is a reference to using a portion of a drive to regenerate lost data. Striping refers to improving hard drive performance and doesn't address fault tolerance. SNMP (Simple Network Management Protocol) has nothing to do with dedicated controller cards.

4. **Answers: A, C, D.** Disk mirroring (RAID 1) requires two hard disks and a single hard disk controller. Disk duplexing, which is a variation of RAID 1, uses two hard disks connected to two separate disk controllers. Although not a fault-tolerant implementation, RAID 0 uses disk striping to provide increased performance. Two disks are required to implement RAID 0. Disk striping with parity (RAID 5) requires a minimum of three disks. Disk shadowing is not a valid RAID implementation.

5. **Answer: B.** An Uninterruptible Power Supply (UPS) is connected in series with a server. The server receives all power from the UPS. A stand-by power supply is used when the main power fails, causing the supply to switch to the SPS. An SPS always has a delay factor that may cause a loss of data during the switching time. Note that both a UPS and an SPS are alternative power supplies. The key to choosing correctly for this question is the hint in the question, "true, continuous power." Only a UPS provides this.

6. **Answers: A, B, C.** With two hard disks and two controllers you can implement RAID 0, RAID 1, and disk duplexing. RAID 5 (disk striping with parity), requires a minimum of three disks to be implemented. RAID 10 is a combination of RAID 1 (disk mirroring) and RAID 0 (disk striping). It requires a minimum of four disks.

7. **Answer: A.** A RAID 5 array consists of at least three hard disks and stripes parity information across all disks in the array.

8. **Answer: D.** Fault tolerance promotes data availability by eliminating a single point of failure. It may reduce the reliance on backups, but they should still be performed. A fault-tolerant system does not help a system be brought back on line more quickly. Fault tolerance does not protect data from accidental deletion.

9. **Answer: A.** Striping means that a block of data is separated and alternately written to sectors on each of the three disks. For example, suppose a 48KB file is written to the disks. RAID 0 will write 16KB to the first drive, 16KB to the second drive, and 16KB to the third drive. In other words, data blocks are striped across the fixed disks.

10. **Answer: B.** RAID 0 doesn't provide for redundancy; therefore, it has no fault tolerance attributes. RAID 0 provides improved throughput without parity. Parity is used with the other levels as a means for regenerating data, if it's lost on any of the fixed disks. If a fixed disk is lost in a RAID 0 system, all data is lost, and there is no means of recovering it; that is, it has no parity for data recovery.

11. **Answer: D.** A technique for avoiding this possibility is to duplex RAID 1 by using separate disk controllers for each fixed disk. Duplexing refers to the practice of using a separate disk controller for each fixed disk.

12. **Answer: D.** RAID 1, in which data on a primary disk is copied to a mirror disk. Mirroring is a RAID term meaning simply that all data written to one hard drive is simultaneously written to a backup—or mirror—hard drive.

13. **Answers: A, B, C.** Installing a UPS, a RAID system, and a mirror server all represent steps aimed at keeping the system going when something breaks down. Performing a backup is an activity designed for disaster recovery instead of continuation.

14. **Answer: A.** Duplexing the RAID 1 system by adding an additional controller removes the controller as a single point of failure.

15. **Answer: B.** Striping with parity means that data is written in stripes of bits, or bytes, usually across multiple hard drives. Parity refers to a section allotted on the drive that's used to regenerate lost data. Striping enhances drive performance; whereas parity provides for fault tolerance. Tape backup provides for fault tolerance only, but doesn't address performance. Mirroring provides for fault tolerance but doesn't necessarily boost performance because writes to the drive must be duplicated to the mirror drive (it typically improves reads from the drive, however). Striping without parity addresses performance but not fault tolerance.

16. **Answer: B.** Because the drive subsystem is duplexed, the drives will remain intact and will operate from the remaining controller. However, the performance will decrease because now only one channel is open for data movement.

17. **Answer: A.** Because the data drives are striped without any sort of parity, when one drive fails, both drives are rendered inoperable. There is no ability to rebuild the drives, so one would have to replace the drive and restore the contents from backup.

18. **Answer: D.** Striping offers no fault tolerance. Mirror and duplexing both require that half the hard drives be used for data redundancy. Striping with parity takes one hard drive's worth of data and uses it for parity purposes.

19. **Answer: D.** RAID 0 offers no fault tolerance. RAID 1 and mirroring both require that half the hard drives be used for data redundancy. Striping with parity takes the equivalent of one hard drive's worth of space and distributes it across all the drives for parity purposes.

20. **Answer: C.** A volume is used to subdivide partitions into smaller units. With four allowable partitions on each disk, you can have up to eight volumes on a disk. Whereas a partition is limited to a single disk, a volume can span multiple disks. A volume is organized into logical groupings, such as user directories for various departments (for example, sales, production, and so on). A volume can also be created to contain application software available across the network.

Objective 3.12

1. **Answers: A, B.** In an incremental and a full backup, files that are copied to the backup media have the archive bit cleared. A differential backup does not clear the archive bit. Periodic is not an accepted backup method.

2. **Answer: C.** Grandfather, Father, Son (GFS) is a backup rotation system that incorporates daily, weekly, and monthly backups. RAID rebuilds are only performed on an as- and a when-needed basis. Tapes should be replaced in a backup cycle periodically, although there is no accepted standard for this action.

3. **Answer: D.** A normal backup, also called a full backup, is used to copy all files on a server or workstation, or files that have been selected for copy.

4. **Answer: B.** An incremental backup is performed only on files that have changed since the last backup. A full backup is used to back up all selected files, regardless of whether they have changed. Differential is incorrect because this method will back up files that have changed since the last backup as well as all other files that have changed since the last full backup. Differential backups are cumulative, whereas incremental backups are selective. A tape backup is a backup technique rather than a backup method.

5. **Answer: B.** A daily normal backup can use as little as one tape. The single tape is used each day to perform a full backup of the server data.

6. **Answer: B.** Although this is subjective, note that as a general rule, a full backup occurs on a weekly basis.

7. **Answer: A.** Differential is used to back up files on a server. The advantage is that it is easier to restore from this because you only need the last full and the latest differential. It is also less time consuming during backups than repeatedly performing full backups. The disadvantage is that with each differential backup, more tape space is needed progressively closer to the requirements of a full backup.

8. **Answer: B.** A weekly normal backup provides a full backup to the server. The daily incremental backups are short because only files that have changed since the last incremental backup are copied.

9. **Answer: D.** Environmental disasters include fire, theft, flooding, or a crash of the server hard drive.

10. **Answers: A, B.** Both the full and incremental backup methods clear the archive bit. This indicates which data does and does not need to be backed up. In a differential backup, the archive bit is not cleared. Sequential is not a type of backup.

11. **Answer: B.** Normal backup, also called a full backup, means that all data on a hard drive is backed up, regardless of the state of the archive bit. Because all data from the hard drive is backed up this backup takes the longest.

12. **Answer: C.** Sometimes a full backup is needed —perhaps once a week—but it should be augmented with more efficient planning.

13. **Answer: D.** Normal backup, also called a full backup, means that all data on a hard drive is backed up, regardless of the state of the archive bit.

14. **Answer: A.** Servers and workstations employ data backups in the event of a disaster that may destroy crucial data. The most common method used to back up data is tape. A tape backup system is used to back up the data stored on fixed disks.

15. **Answer: D.** A differential backup occurs for all files that have changed since the last full backup, regardless of whether they changed since the last differential backup. The archive bit is set to 1 when the file is modified and not reset after the backup.

16. **Answer: B.** Incremental backup occurs only on files that have changed since the last full backup. A change to a file will set the archive bit to 1, thus flagging it for the backup.

17. **Answer: C.** The only reliable way to be certain that a backup system will perform correctly in the event of a failure is to actually perform a Restore operation in a test environment when no actual problem exists.

4

Network Support

Practice Questions

Quick Check

Objective 4.1: Given a Troubleshooting Scenario, Select the Appropriate Network Utility

1. You are troubleshooting a connectivity problem on a workstation that is unable to connect to the network. You have verified that the physical connectivity of the system is okay, and you suspect that the problem is related to the bindings of the protocols to the network cards. You decide to use the local loopback feature of the TCP/IP stack to test the configuration. Which of the following commands could you use to do this?

   Quick Answer: **217**
   Detailed Answer: **221**

   - ❑ A. Ping 127.0.0.1
   - ❑ B. Ping localhost
   - ❑ C. Ping the router
   - ❑ D. Ping another workstation on the same segment

2. Which Windows 2000-based utility displays detailed protocol connection information for TCP connections?

   Quick Answer: **217**
   Detailed Answer: **221**

   - ❑ A. NetBIOS
   - ❑ B. Nbtstat
   - ❑ C. Netstat
   - ❑ D. Ping

Quick Check

3. A user is experiencing connectivity problems to a remote system. While sitting at the user's computer, you determine that the TCP/IP configuration of the workstation is correct and that you are able to ping the local loopback, the IP address of the system itself, and the IP address of the default gateway. What is the next step in the troubleshooting process?

Quick Answer: **217**
Detailed Answer: **221**

- ❑ A. Reinitialize the TCP/IP stack
- ❑ B. Remove and reinstall the TCP/IP protocol
- ❑ C. Change the IP address to one in another range
- ❑ D. Ping the remote host

4. Which of the following protocol suites provides the Ping utility for use in troubleshooting situations?

Quick Answer: **217**
Detailed Answer: **221**

- ❑ A. TCP/IP
- ❑ B. NetBEUI
- ❑ C. RTMP
- ❑ D. IPX/SPX

5. What does the command arp -a do when executed on a Windows 2000 system?

Quick Answer: **217**
Detailed Answer: **221**

- ❑ A. It displays the list of IP addresses that have been resolved to MAC addresses.
- ❑ B. It displays the list of NetBIOS names that have been resolved to IP addresses.
- ❑ C. It removes all the current entries from the ARP table.
- ❑ D. It allows a static entry to be added to the ARP table.

6. Which command can you use to view a list of the NetBIOS names and the associated IP addresses that have been resolved by the system?

Quick Answer: **217**
Detailed Answer: **221**

- ❑ A. netstat
- ❑ B. nbtstat -c
- ❑ C. arp -a
- ❑ D. tracert

7. To view the IP address of a workstation, which of the following is the best tool to use?

Quick Answer: **217**
Detailed Answer: **222**

- ❑ A. Netstat
- ❑ B. Tracert
- ❑ C. Ipconfig
- ❑ D. FTP

Quick Check

8. To check the connection to a remote server, which TCP/IP utility will show all routers to the remote server?
   - ❑ A. Tracert
   - ❑ B. Telnet
   - ❑ C. Netstat
   - ❑ D. Ping

Quick Answer: 217
Detailed Answer: 222

9. The IP address of a workstation is 192.168.20.2. It's connected to a hub with an IP address of 192.168.20.3. Which of the following will check the connection status between workstation and hub?
   - ❑ A. ipconfig/all
   - ❑ B. Ping 192.168.20.3
   - ❑ C. arp 192.168
   - ❑ D. tracert 192.168.20.3

Quick Answer: 217
Detailed Answer: 222

10. An installed NIC card is working properly. What will happen if you ping the card using 127.0.0.1?
    - ❑ A. The screen shows the IP of the host in which the card is installed.
    - ❑ B. The screen echoes the IP of the default gateway.
    - ❑ C. The screen shows the return of four, 32-byte packets.
    - ❑ D. It will time-out.

Quick Answer: 217
Detailed Answer: 222

11. What TCP/IP utility displays all current connections and ports?
    - ❑ A. Netstat
    - ❑ B. Nbtstat
    - ❑ C. Arp
    - ❑ D. Tracert

Quick Answer: 217
Detailed Answer: 222

12. What command would you use to delete entries host file?
    - ❑ A. arp -d
    - ❑ B. nbtstat -R
    - ❑ C. ipconfig /renew
    - ❑ D. netstat -n

Quick Answer: 217
Detailed Answer: 222

13. You have been called by a user who complains that access to a Web page is very slow. What utility can you use to find the bottleneck?
    - ❑ A. Ping
    - ❑ B. Telnet
    - ❑ C. Tracert
    - ❑ D. Nbtstat

Quick Answer: 217
Detailed Answer: 222

Quick Check

14. What utility do you use to check your IP configuration on a Windows 95/98 workstation?

Quick Answer: **217**
Detailed Answer: **222**

- ❑ A. Winipcfg
- ❑ B. Netstat
- ❑ C. Ping
- ❑ D. Ipconfig

15. You are troubleshooting a server connectivity problem on your network. A Windows 95 system is having trouble connecting to a Windows 2000 Server. Which of the following commands would you use to display per protocol statistics on the workstation system?

Quick Answer: **217**
Detailed Answer: **223**

- ❑ A. netstat -s
- ❑ B. arp -A
- ❑ C. nbtstat -s
- ❑ D. ping

16. You are experiencing a problem with a workstation and want to ping the localhost. Which two of the following are valid ways to check your local TCP/IP connection?

Quick Answer: **217**
Detailed Answer: **223**

- ❑ A. ping 127.0.0.1
- ❑ B. ping localhost
- ❑ C. ping host
- ❑ D. ping 127.0.0.0

17. While troubleshooting a network connectivity problem on a Windows 2000 Server, you need to view a list of the IP addresses that have been resolved to MAC addresses. Which of the following commands would you use to do this?

Quick Answer: **217**
Detailed Answer: **223**

- ❑ A. arp -s
- ❑ B. nbtstat -a
- ❑ C. arp -d
- ❑ D. arp –a

18. While troubleshooting a sporadic network connectivity problem on a Windows 2000 system, a fellow technician suggests that you run the ping -t command. What is the purpose of this command?

Quick Answer: **217**
Detailed Answer: **223**

- ❑ A. It allows the number of Ping messages to be specific.
- ❑ B. It shows the time, in seconds, that the packet takes to reach the destination.
- ❑ C. It pings the remote host continually until it is stopped.
- ❑ D. It shows the route taken by a packet to reach the destination host.

Quick Check

19. What utility would you use to view the TCP connections that have been established between two systems?

❑ A. Ipconfig
❑ B. Nbtstat
❑ C. Tracert
❑ D. Netstat

Quick Answer: 217
Detailed Answer: 223

20. Which TCP/IP utility is used to show IP addresses?

❑ A. Ping
❑ B. Netstat
❑ C. Ipconfig
❑ D. Tracert

Quick Answer: 217
Detailed Answer: 223

21. What utility do you use to check your IP configuration on a Windows 95 workstation?

❑ A. Ipconfig
❑ B. Netstat
❑ C. Ping
❑ D. Winipcfg

Quick Answer: 217
Detailed Answer: 223

22. To determine the computer name of a remote server, you would ______.

❑ A. start a Telnet session with the remote server
❑ B. use the tracert command to perform a trace to the IP address of the server
❑ C. use the ping command to loopback the IP address of the server
❑ D. use the nbtstat command to resolve the name of the remote server to its IP address

Quick Answer: 217
Detailed Answer: 223

23. Which TCP/IP utility is used for determining NetBIOS names?

❑ A. Tracert
❑ B. Nbtstat
❑ C. Netstat
❑ D. Ping

Quick Answer: 217
Detailed Answer: 224

24. Users on a LAN are unable to connect to the server. To isolate the problem between workstations and server, which of the following should be run?

❑ A. Nbtstat
❑ B. Ipconfig
❑ C. Netstat
❑ D. Ping

Quick Answer: 217
Detailed Answer: 224

Quick Check

25. Which TCP/IP utility is used to show the number of packets sent and received on a workstation?
    - ❑ A. Nbtstat
    - ❑ B. Netstat
    - ❑ C. Nptstat
    - ❑ D. Arp

Quick Answer: **217**
Detailed Answer: **224**

26. The IP address of a workstation is 192.168.20.2. It's connected to a hub with an IP address of 192.168.20.3. Which of the following will check the connection status between workstation and hub?
    - ❑ A. ping 192.168.20.3
    - ❑ B. ipconfig /all
    - ❑ C. arp 192.168
    - ❑ D. tracert 192.168.20.3

Quick Answer: **217**
Detailed Answer: **224**

27. Which commands will NOT display the MAC address of the workstation?
    - ❑ A. ifconfig
    - ❑ B. ipconfig
    - ❑ C. ifconfig /all
    - ❑ D. winipcfg

Quick Answer: **217**
Detailed Answer: **224**

28. You are working on one of the network's servers and you want to check connectivity to the workstations via NetBIOS names. What command would you use to do this?
    - ❑ A. nbtstat
    - ❑ B. nslookup
    - ❑ C. netstat
    - ❑ D. netwatch

Quick Answer: **217**
Detailed Answer: **224**

29. Network users report that they have slow Internet connections. You check the network with the Network Monitor utility, which reports high activity, although no users are accessing the network. What tool would you use to list the active network connections?
    - ❑ A. netstat
    - ❑ B. traceroute
    - ❑ C. nslookup
    - ❑ D. ping

Quick Answer: **217**
Detailed Answer: **224**

Quick Check

30. Your remote office has changed location and all of the network devices have been assigned new addresses. Local users have no problems accessing the resources, but remote users can only access these devices by IP address. Which utility would you use first to get a better understanding of the problem from a DNS perspective?

Quick Answer: **217**
Detailed Answer: **224**

- ❑ A. Arp
- ❑ B. Netstat
- ❑ C. Tracert
- ❑ D. Nslookup

31. When running the Ping command, you receive a report that says: "Destination Unreachable." What is the most likely cause of this response?

Quick Answer: **217**
Detailed Answer: **224**

- ❑ A. The Host is in another country.
- ❑ B. The Host is on the same subnet.
- ❑ C. There is a misconfigured router.
- ❑ D. The router is the default gateway.

32. You are experiencing problems with the network connectivity of a Windows 2000 system, and you suspect that there might be a problem with an incorrect route in the routing table. Which two of the following TCP/IP utilities can you use to view the routing table?

Quick Answer: **217**
Detailed Answer: **224**

- ❑ A. Tracert
- ❑ B. Netstat
- ❑ C. Route
- ❑ D. Nbtstat
- ❑ E. Ping

Quick Check

Objective 4.2: Given Output from a Diagnostic Utility (Tracert, Ping, Ipconfig, and so on), Identify the Utility and Interpret the Output

1. Examine the following output:

    Reply from 24.67.184.1: bytes=32 time=20ms TTL=64
    Reply from 24.67.184.1: bytes=32 time=60ms TTL=64
    Reply from 24.67.184.1: bytes=32 time=10ms TTL=64
    Reply from 24.67.184.1: bytes=32 time=10ms TTL=64

    Which utility generated this output?

    ❑ A. Ping
    ❑ B. Tracert
    ❑ C. Netstat
    ❑ D. Nbtstat

Quick Answer: 217
Detailed Answer: 224

2. Examine the following output:

    1 10 ms 10 ms 20 ms 24.67.184.1
    2 20 ms 20 ms 20 ms rd1ht-ge3-0.ok.shawcable.net [24.67.224.7]
    3 20 ms 20 ms 30 ms rd2ht-ge4-0.ok.shawcable.net [204.209.214.238]
    4 60 ms 30 ms 30 ms rc2wh-atm0-2-1.vc.sha.net [204.209.214.205]
    5 30 ms 31 ms 230 ms rc2wt-pos2-0.wa.shawcable.net [66.163.76.37]
    6 30 ms 40 ms 40 ms c1-pos6-3.sttlwa1.home.net [24.7.70.37]

    Which command generated this output?

    ❑ A. ping
    ❑ B. tracert
    ❑ C. netstat
    ❑ D. nbtstat

Quick Answer: 217
Detailed Answer: 224

3. Which of the following utilities returns the number of errors generated during a connection?

    ❑ A. Ipconfig
    ❑ B. Ping
    ❑ C. Netstat
    ❑ D. Telnet

Quick Answer: 217
Detailed Answer: 224

Quick Check

4. Which of the following utilities would you typically use to determine the number of hops to a specific destination?

Quick Answer: 217
Detailed Answer: 225

- ❑ A. Nbtstat
- ❑ B. Netstat
- ❑ C. Ping
- ❑ D. Tracert

5. Which TCP/IP command produces the following output?

Quick Answer: 217
Detailed Answer: 225

Proto	Local Address	Foreign Address	State
TCP	laptop:1028	LAPTOP:0	LISTENING
TCP	laptop:1031	LAPTOP:0	LISTENING
TCP	laptop:1093	LAPTOP:0	LISTENING
TCP	laptop:50000	LAPTOP:0	LISTENING
TCP	laptop:5000	LAPTOP:0	LISTENING
TCP	laptop:1031	n218.audiogalaxy.com:ftp	ESTABLISHED
TCP	laptop:1319	h24-67-184-65.ok.shawcable.net:nbsess	

- ❑ A. netstat
- ❑ B. nbtstat
- ❑ C. ping
- ❑ D. tracert -R

6. Which of these commands generates the following output?

Quick Answer: 217
Detailed Answer: 225

7	60 ms	30 ms	40 ms	home-gw.st6wa.ip.att.net [192.205.32.249]
8	30 ms	40 ms	30 ms	gbr3-p40.st6wa.ip.att.net [12.123.44.130]
9	50 ms	50 ms	60 ms	gbr4-p10.sffca.ip.att.net [12.122.2.61]
10	60 ms	60 ms	60 ms	gbr3-p10.la2ca.ip.att.net [12.122.2.169]
11	90 ms	60 ms	70 ms	gbr6-p60.la2ca.ip.att.net [12.122.5.97]

- ❑ A. ping
- ❑ B. netstat
- ❑ C. tracert
- ❑ D. ipconfig

Quick Check

7. A user calls to inform you that she can't access the Internet from her system. When you visit the user, you run the ipconfig /all utility and see the following information. What is the most likely reason the user is having problems accessing the Internet?

Quick Answer: 217
Detailed Answer: 225

```
C:\>ipconfig /all
Windows 2000 IP Configuration
    Host Name . . . . . . . . . . . . : LAPTOP
    Primary DNS Suffix . . . . . . . :
    Node Type . . . . . . . . . . . . : Broadcast
    IP Routing Enabled. . . . . . . . : No
    WINS Proxy Enabled. . . . . . . . : No
Ethernet adapter Local Area Connection:
    Connection-specific DNS Suffix . :
    Description . . . . . . . . . . . : Intel 8255x-based PCI Ethernet
    Physical Address. . . . . . . . . : 00-D0-59-09-07-51
    DHCP Enabled. . . . . . . . . . . : No
    IP Address. . . . . . . . . . . . : 192.168.2.1
    Subnet Mask . . . . . . . . . . . : 255.255.255.0
    Default Gateway . . . . . . . . . :
    DNS Servers . . . . . . . . . . . : 192.168.2.10
                                        192.168.2.20
```

- ❑ A. DHCP is not enabled.
- ❑ B. The default gateway setting is not configured.
- ❑ C. The subnet mask is incorrect.
- ❑ D. The system is on a different subnet than the DNS servers.

8. To determine delays from a local machine to a remote server on the Internet, you would ________.

Quick Answer: 217
Detailed Answer: 225

- ❑ A. nbtstat the IP address of the remote server
- ❑ B. ping the IP address of the server
- ❑ C. tracert to the IP address of the server
- ❑ D. start a Telnet session with the remote server

Quick Check

9. Which of the following TCP/IP commands generates the following output?

Quick Answer: 217
Detailed Answer: 225

Interface: 192.168.0.2 --- 0x2

Internet Address	Physical Address	Type
192.168.0.1	00-0d-44-b2-a5-c3	static
192.168.0.10	00-0b-47-a5-19-43	dynamic

- ❑ A. ping
- ❑ B. arp -a
- ❑ C. nbstat
- ❑ D. tracert

10. Which of the following TCP/IP commands generates the following output?

Quick Answer: 217
Detailed Answer: 225

1 15 ms <10 ms <10 ms 192.168.2.1

2 31 ms 32 ms 31 ms wbar8.sea1-4-4-064-001.sea1.dsl-verizon.net [4.4.64.1]

3 31 ms 31 ms 47 ms 4.9.0.161

4 31 ms 31 ms 47 ms vnsc-pri.sys.gtei.net [4.2.2.1]

Trace complete.

- ❑ A. tracert
- ❑ B. pathping
- ❑ C. netstat
- ❑ D. arp -d

11. Which of these TCP/IP commands generates the following output?

Quick Answer: 217
Detailed Answer: 225

Connection-specific DNS Suffix . : server.isp.com
IP Address. . . . .: 192.168.0.2
Subnet Mask . . . .: 255.255.255.0
Default Gateway . . . .: 192.168.0.1

- ❑ A. ping
- ❑ B. ipconfig
- ❑ C. tracert
- ❑ D. arp -d

Quick Check

12. Which TCP/IP utility generates the following output?

Quick Answer: **217**
Detailed Answer: **225**

Local Area Connection:
Node IpAddress: [192.168.0.1] Scope ID: []

NetBIOS Remote Machine Name Table

Name		Type	Status
Computername	<00>	UNIQUE	Registered
DOMAIN	<00>	GROUP	Registered
Computername	<20>	UNIQUE	Registered
USER	<03>	UNIQUE	Registered

MAC Address = 00-10-AB-1D-A1-FF

- ❑ A. Nbtstat
- ❑ B. Ipconfig
- ❑ C. Tracert
- ❑ D. Arp -d

Objective 4.3: Given a Network Scenario, Interpret Visual Indicators (Link Lights, Collision Lights, and so on) to Determine the Nature of the Stated Problem

1. You are troubleshooting a problem in which a workstation is experiencing intermittent connectivity problems. You arrive at the workstation and notice that the link light on the network card flashes intermittently. Which three of the following troubleshooting steps might you try?

Quick Answer: **218**
Detailed Answer: **225**

- ❑ A. Plug the workstation into a different port on the network hub.
- ❑ B. Change the network card in the workstation.
- ❑ C. Try a known working cable on the connection to see whether it works.
- ❑ D. Change the IP address to a different one in the same subnet.

2. A workstation NIC link light isn't illuminated. After replacing the NIC, the light still isn't lit. What should be done next?

Quick Answer: **218**
Detailed Answer: **226**

- ❑ A. Reboot the server.
- ❑ B. Replace the cable connecting the NIC to the hub.
- ❑ C. Replace the hub.
- ❑ D. Replace the workstation.

Quick Check

3. What is the value of NIC card LEDs?

Quick Answer: 218
Detailed Answer: 226

- ❑ A. They tell you whether the NIC is sending and receiving.
- ❑ B. They are a good indicator of the status of a router.
- ❑ C. They tell you whether the network is operational.
- ❑ D. They tell you whether the workstation system board is working.

4. You are troubleshooting a problem in which a workstation is experiencing intermittent connectivity problems. You notice that the link light on the network card flashes intermittently. Which three of the following are valid next troubleshooting steps?

Quick Answer: 218
Detailed Answer: 226

- ❑ A. Plug the workstation into a different port on the network hub.
- ❑ B. Change the network card in the workstation.
- ❑ C. Try a known working cable on the connection to see if it works.
- ❑ D. Change the IP address to a different one in the same subnet.

5. After installing a NIC card and properly setting up the workstation, there's no link light on the NIC. You test the network cable and it is good. What action should be taken next?

Quick Answer: 218
Detailed Answer: 226

- ❑ A. Run diagnostics on the NIC such as a hardware loopback.
- ❑ B. Replace the NIC.
- ❑ C. Attach a network analyzer to the server and check all connections.
- ❑ D. Replace the hub.

6. A group of clients on a network segment complains that they are unable to access a remote web server, which is the only thing they are allowed to access outside of their network. The technician notes that the red LED of the Link light of the router that services the clients' network is lit solid. The web server can be accessed successfully through another router on a different remote network. What is the problem with the first router?

Quick Answer: 218
Detailed Answer: 226

- ❑ A. The router is possibly being attacked from the WAN side.
- ❑ B. The router is detecting too many packet collisions.
- ❑ C. The hub that the clients use is damaged.
- ❑ D. The router is disconnected.

Quick Check

7. A user connects both a modem and a laptop to a switch, using straight Ethernet cabling for both devices. The LED is not lit on the switch connection to the modem. Which of the following is the likely cause of this condition?

Quick Answer: 218
Detailed Answer: 226

- ❑ A. The Ethernet port is broken on the laptop.
- ❑ B. The cable is defective between the laptop and the switch.
- ❑ C. The switch needs to be set to MDIX.
- ❑ D. The switch needs to be set to MDI.

8. You move a computer to a new network, using the original ethernet cable that came with the computer. However, when you start it up you notice that nothing is being displayed from the activity light on the back of the NIC. What is the most likely cause of this condition?

Quick Answer: 217
Detailed Answer: 226

- ❑ A. The NIC has failed.
- ❑ B. The hub port is bad.
- ❑ C. The cabling to the hub is bad.
- ❑ D. The DHCP Server is down.

Objective 4.4: Given a Troubleshooting Scenario Involving a Client Accessing Remote Network, Identify the Cause of the Problem (File Services, Print Services, Authentication Failure, Protocol Configuration, Physical Connectivity and SOHO Router)

1. A remote user calls you to report a problem connecting to the corporate network over his DSL connection. The user can connect to the Internet and browse web pages, but can't connect to the corporate remote access gateway. Which of the following troubleshooting steps would you perform first?

Quick Answer: 218
Detailed Answer: 226

- ❑ A. Have the user reconfigure the IP address on his system to one of the address ranges used on the internal corporate network, and try again.
- ❑ B. Have the user reboot his system.
- ❑ C. Check the corporate remote access gateway to see whether it is running and operating correctly.
- ❑ D. Have the user power cycle the DSL modem and try again.

Quick Check

2. A client has a wireless home network using IEEE 802.11b standard. When the laptop is more than 150 feet away from the wireless AP sending data is slow. What is causing this?

Quick Answer: 218
Detailed Answer: 226

- ❑ A. The farther away from the AP you are the slower the data rate will be.
- ❑ B. The batteries are dead.
- ❑ C. The antenna is loose.
- ❑ D. The cable is disconnected.

3. Prior to installing a firewall, your network clients are able to access remote files with no problem. After the firewall is installed, they can no longer access the remote files. What should be done to correct this problem?

Quick Answer: 218
Detailed Answer: 226

- ❑ A. Reboot the client computers.
- ❑ B. Ask the Administrator to reboot the server.
- ❑ C. Ask the Administrator to open the correct ports in the firewall.
- ❑ D. Change the client TCP/IP configuration to accept the new firewall.

4. A user reports that he cannot reach remote servers using his domain name, but can reach them using their numerical IP addresses. In the past, he was able to reach remote servers using his domain name. What is the most likely cause of this problem?

Quick Answer: 218
Detailed Answer: 226

- ❑ A. The address resolution protocol is not working.
- ❑ B. The domain name server needs to be repaired.
- ❑ C. The computers need to be configured with the DHCP client service.
- ❑ D. The computers need to be configured with the DNS client service.

5. You have clients who cannot access remote networks. Their IP configuration is valid. What should you check first?

Quick Answer: 218
Detailed Answer: 227

- ❑ A. The HOST file
- ❑ B. The DNS configuration
- ❑ C. The Default Gateway to determine that it is active
- ❑ D. The LMHOST file

Quick Check

6. You receive a "Forbidden…" error message after changing the directory where the file is stored. What should be done to correct this situation?

   ❑ A. Change the symbolic link.

   ❑ B. Change permissions to the directory.

   ❑ C. Reinstall the Operating System, as it has been corrupted.

   ❑ D. Rename the file.

Quick Answer: **218**
Detailed Answer: **227**

7. The network administrator from the outside world can ping www.mic-inc.com, but he cannot ping one of the clients that are a part of the mic-inc.com network. In addition, that client cannot access the Internet. What is the most likely cause of this problem?

   ❑ A. The user is on a different network segment than the web server, and that specific segment is unable to connect to the internet.

   ❑ B. The web server is disconnected.

   ❑ C. The network administrator has incorrectly configured WINS settings.

   ❑ D. The www.mic-inc.com clients are on a wireless network, and therefore cannot be pinged.

Quick Answer: **218**
Detailed Answer: **227**

8. A user calls you to help him troubleshoot a dial-up modem problem. The modem dials the number and is answered but is disconnected shortly thereafter. Which two of the following troubleshooting steps might you suggest?

   ❑ A. Reinstall the device drivers for the modem.

   ❑ B. Check the configuration for the dial-up connection.

   ❑ C. Replace the cable that connects the modem to the phone socket.

   ❑ D. Check the authentication information.

Quick Answer: **218**
Detailed Answer: **227**

9. You are troubleshooting a connectivity problem on a workstation in which the system is able to communicate with other devices on the same segment, but is unable to communicate with devices on other segments. Other devices on the segment can communicate with remote systems. Which of the following are valid reasons for this scenario?

   ❑ A. The IP address of the workstation is incorrect.

   ❑ B. The router acting as the default gateway is misconfigured or not running.

   ❑ C. The default gateway setting on the workstation is incorrect or missing.

   ❑ D. The subnet mask of the workstation is incorrect.

Quick Answer: **218**
Detailed Answer: **227**

Quick Check

10. You receive a call from a user who says she can't establish a remote connection to her ISP. The user describes her connection as SLIP for a network running AppleTalk. Which of the following represents the best solution to establish the remote connection?

Quick Answer: 218
Detailed Answer: 227

- ❑ A. Change the network protocol to IPX/SPX.
- ❑ B. Change the client's computers to run Windows 95 or 98.
- ❑ C. Change the access protocol to PPP.
- ❑ D. Change the access method to ISDN.

11. A user calls you from a motel room. He has tried numerous times to dial in to the corporate RAS server, but the modem in his system is reporting a no dial tone error. What is the most likely cause of the problem?

Quick Answer: 218
Detailed Answer: 227

- ❑ A. The phone line in the room is digital.
- ❑ B. The phone line in the room is faulty.
- ❑ C. The modem is faulty.
- ❑ D. The phone line in the room is analog.

12. Client computers on a network can exchange files but none can access the Internet. What is the likely problem?

Quick Answer: 218
Detailed Answer: 227

- ❑ A. TCP/IP has been installed on the network.
- ❑ B. The hub isn't functioning.
- ❑ C. The NIC cards don't have MAC addresses.
- ❑ D. The default gateway isn't configured correctly.

13. After installing a new Proxy server system, users cannot connect to another system using FTP. Your manager asks you to reconfigure the Proxy server to correct this problem. Which port on the Proxy server would you allow to facilitate FTP connections?

Quick Answer: 218
Detailed Answer: 227

- ❑ A. 21
- ❑ B. 23
- ❑ C. 81
- ❑ D. 110

Quick Check

14. A number of users have called to report problems printing. Upon investigation, you find the cause to be a network printer connected to a network server. The printer is connected, online, and it appears to perform a test print without any problems. You check the network connectivity and that seems to be okay as well. Which of the following troubleshooting steps would you perform next?

Quick Answer: 218
Detailed Answer: 228

- ❑ A. Remove and reinstall the printer drivers.
- ❑ B. Reboot the server that is acting as the print server.
- ❑ C. Examine the log files on the server to see if there are any printing related events.
- ❑ D. Change the network cable that connects the printer to the network.

15. After creating a new secure page for your website, external users complain that they cannot access it, but they can access other areas of the site. When you try to access it from a workstation internally, everything seems fine. What is the most likely explanation of the problem?

Quick Answer: 218
Detailed Answer: 228

- ❑ A. Your firewall is blocking all traffic.
- ❑ B. Your firewall is blocking port 80.
- ❑ C. Your firewall is blocking port 110.
- ❑ D. Your firewall is blocking port 443.

16. None of the users on a network can log on to the server. The link lights on all client NICs are lit, and the same lights are lit at the hub. The server NIC link light and the corresponding hub port light are not lit. When one of the workstation cables is inserted into the server port at the hub, the hub link light is lit. What is the likely problem?

Quick Answer: 218
Detailed Answer: 228

- ❑ A. The cable from hub to workstations.
- ❑ B. The hub is bad.
- ❑ C. The server cable is bad.
- ❑ D. The hub port is bad.

Quick Check

Objective 4.5: Given a Troubleshooting Scenario Between a Client and the Following Server Environments (UNIX/Linux/MAC OS X, NetWare, Windows, and Appleshare IP), Identify the Cause

1. You have been given the task of installing a number of new PCs on your Novell NetWare-based network. You are using DHCP to automatically assign IP address information. Which two of the following pieces of information would you enter into the configuration of the workstation?

   Quick Answer: **218**
   Detailed Answer: **228**

   - ❑ A. DNS server address
   - ❑ B. The DNS tree name to which the workstation should connect
   - ❑ C. The DNS context in which the user object resides
   - ❑ D. IP address of the default gateway
   - ❑ E. The workstation IP address
   - ❑ F. DHCP server address

2. As the system administrator, you have been asked to install a NetWare 5.x server system on your network. You have 20 Windows 98 workstations and 4 Linux systems that are used as clients. Which two of the following can you install on the Windows 98 systems to allow you to connect to the NetWare server?

   Quick Answer: **218**
   Detailed Answer: **228**

   - ❑ A. Novell Client for Windows 95/98
   - ❑ B. Microsoft Client for NetWare Networks
   - ❑ C. Novell CAFS Client
   - ❑ D. Nothing, as long as TCP/IP is the default protocol

3. You have been tasked with installing five new Windows 95 client systems, including the Novell Client software. Which two pieces of information will you need during the Novell Client install to configure the connection to the NetWare server?

   Quick Answer: **218**
   Detailed Answer: **228**

   - ❑ A. The context in which the user resides
   - ❑ B. Domain name
   - ❑ C. Username
   - ❑ D. Target NDS replica name NDS tree name
   - ❑ E. Password
   - ❑ F. Target NDS replica

Quick Check

4. You are working as a network administrator for a UNIX system. The system uses dynamic name resolution. What is used to dynamically resolve a host name on a UNIX server?

   Quick Answer: 218
   Detailed Answer: 229

   - ❑ A. BIND (DNS)
   - ❑ B. ARP
   - ❑ C. WINS
   - ❑ D. LMHOSTS

Objective 4.6: Given a Scenario, Determine the Impact of Modifying, Adding, or Removing Network Services (DHCP, DNS, WINS, and so on) on Network Resources and Users

1. Users connected to an NT server cannot communicate outside their LAN. When their computers are pinged by name, the result is negative; but when they're pinged by IP, it works. Which of the following is the likely cause?

   Quick Answer: 219
   Detailed Answer: 229

   - ❑ A. Incorrect NDS configuration
   - ❑ B. Incorrect WINS configuration
   - ❑ C. Incorrect HOST configuration
   - ❑ D. Incorrect DHCP configuration

2. You can connect to an Internet site using the IP address but not with the domain name for that site. What is the problem?

   Quick Answer: 219
   Detailed Answer: 229

   - ❑ A. Incorrect WINS configuration
   - ❑ B. Incorrect HOST configuration
   - ❑ C. Incorrect DNS configuration
   - ❑ D. Incorrect DHCP configuration

3. A client is configured for a dynamic IP address. When the user turns on the computer, they are unable to access the network. What is the most likely cause of the problem?

   Quick Answer: 219
   Detailed Answer: 229

   - ❑ A. The server on the network segment has not been configured for DHCP.
   - ❑ B. The client has no entries in the LMHOST file.
   - ❑ C. The server does not have a properly configured DNS server.
   - ❑ D. The server is only using the TCP/IP protocol, not NetBEUI.

Quick Check

4. What will happen if a client is given a static IP address when the server is using DHCP to assign IP addresses?

Quick Answer: 219
Detailed Answer: 229

- ❑ A. The client will be the sole owner of that static IP address.
- ❑ B. The client will have two IP addresses.
- ❑ C. The client with the static IP address will become the server of the network.
- ❑ D. Another client may try to use the same IP address.

5. Your company network has a mixture of Windows 2000 and NetWare servers. When you install a new group of Windows XP client machines, they can connect to the Windows servers but not to the NetWare servers. What is the most likely reason for this?

Quick Answer: 219
Detailed Answer: 229

- ❑ A. TCP/IP has not been configured on the clients.
- ❑ B. NDS has not been configured on the clients.
- ❑ C. Client Services for NetWare has not been installed on the clients.
- ❑ D. LMHOSTS has not been installed on the clients.

6. The network slows down noticeably after the office building is remodeled. Which of the following is the most possible cause?

Quick Answer: 219
Detailed Answer: 229

- ❑ A. Disconnected network
- ❑ B. EMI
- ❑ C. Faulty NIC card
- ❑ D. No DNS server

7. During a meeting with your ISP Account Manager, he suggests that it might be appropriate for you to install a DNS server internally. Which of the following functions will the DNS server provide?

Quick Answer: 219
Detailed Answer: 229

- ❑ A. It will perform network address translation services.
- ❑ B. It will streamline the resolution of NetBIOS names to IP addresses.
- ❑ C. It will allow some hostname to IP address resolutions to occur internally.
- ❑ D. It will allow users to retrieve Internet web pages more quickly.

8. DNS is to be set up on a workstation. The host and domain name is entered. Which of the following is the next step?

Quick Answer: 219
Detailed Answer: 229

- ❑ A. The DNS Server Search Order must be entered.
- ❑ B. This is all the information that's needed.
- ❑ C. NetBEUI must be running on the workstation.
- ❑ D. The Domain Suffix Search Order must be entered.

Quick Check

9. A client is going to add another 20 nodes to the network before the end of next month. These PCs will be running I/O-intensive CAD/CAM applications. What PC bus architecture would you recommend?

Quick Answer: **219**
Detailed Answer: **230**

- ❑ A. PCMCIA
- ❑ B. EISA
- ❑ C. MCA
- ❑ D. PCI

10. If a DNS server suffers a catastrophic failure, what happens to the clients being served by it?

Quick Answer: **219**
Detailed Answer: **230**

- ❑ A. They will be unable to automatically renew their IP address.
- ❑ B. They will be unable to connect to a server using a Host name.
- ❑ C. They will be unable to connect to the server using a NetBIOS name.
- ❑ D. They will be unable to connect to a server using its IP address.

11. Your company has two subnets on its network. Subnet A uses 192.168.1.X, subnet B uses 192.168.2.X. An Administrator installs a new server on subnet A and assigns it the address of 192.168.1.2, with a DHCP scope of 192.168.2.2–192.168.2.100. The users on subnet A complain that they cannot connect to company resources. The users on subnet B have no problems. How would you correct this problem?

Quick Answer: **219**
Detailed Answer: **230**

- ❑ A. Add a DHCP Relay Agent
- ❑ B. Add a second DHCP Scope
- ❑ C. Add an Alias record for subnet A to the DNS server
- ❑ D. Have the users on Subnet A reboot their machines

12. The DHCP scope has been adjusted so that the leases will be changed every day instead of every two weeks. What effect will this have on users?

Quick Answer: **219**
Detailed Answer: **230**

- ❑ A. No change will be noticed by the users
- ❑ B. Users will have to log in every day
- ❑ C. Users will have to use IPConfig /release and /renew daily
- ❑ D. Users will be required to manually update their IP lease information every day

Quick Check

13. You add a new Windows Server 2003 server acting as a mail server to your network and you want to update the A records. Who should be contacted?

Quick Answer: 219
Detailed Answer: 230

- ❑ A. Any ISP.
- ❑ B. No one, they should be updated automatically.
- ❑ C. The Domain Registrar.
- ❑ D. The ISP who hosts the domain.

14. You are adding a router with a new subnet and you want to accommodate NetBIOS. What will have to be installed?

Quick Answer: 219
Detailed Answer: 230

- ❑ A. The DHCP service
- ❑ B. The WINS service
- ❑ C. The NTP service
- ❑ D. The DNS service

15. You connect your network to another company network through a router. Your original network employs a DHCP server to generate IP addresses for its clients. When you start the network up again, you discover that the server is not configuring clients on the additional network segment. What action is required to get everyone working together in this extended network?

Quick Answer: 219
Detailed Answer: 230

- ❑ A. Set up DHCP in the additional network segment clients
- ❑ B. Install a DHCP relay agent
- ❑ C. Set up APIPA configuration in the additional network segment clients
- ❑ D. Move the DHCP server so that it acts as the center of the two networks

16. Users call the Help Desk and complain that they cannot connect to remote file shares. The System Administrator troubleshoots the problem and discovers he can only connect to the shares by IP and not by the URL of the server. What is the problem?

Quick Answer: 219
Detailed Answer: 230

- ❑ A. The DCHP server is issuing the wrong subnet.
- ❑ B. The DHCP server is offline.
- ❑ C. The DNS server is offline.
- ❑ D. The WINS server is offline.

Quick Check

Objective 4.7: Given a Troubleshooting Scenario Involving a Network with a Particular Physical Topology (Bus, Star, Mesh, or Ring) and Including a Network Diagram, Identify the Network Area Affected and the Cause of the Stated Failure

1. A workstation can ping the local server but cannot do the same to the ISP. From the diagram, choose which component is the cause of the problem.

Quick Answer: 219
Detailed Answer: 230

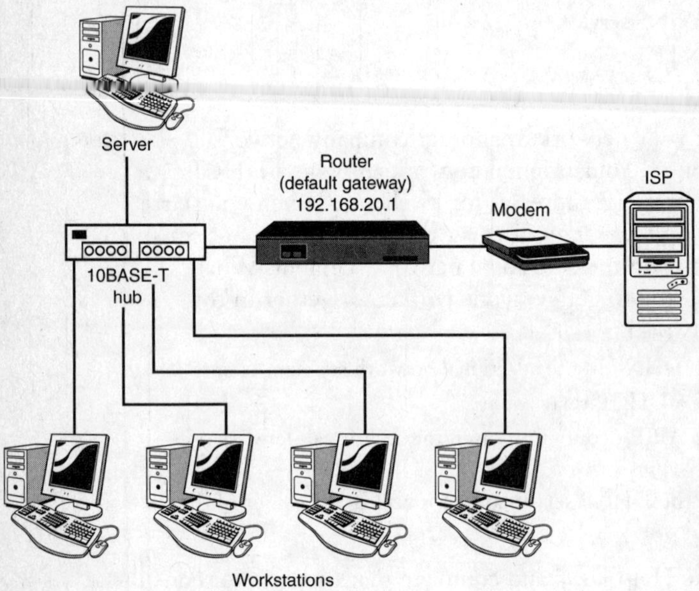

- ❑ A. Hub
- ❑ B. Router
- ❑ C. Modem
- ❑ D. ISP

Quick Check

2. From a workstation a network administrator notices that the same data being sent to and from the Internet is much slower when sent to and from the server. Using the diagram choose one of the following components in the network that best identifies the problem.

Quick Answer: 219
Detailed Answer: 230

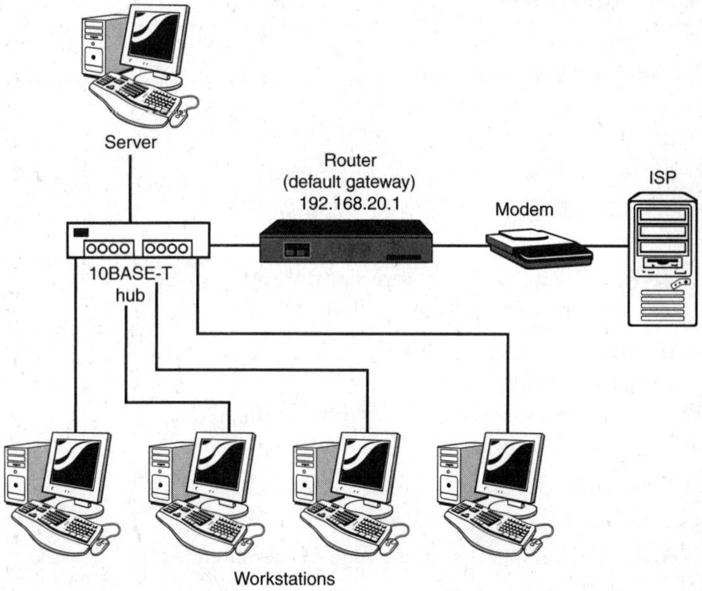

- ❑ A. Hub
- ❑ B. Router
- ❑ C. Modem
- ❑ D. ISP

3. Your assistant installs a Token Ring network and hooks up the client stations to a 100BaseT hub. When you start up the network, users cannot connect. What needs to be done to correct this problem?

Quick Answer: 219
Detailed Answer: 230

- ❑ A. Make the end node connections to a MSAU
- ❑ B. Make the end node connections to a Router
- ❑ C. Replace the 10BaseT hub
- ❑ D. Make the end node connections to a Bridge

Quick Check

Objective 4.8: Given a Network Troubleshooting Scenario Involving an Infrastructure Problem (Wired or Wireless), Identify the Cause of the Problem (Bad Media, Interference, Network Hardware or Environment)

1. A server in a 10BASE-T network has begun to reboot each afternoon. The server performance data indicates the problem isn't with the server. At the time of the reboot, the temperature in the server room is 92 degrees F, and the relative humidity is 45 percent.

   Quick Answer: 219
   Detailed Answer: 230

   Required Result: Eliminate external events that cause the server to reboot.

   Optional Desired Result: Provide uninterruptible AC power to external devices that may contribute to the problem.

   Proposed Solution: Install a separate air conditioning unit for the server room that will maintain the temperature at 72 degrees and the humidity at 50 percent. Attach a dedicated UPS to the air conditioning unit.

   Evaluation of Proposed Solution: Which of the following statements best describes the proposed solution?

   ❑ A. The proposed solution meets both the required result and optional desired result.

   ❑ B. The proposed solution meets only the required result.

   ❑ C. The proposed solution does not meet the required result or the optional desired result.

   ❑ D. The proposed solution meets only the optional desired result.

Quick Check

2. A client in a 100BASE-T LAN using category 5 UTP experiences intermittent server access. The hub is located 70 meters from a patch panel. The distance from the patch panel to the wall outlet is 20 meters. The patch cable from wall outlet to client is 15 meters.

Quick Answer: **219**
Detailed Answer: **231**

Required Result: To provide consistent access to the server from the client workstation.

Optional Desired Results: To reduce collisions on the network. To reduce the number of service calls.

Proposed Solution: Reduce the length of the patch cable from wall outlet to client workstation to 10 meters.

Evaluation of Proposed Solution: Which of the following statements best describes the proposed solution?

- ❑ A. The proposed solution produces the required result and one of the optional desired results.
- ❑ B. The proposed solution produces the required result and both of the optional desired results.
- ❑ C. The proposed solution produces the required result but neither of the optional desired results.
- ❑ D. The proposed solution does not produce the required result but produces both of the optional desired results.

3. None of the users on a network can log on to the server. The link lights on all client NICs are lit, and the same lights are lit at the hub. The server NIC link light and the corresponding hub port light are not lit. When one of the workstation cables is inserted into the server port at the hub, the hub link light is lit. What is the likely problem?

Quick Answer: **219**
Detailed Answer: **231**

- ❑ A. The cable from hub to workstations
- ❑ B. The workstations or hub
- ❑ C. The server NIC or cable
- ❑ D. The hub

Quick Check

4. The number of collisions on a network has increased substantially as new user workstations are added. What's the next step in determining the nature of the problem?

Quick Answer: 219
Detailed Answer: 231

- ❑ A. Limit the size of files that may be sent on the network.
- ❑ B. Replicate network traffic on a test network and compare the number of collisions.
- ❑ C. Schedule times that users are permitted to send files across the network.
- ❑ D. Disconnect users from the network until the number of collisions drops to a normal level.

5. Users on a LAN complain that server access slows in the afternoon. You compare their complaints to benchmark data that shows the access times and determine that their complaints are valid but all tests and diagnostics show the server and hub are working normally. When you check the server closet, the temperature reads 94 degrees, the humidity is 58 percent, and the cabling infrastructure is category 5 UTP.

Quick Answer: 219
Detailed Answer: 231

Required Result: To return server access times to the benchmark norm.

Optional Desired Results: To speed access times beyond the benchmark. To increase Internet availability.

Proposed Solution: Replace the category 5 UTP with shielded coaxial cable.

Evaluation of Proposed Solution: Which of the following best describes the proposed solution?

- ❑ A. The proposed solution produces the required result and both of the optional desired results.
- ❑ B. The proposed solution produces the required result but neither of the optional desired results.
- ❑ C. The proposed solution produces the required result but only one of the optional desired results.
- ❑ D. The proposed solution doesn't produce the required result or either of the optional desired results.

Quick Check

6. A new client is added to the 100BASE-T network. When the client is booted, it connects to the hub, but the connection is erratic. Suspecting the problem is in the cabling, you use a cable checker to determine the following lengths: hub-to-patch panel, 5m; patch panel-to-wall outlet, 90m; wall outlet-to-client computer, 10m. Which of the following is the best solution for addressing the cable lengths?

Quick Answer: **219**
Detailed Answer: **231**

- ❑ A. Reduce the client-to-wall outlet length to 3m.
- ❑ B. Reduce the hub-to-patch panel length to 3m.
- ❑ C. Reduce the patch panel-to-wall outlet length to 87m.
- ❑ D. Reduce the client-to-wall outlet length to 7m.

7. Which of the following utilities can be used to view the current protocol connections on a system?

Quick Answer: **219**
Detailed Answer: **231**

- ❑ A. Ping
- ❑ B. Netstat
- ❑ C. Telnet
- ❑ D. Tracert

8. A server located in a room with a controlled temperature of 70 degrees and humidity of 50% crashes at a specific time in the evening. The room has fluorescent lighting, and category 5 UTP ran through the ceiling and under the floor. Heat for the room is provided by a space heater located in the center of the room. Baseline and diagnostic data has eliminated the server as the problem of the crashes. Which of the following statements best describes the proposed solution?

Quick Answer: **219**
Detailed Answer: **231**

Required Results: Eliminate the server crash.

Optional Desired Results: Decrease the time required for the server to process file requests.

Proposed Solution: Remove the space heater and replace with a unit located a distance from the server room.

- ❑ A. The proposed solution does not meet the required results.
- ❑ B. The proposed solution meets the required results.
- ❑ C. The proposed solution doesn't meet the required results or the optional desired results.
- ❑ D. The proposed solution meets the optional desired results.

Quick Check

9. Which of the following is a disadvantage of using SPS as an alternative power supply?
   - ❑ A. Small capacity
   - ❑ B. Too expensive
   - ❑ C. Switch-over time
   - ❑ D. Over heat

Quick Answer: **219**
Detailed Answer: **232**

10. Which of the following provides truly continuous power to the server if the commercial power system fails?
    - ❑ A. Generator
    - ❑ B. Power Strip
    - ❑ C. BBC
    - ❑ D. UPS

Quick Answer: **219**
Detailed Answer: **232**

11. Maintenance has just installed new ceiling fans in your offices and now users complain of a slowdown in network performance. Nothing in the network topology has changed. What is the cause of the slowdown?
    - ❑ A. AMI (Alternate Mark Inversion)
    - ❑ B. EMI (Electromagnetic Interference)
    - ❑ C. MIB (Management Information Block)
    - ❑ D. FDM (Frequency Dividing Multiplex)

Quick Answer: **219**
Detailed Answer: **232**

12. One of your network technicians has made up 10 new network cables and installed them throughout the building. One of the new cable drops has bad connectivity. The network drop cable is 80 meters over a drop ceiling. What is the most likely cause of this problem?
    - ❑ A. The cable length is too long.
    - ❑ B. CAT6 cable is required.
    - ❑ C. Fluorescent lights are causing interference.
    - ❑ D. CAT3 cable is required.

Quick Answer: **219**
Detailed Answer: **232**

13. You are the administrator of a mixed wired/wireless network. Periodically your wireless clients lose connectivity, but the wired clients never do. The wireless clients all lose communications with the network and each other at the same time. What should you do to correct this problem?
    - ❑ A. Check the connection from the WAP to the wired network
    - ❑ B. Change the SSID setting for the WAP
    - ❑ C. Check the signal strength to the WAP
    - ❑ D. Check the WEP settings on the clients

Quick Answer: **219**
Detailed Answer: **232**

Quick Check

14. Computer A in Network A is configured with the following settings:

    IP Address: (130.0.0.2)

    Subnet Mask: 255.255.0.0

    Default Gateway:130.0.0.1

    Likewise, Computer B in Network B is configured with the following settings:

    IP Address: (193.100.100.2)

    Subnet Mask: 255.255.255.0

    Default Gateway: 130.0.0.1

    Computer A cannot communicate with Computer B across the network. What should you do to enable this to occur?

    - ❑ A. Change the IP address for Computer A to 193.100.100.2
    - ❑ B. Change the Subnet Mask for Computer B to 255.255.0.0
    - ❑ C. Change the Default Gateway for Computer B to 193.100.100.1
    - ❑ D. Change the Default Gateway setting for Computer A to 193.100.100.2

Quick Answer: 219
Detailed Answer: 232

Objective 4.9: Given a Network Problem Scenario, Select an Appropriate Course of Action Based on a General Logical Troubleshooting Strategy

1. A user is complaining of problems connecting to the server. You have not received any other calls as of yet from other users with problems. Which three of the following are valid next steps in this scenario?

    - ❑ A. Call another user who is connected to the same segment and ask him whether he is experiencing any problems accessing that server.
    - ❑ B. Call another user on a remote segment and ask him whether he can connect.
    - ❑ C. Try to connect to the server yourself to see whether there are any connectivity issues.
    - ❑ D. Replace the NIC in the system that is having the problem.

Quick Answer: 219
Detailed Answer: 232

Quick Check

2. The NIC link light on a workstation isn't lit. The cable from patch panel to hub checks good, as does the cabling from wall outlet to patch panel. From the following options, choose the next step.

   Quick Answer: 219
   Detailed Answer: 232

   - ❑ A. Reinstall the NOS.
   - ❑ B. Check the cable from the workstation NIC to the wall jack.
   - ❑ C. Replace the hub.
   - ❑ D. Replace all cabling from NIC to hub.

3. A workstation cannot connect with the rest of the network. What's the next step to take?

   Quick Answer: 219
   Detailed Answer: 233

   - ❑ A. Reinstall networking software on the workstation.
   - ❑ B. Check the connection to remote servers.
   - ❑ C. Check the NOS configuration settings at the server.
   - ❑ D. Check other workstations to determine whether they have a similar problem.

4. You receive a call from a user who says an error message pops up on the screen when a document is sent to a print server. A co-worker has tried to print from his workstation and the document printed successfully. What should be done now?

   Quick Answer: 219
   Detailed Answer: 233

   - ❑ A. Have the user's co-worker attempt to print from the original workstation.
   - ❑ B. Reinstall the printer drivers for both workstations.
   - ❑ C. Replace the print server.
   - ❑ D. Refer the user to a standard operating procedure that describes how to print to a print server.

5. A network has recently been infected with viruses that are irritating but not devastating. Before a devastating virus cripples the network, antivirus software is installed on the server. Which of the following is true?

   Quick Answer: 219
   Detailed Answer: 233

   - ❑ A. The server is not protected.
   - ❑ B. The network is adequately protected.
   - ❑ C. Antivirus software should also be installed on all patch panels.
   - ❑ D. Antivirus software should also be installed on all workstations.

Quick Check

6. A user complains of connectivity problems to the server and other members of his workgroup. You have him ping the local server but he doesn't receive a response. Thinking he may be entering the ping IP incorrectly, you ask him to have another operator enter the ping IP at a second workstation. The ping echoes the correct response. What is the next step?

 - ❑ A. Determine whether operators are following standard operating procedures.
 - ❑ B. Have a second operator perform the task on another workstation.
 - ❑ C. Have a second operator perform the task on the original workstation.
 - ❑ D. Formulate a correction.

Quick Answer: **219**
Detailed Answer: **233**

7. A user can't connect to the Internet from her workstation. What should be done next?

 - ❑ A. Run diagnostics on the server.
 - ❑ B. Isolate her computer from the rest of the network.
 - ❑ C. Have another user attempt to connect at his workstation.
 - ❑ D. Change the NIC in her computer.

Quick Answer: **219**
Detailed Answer: **233**

8. What is the purpose of a software patch?

 - ❑ A. To connect a workstation to a wall outlet
 - ❑ B. To fix a software weakness discovered after the software was formally released
 - ❑ C. To back up hard drive data to a duplicate hard drive
 - ❑ D. To correct a hard drive corrupted with a virus

Quick Answer: **219**
Detailed Answer: **233**

9. You cannot connect to a network server. The light in the back of the NIC card is not flashing. You change the patch cable and it is still not flashing. You go into the wiring closet and switch the connector from one connection on the hub to another. You check the NIC light and it is now blinking. What should you do next?

 - ❑ A. Document your findings
 - ❑ B. Replace the NIC
 - ❑ C. Replace the cable
 - ❑ D. Log in and try to transfer a file

Quick Answer: **219**
Detailed Answer: **233**

Quick Check

10. During a busy administrative week, you install a new virus suite on your network of 55 computers, a new RAID array in one of the servers, and a new office suite on 25 of the computer systems. After all the updates, you are experiencing system errors throughout the entire network. Which of the following activities would you perform to help isolate the problem?

Quick Answer: **220**
Detailed Answer: **233**

- ❑ A. Uninstall the office suite.
- ❑ B. Check the virus vendor's website for system patches or service packs.
- ❑ C. Disable the RAID array.
- ❑ D. Reinstall the virus software.

11. During the night, one of your servers powers down. Upon reboot, print services will not load. Which of the following would be the first step in the troubleshooting process?

Quick Answer: **220**
Detailed Answer: **233**

- ❑ A. Reinstall the printer
- ❑ B. Reboot the server
- ❑ C. Examine the server log files
- ❑ D. Reinstall the printer software

12. Users on server EAST1 can communicate with the server but none can access the Internet. The problem is suspected to lie with the default router for the LAN. What's the next step?

Quick Answer: **220**
Detailed Answer: **234**

- ❑ A. Change the server network protocol.
- ❑ B. Connect an outside workstation to the suspect default router to see whether the problem occurs.
- ❑ C. Install a modem and configure a dial-up connection to an ISP to see whether a workstation can access the Internet.
- ❑ D. Change the configuration so that Internet access is denied.

13. The NIC link light on a workstation isn't lit. The cable from patch panel to hub checks good, as does the cabling from wall outlet to patch panel. Which of the following is the next step?

Quick Answer: **220**
Detailed Answer: **234**

- ❑ A. Check the cable from the workstation NIC to the wall jack.
- ❑ B. Reinstall the NOS.
- ❑ C. Replace the hub.
- ❑ D. Replace all cabling from NIC to hub.

Quick Check

14. A number of users have called to report printing problems. Upon investigation, you find the cause to be a network printer connected to a server system. You arrive at the printer to find that it is connected, online, and performs a test print without any problems. You check the network connectivity and that seems to be okay as well. Which of the following troubleshooting steps would you perform next?
    - ❑ A. Remove and reinstall the printer drivers.
    - ❑ B. Reboot the server that is acting as the print server.
    - ❑ C. Examine the log files on the server to see whether there are any printing related events.
    - ❑ D. Change the network cable that connects the printer to the network.

Quick Answer: **220**
Detailed Answer: **234**

15. The number of collisions on a network has increased substantially as new user workstations are added. What's the first step in determining the nature of the problem?
    - ❑ A. Apply proven troubleshooting techniques.
    - ❑ B. Localize the extent of the problem to an area of the network.
    - ❑ C. Attempt to duplicate the problem.
    - ❑ D. Determine whether the entire network is affected.

Quick Answer: **220**
Detailed Answer: **234**

16. Antivirus software is installed on all client computers in the network. Which of the following is true?
    - ❑ A. The server isn't protected.
    - ❑ B. Virus protection isn't needed in a LAN.
    - ❑ C. The network is protected against viruses.
    - ❑ D. None of the network components are protected.

Quick Answer: **220**
Detailed Answer: **234**

17. A user cannot access computers in a remote workgroup subnet, but can access computers within his local subnet. Other users in the local subnet can access the remote subnet without any problems. The first step in troubleshooting this problem is to:
    - ❑ A. Implemented an Action Plan
    - ❑ B. Test the result
    - ❑ C. Identify the affected area
    - ❑ D. Document the solution

Quick Answer: **220**
Detailed Answer: **234**

Quick Check

18. You receive an error message saying: "A duplicate IP address has been detected." After implementing an Action Plan, what standard troubleshooting model action should you perform next?

 - ❑ A. Document the results
 - ❑ B. Test the result
 - ❑ C. Identify the effected area
 - ❑ D. Document the solution

Quick Answer: 220
Detailed Answer: 234

Quick Check Answer Key

Objective 4.1: Given a Troubleshooting Scenario, Select the Appropriate Network Utility

1. A, B
2. C
3. D
4. A
5. A
6. B
7. C
8. A
9. B
10. C
11. A
12. A
13. C
14. A
15. A
16. A, B
17. D
18. C
19. D
20. C
21. D
22. D
23. B
24. C
25. B
26. A
27. B
28. A
29. A
30. D
31. C
32. B, C

Objective 4.2: Given Output from a Diagnostic Utility (tracert, ping, ipconfig, and so on), Identify the Utility and Interpret the Output

1. A
2. A
3. C
4. D
5. A
6. C
7. B
8. C
9. B
10. A
11. B
12. A

Quick Check Answer Key

Objective 4.3: Given a Network Scenario, Interpret Visual Indicators (Link Lights, Collision Lights) to Determine the Nature of the Stated Problem

1. A, B, C
2. B
3. D
4. A
5. A
6. B
7. C
8. B

Objective 4.4: Given a Troubleshooting Scenario Involving a Client Accessing Remote Network Services, Identify the Cause of the Problem (File Services, Print Services, Authentication Failure, Protocol Configuration, Physical Connectivity and SOHO Router)

1. C
2. A
3. C
4. B
5. C
6. B
7. A
8. B, D
9. C
10. C
11. A
12. D
13. A
14. C
15. D
16. C

Objective 4.5: Given a Troubleshooting Scenario Between a Client and the Following Server Environments (UNIX/Linux/MAC OS X, NetWare, Windows, and Appleshare IP), Identify the Cause

1. B, C
2. A, B
3. A, D
4. A

Quick Check Answer Key

Objective 4.6: Given a Scenario, Determine the Impact of Modifying, Adding, or Removing Network Services (DHCP, DNS, WINS, and so on)

1. B
2. C
3. A
4. A
5. C
6. A
7. C
8. A
9. D
10. B
11. A
12. A
13. B
14. B
15. B
16. C

Objective 4.7: Given a Troubleshooting Scenario Involving a Network with a Particular Physical Topology (Bus, Star, Mesh, or Ring) and Including a Network Diagram, Identify the Network Area Affected and the Cause of the Stated Failure

1. B
2. C
3. A

Objective 4.8: Given a Network Troubleshooting Scenario Involving an Infrastructure Problem (Wired or Wireless), Identify the Cause of the Problem (Bad Media, Interference, Network Hardware or Environment)

1. A
2. A
3. C
4. B
5. D
6. A
7. B
8. B
9. C
10. D
11. B
12. C
13. A
14. C

Objective 4.9: Given a Network Problem Scenario, Select an Appropriate Course of Action Based on a General Logical Troubleshooting Strategy

1. A, B, C
2. B
3. D
4. A
5. D
6. C
7. A
8. B
9. D

Quick Check Answer Key

10. B

11. C

12. B

13. A

14. C

15. D

16. A

17. C

18. B

Answers and Explanations

Objective 4.1

1. **Answers: A, B.** In TCP/IP, a local loopback function is built into the TCP/IP protocol stack, and the address range 127.x.x.x is reserved for its use. The localhost entry corresponds to the IP address of the system itself, not to the loopback functionality. However, most operating systems resolve the localhost option to 127.0.0.1. Pinging the router would prove whether the TCP/IP protocol stack is functioning, but the intention is to start the troubleshooting process with the local loopback. Pinging another workstation would prove whether or not the TCP/IP protocol stack is functioning, but the intention is to start the troubleshooting process with the local loopback.

2. **Answer: C.** The netstat command can be used to view information on what TCP connections have been established as well as a range of other information. Nbtstat is used to view information related to NetBIOS over TCP/IP connections. NetBIOS is a network protocol, not a utility. The Ping utility is used to test network connectivity.

3. **Answer: D.** After establishing that the local loopback, the host's IP address, and the default gateway can be pinged, the next step is to ping the remote host to see whether it responds. Removing and reinstalling the TCP/IP protocol may be a valid troubleshooting step, but you would not perform this step before trying to ping the remote host. Changing the IP address to one in another range is not a valid troubleshooting step and in fact would certainly make the problem worse, not better. Reinitializing the TCP/IP stack may be a valid troubleshooting step, but you would not perform it before trying to ping the remote host.

4. **Answer: A.** Ping is a troubleshooting utility that can be used to test connectivity on networks that use the TCP/IP protocol suite. The Ping utility cannot be used with the NetBEUI protocol. RTMP is a routing protocol that is part of the AppleTalk protocol suite. There is a Ping-like utility for the IPX/SPX protocol suite, but it is called Ipxping and is available only on Novell NetWare.

5. **Answer: A.** The arp -a command lists all the IP addresses that have been resolved to MAC addresses. The nbtstat command displays the list of NetBIOS names that have been resolved to IP addresses. The arp - d * command removes all the current entries from the ARP table. The arp -s command allows you to add a static entry to the ARP table.

6. **Answer: B.** The nbtstat command, when used with the -c switch, displays the addresses that have been resolved by the system. The netstat command is used to view the protocol connections that have been established by the system

along with other associated statistics. The arp -a command can be used to view the IP address to MAC address resolutions that have been performed by the system. The tracert command is used to track the path of a packet between two destinations.

7. **Answer: C.** Ipconfig is the most commonly used utility for viewing addressing information on a workstation. Netstat is used to view statistical information concerning a session between workstations or servers. Tracert, or traceroute, is used to view all hops to a remote server. FTP is used to copy files for downloading.

8. **Answer: A.** Tracert, or traceroute, displays each router connection from the local machine to the final destination. Telnet is incorrect because it doesn't display router information. Netstat is a tool used to gather statistical data on a session. Ping is used to check connectivity between two network devices.

9. **Answer: B.** Ping is a TCP/IP utility used to check connectivity between two nodes that have an IP address.

10. **Answer: C.** This is the address of the local loopback test used for checking communications to and from a network card. The Ping utility sends four packets to the card and retransmits them. The utility checks the ability of the card to send and receive, as well as to respond to Network layer software—TCP/IP in this case.

11. **Answer: A.** The netstat command displays packet statistics such as how many packets have been sent and received as well as other related protocol information.

12. **Answer: A.** arp -d is used to delete entries from the host file.

13. **Answer: C.** tracert is a Windows command that can be used to display the full path between two systems including the number of hops between the systems. The Ping utility can be used to test connectivity between two devices but it only reports the time taken for the round trip, it does not give information about the time it takes to complete each hop in the route. The Telnet utility is used to open a virtual terminal session on a remote host. The nbtstat command is used to view statistical information about the NetBIOS status of a system.

14. **Answer: A.** On Windows client-based systems such as Windows 95/98/Me, the Winipcfg utility can be used to verify the TCP/IP configuration of the system. The same command does not work on Windows server systems. The Netstat utility is used to view protocol statistic information. The Ping utility is used to test the connectivity between two systems on a TCP/IP network. The Ipconfig utility is used to view the TCP/IP configuration on a Windows NT or Windows 2000 system.

15. **Answer: A.** The netstat –s command can be used to display per protocol statistics. The arp command is used to view a list of the IP address to MAC address resolutions performed by the system. The Nbtstat utility is used to view protocol statistics for the NetBIOS protocol.

16. **Answers: A, B.** To verify the IP configuration on a local computer system you can either ping the localhost or the IP address of 127.0.0.1. The default hostname for a system is localhost, not host. 127.0.0.0 is the network address for the class A loopback address, not a valid node loopback address.

17. **Answer: D.** The arp -a protocol is used to display the IP addresses that have been resolved to MAC addresses. The nbtstat command is used to view protocol statistics for NetBIOS connections. arp -d is not a valid command. The arp -s command allows you to add static entries to the ARP cache.

18. **Answer: C.** The function of the ping -t command is used to send continuous ping requests to a remote system. The ping request continues until manually stopped. The Traceroute utility shows the route taken by a packet to reach the destination host. The ping command shows the amount of time a packet takes to complete the round trip from host to destination. The ping -n command allows the number of Ping messages to be specific.

19. **Answer: D.** The Netstat utility allows you to view the TCP/IP connections between two systems. The Nbtstat utility is used to see the status of NetBIOS over TCP/IP connections. The Tracert utility is used to track the path a packet of data takes between two hosts. The Ipconfig utility is used to view the IP addressing configuration information on a system.

20. **Answer: C.** Ipconfig is a utility that provides addressing information for the workstation where the utility is entered.

21. **Answer: D.** On Windows client-based systems such as Windows 95/98/Me, the Winipcfg utility can be used to verify the TCP/IP configuration of the system. The same command does not work on Windows server systems. The Netstat utility is used to view protocol statistic information. The Ping utility is used to test the connectivity between two systems on a TCP/IP network. The Ipconfig utility is used to view the TCP/IP configuration on a Windows NT or Windows 2000 system.

22. **Answer: D.** The Nbtstat utility (NetBIOS over a TCP connection) is used with Windows machines to provide NetBIOS name information about the remote connection.

23. **Answer: B.** When entered, it shows information about workstation NetBIOS names and their corresponding IP addresses. In addition, Nbtstat can be used to determine the status of a remote connection—whether or not it's active. The Nbtstat utility (NetBIOS over a TCP connection) is used with Windows machines to provide NetBIOS name information about the remote connection.

24. **Answer: C.** Netstat is a tool used to display all current Network layer connections. This means you'll see TCP/IP or UDP protocols that are active at the time the tool is used. Netstat lists the network connections.

25. **Answer: B.** You will see the number of bytes received and transmitted, the type of packets, and, of particular interest, the number of errors generated.

26. **Answer: A.** Ping is a TCP/IP utility used to check connectivity between two nodes that have an IP address.

27. **Answer: B.** ipconfig /all, ifconfig, and winipcfgw will display the MAC address of your workstation.

28. **Answer: A.** Nbtstat is used to list all connections via NetBIOS names.

29. **Answer: A.** Netstat is used to list all active network connections.

30. **Answer: D.** Nslookup pertains to DNS information. This would allow you to determine if a DNS record locally or remotely is incorrectly configured.

31. **Answer: C.** If the router is misconfigured, you will be unable to ping outside IP addresses.

32. **Answers: B, C.** Both the route and the netstat commands can be used to view the routing table on a Windows 2000 system. The Tracert utility is used to track the route a packet takes between two destinations. The nbtstat command is used to view statistical information for NetBIOS connections. The Ping utility is used to test network connectivity.

Objective 4.2

1. **Answer: A.** The output is from a ping command executed on a Windows 2000 system. The output from the tracert, netstat, or nbtstat command is different from that shown.

2. **Answer: A.** The output is from a tracert command run on a Windows 2000 system. Ping, netstat, and nbtstat provide different output from that shown.

3. **Answer: C.** The netstat -e command displays packet statistics, such as how many packets have been sent and received, as well as other related protocol information, such as the number of errors. This should be a low number. If it is not, it could indicate a problem with the NIC.

4. **Answer: D.** Tracert is a remote access utility that's used to determine whether a remote server is active.

5. **Answer: A.** The Netstat utility can be used to display protocol statistics and TCP/IP network connections. The Nbtstat utility shows statistical information about the NetBIOS over TCP/IP connections. The Ping utility is used to test the connectivity between two devices on a TCP/IP network. The Tracert utility allows the path between two hosts on a TCP/IP network.

6. **Answer: C.** The output displayed in this question is from the Windows Tracert utility. Netstat, ping. and ipconfig produce output different from that shown.

7. **Answer: B.** The most likely cause of the problem is that the default gateway is not configured. The DNS servers are on the same subnet as this system. Addressing is configured statically, so there is no DHCP service. This is not a problem, however. The subnet mask is the default subnet mask for a class C network and so is not correct.

8. **Answer: C.** When an IP address is specified, tracert lists the number of hops to the destination, along with the IP addresses of each router along the way. You can specify the number of hops to the destination to determine the most efficient route. It's also a good tool to use to determine whether a problem lies at the remote address or within the route to the destination.

9. **Answer: B.** The output displayed in this question is from the Arp utility using the –a switch. Nbstat, Ping and Tracert produce output different from that shown.

10. **Answer: A.** The output displayed in this question is from the Tracert utility. Netstat, Pathping, and Arp produce output different from that shown.

11. **Answer: B.** The output displayed in this question is from the Windows IPconfig utility. Ping, Tracert and Arp -d produce output different from that shown.

12. **Answer: A.** The output displayed in this question is from the Windows Nbstat utility. Tracert, Arp -d and Ipconfig produce output different from that shown.

Objective 4.3

1. **Answers: A, B, C.** Link lights should be continually lit. The fact that a light is flashing indicates a physical connectivity problem. The hub, the cable, or the network card could be at fault. IP address assignments won't affect the link light status.

2. **Answer: B.** For physical connectivity problems, it's far less disruptive to all network users to replace a single cable than to replace a hub. If, however, the link light still isn't lit, replacing the hub would be the next choice.

3. **Answer: D.** They indicate whether the client is transmitting and receiving data frames and, by extension, whether the user is in the network.

4. **Answer: A.** Link lights should be continually lit. The fact that a light is flashing indicates a physical connectivity problem. The hub, the cable, or the network card could be at fault. IP address assignments won't affect the link light status.

5. **Answer: A.** Ping is a versatile tool used to verify connections to a remote host. This test will verify your connectivity to a particular piece of equipment, such as a server or router.

6. **Answer: B.** Because other sources are able to access the web server, it's most likely that the source of the problem is that there's too many connections for the router to handle.

7. **Answer: C.** The MDIX port is used to connect devices together.

8. **Answer: B.** If a hub port has been damaged, the link light will not turn on. Because we're using the original cabling that came with the computer, it's unlikely that there's any damage associated with that cable.

Objective 4.4

1. **Answer: C.** In this scenario, you would first check the remote access gateway to see whether it is running and operating correctly. Because the user can browse web pages, it is not a connectivity problem. Rebooting the system may help, but as the system appears to be working correctly this is unlikely to cure the problem. The IP address configuration would appear to be working, as the user can access web pages. The Internet connection would appear to be working, so cycling the power on the DSL modem is unlikely to help.

2. **Answer: A.** An 802.11b has a maximum data rate of 11Mbps at a minimum length of 150 feet. The further away from the AP, the slower the data rate. The minimum data rate is 1Mbps.

3. **Answer: C.** Unless the firewall has been configured to allow certain ports to be accessed, programs that you were originally able to access remotely will be blocked.

4. **Answer: B.** The Domain Name Server is used to resolve URLs to IP addresses and vice versa. The fact that it was working before suggests that the client service does not need to be installed.

5. **Answer: C.** The Gateway needs to be functional for users to access the Internet, even if the client computers have been properly setup.

6. **Answer: B.** The folder that the file is located in has to have proper permissions setup so that the file can be accessed, otherwise users will be forbidden from accessing them.

7. **Answer: A.** If the user is on a different network segment, while they are all a part of the mic-inc.com domain, they can be unable to connect to the internet or be pinged, while the web server can be on a segment that is connected to the internet and able to be pinged.

8. **Answers: B, D.** The fact that the modem connects and then disconnects suggests that either the configuration information or the authentication parameters are incorrect. Because the connection is being established, it is unlikely that the cable is at fault. The drivers are unlikely to be the source of the problem in this scenario because the connection is being established, proving that the modem is working.

9. **Answer: C.** The most likely explanation of the problem is that the default gateway setting on the workstation is wrong or misconfigured. The fact that the other workstations can communicate with remote systems indicates that the router acting as the default gateway is operating correctly. If the IP address of the workstation were incorrect, it would not be able to communicate with the other workstations on the segment. If the subnet mask setting of the workstation were incorrect, it would not be able to communicate with the other workstations on the segment.

10. **Answer: C.** The problem is that SLIP only supports TCP/IP at the Network layer. Although the other three choices represent solutions, they simply aren't viable compared to the ease and lack of expense of changing serial protocols.

11. **Answer: A.** Most modern phone systems are digital and as such, regular analog modems that require analog lines will not work. If the phone line in the room were analog, the modem would probably work. The phone line in the room is not faulty as the user can use it to call you and report the problem. If the modem can get as far as reporting a no dial tone error, it is most likely working correctly.

12. **Answer: D.** A default gateway is synonymous with a router. The network workstation requires a router to access the Internet.

13. **Answer: A.** FTP uses TCP/IP port 21 for its communications. Telnet uses Port 23. Port 80 is used by HTTP. Port 110 is used by POP3.

14. **Answer: C.** Log files often record information on errors that can be vital to the troubleshooting process. It is also a step that has little or no impact on network services. Rebooting the server is a last resort troubleshooting step. Removing and reinstalling the printer drivers may be a valid step, but it would not be the first choice of those listed. Changing the network cable may be a valid troubleshooting step, but because it has been verified that the network connectivity is working, this should not be necessary.

15. **Answer: D.** Secure web pages are viewed using HTTPS. HTTPS uses port 443, which is different from a normal web page that uses HTTP over port 80. Therefore, in this scenario, the most likely explanation is that port 443 is being blocked by the firewall, preventing people from accessing any pages that use HTTPS. Standard web pages use HTTP, which uses port 80 by default. Because users can access other areas of the website, this is not the problem. Port 110 is used by POP3, an email retrieval protocol, and is therefore unrelated to this problem. Because users still can access other areas of the website, it does not block all traffic.

16. **Answer: C.** The hub checks okay when a workstation is switched to the port connected to the server.

Objective 4.5

1. **Answers: B, C.** If the network has a DHCP server on it, the only information that needs to be supplied to a client workstation on a NetWare server is the name of the tree to which the user is to be connected and the context in which the user's ID can be found. The DNS server address, IP address of the default gateway, and the workstation IP address are supplied by the DHCP server and need not be entered manually. DHCP is a broadcast-based system and therefore the IP address of the DHCP server is not needed.

2. **Answers: A, B.** The Microsoft Client for NetWare Networks NetWare or the Novell Client for Windows 95/98 can be installed on the Windows 98 systems to facilitate connectivity. There is no such thing as the Novell CAFS client. Although TCP/IP can be used to connect to certain versions of Novell NetWare, client software is needed unless NetWare 6 is being used.

3. **Answers: A, D.** To configure the client software you will need to have the context and the NDS tree name. Username and password are not needed during the client configuration but they are to actually log on. You do not need to specify the target NDS replica or the domain name to connect to a NetWare server. The username is only needed when the user actually wants to authenticate to the server. The password is only needed when the user actually wants to authenticate to the server.

4. **Answer: A.** The main UNIX implementation of the Domain Name System (DNS), called BIND, is used on UNIX-based systems to resolve host names. The address resolution protocol resolves IP addresses to MAC addresses. The LMHOSTS file is used on Windows systems to resolve NetBIOS names to IP addresses.

Objective 4.6

1. **Answer: B.** More than likely WINS hasn't been set up correctly, if at all, at the clients.
2. **Answer: C.** Without DNS, the user won't be able to reconcile domain names to IP addresses.
3. **Answer: A.** When changes are made to a network client configuration, the client user cannot utilize the network resources appropriately. DHCP is used to dynamically assign an IP address from a network server to a network client. If the DHCP server is missing or has failed, the clients will not receive any DNS configuration information.
4. **Answer: A.** If the client is given a static IP address when the server is using DHCP to assign IP addresses, it's possible that two clients may try to use the same IP address. When this happens, one of the clients may be rejected from using the network.
5. **Answer: C.** More than likely Client Services for NetWare (CSNW) hasn't been set up on the clients.
6. **Answer: A.** EMI can be a problem with any copper-based wiring infrastructure. EMI can degrade or destroy long runs of digital data. Since a receiving node will reject garbled packets, the source node must resend the packets, which will cause network throughput to suffer and the network to slow down. The interference is caused by electromagnetic radiation emanating from electrical equipment.
7. **Answer: C.** DNS will allow host name resolutions to occur internally. In most cases companies will use a DNS server provided by the ISP. In some cases, however, it may be appropriate to have a DNS server on the internal network. Network address translation is normally a function of firewall or proxy servers. A WINS server streamlines the resolution of NetBIOS names to IP addresses. A Proxy server allows users to retrieve Internet web pages more quickly.
8. **Answer: A.** Optionally, you can enter the domain that you want the DNS server to search first in the Domain Suffix Search Order field. This field is used to specify which domain name is to be searched first for this client computer.

9. **Answer: D.** The PCI bus uses a 32-bit bus. PCI video cards are generally faster than VLB for graphics intensive operations and are Plug and Play. PCI is a 32-bit local-bus used in most Pentium computers and in the Apple Power Macintosh.

10. **Answer: B.** A DNS server that crashes will be unable to process any domain name translations.

11. **Answer: A.** A DHCP Relay Agent forwards requests from one segment, and relays them to the DHCP server on the other segment, allowing multiple segments to access resources.

12. **Answer: A.** A DHCP renew is done transparently to the user. As a result, the user will not experience any sort of change.

13. **Answer: B.** When a change is made to DNS, it propagates up to the root directory over time, not requiring notification.

14. **Answer: B.** A WINS server is required to resolve NetBIOS names.

15. **Answer: B.** A DHCP Relay Agent forwards requests from one segment, and relays them to the DHCP server on the other segment, allowing multiple segments to access resources.

16. **Answer: C.** A DNS server is required to resolve URLs to IP addresses.

Objective 4.7

1. **Answer: B.** A router will discard any unknown addresses and ignore corrupt frames or broadcast messages. To successfully transfer data across networks, a router relies on logical addresses. The most common logical address used by routers is an IP (Internet Protocol) address. The router must have the correct ISP address to ping.

2. **Answer: C.** A modem has to convert transmitted data and work with a limited bandwidth that was designed for voice communications, and not data communications such as text, video, and graphics.

3. **Answer: A.** Connections should be made to an MSAU, or a Multistation Access Device, which is a hub-like object which helps to maintain the ring structure.

Objective 4.8

1. **Answer: A.** The addition of a separate air conditioner and UPS will regulate temperature in the room as well as maintain server power. The key point in the scenario is the temperature in the room. At 92 degrees, the server is likely to behave abnormally. Note that the humidity, at 45 percent, is the borderline.

Low levels of humidity cause static to increase, which may cause intermittent operation of the server.

2. **Answer: A.** The maximum length of a 10BASE-T segment is 100 meters. The segment length in the question is 105 meters. By reducing the length of the NIC-to-wall outlet patch cable, the total segment length meets the standard. This reduces the number of service calls to this particular workstation because the connection should no longer be intermittent. It's not likely to have an effect on collisions because network collisions are more affected by the volume of network traffic than by segment length.

3. **Answer: C.** The hub checks okay when a workstation is switched to the port connected to the server.

4. **Answer: B.** It's the second step in the Network+ troubleshooting model: Re-create the problem. Note that the first step is identified in the question as "collisions have increased." All the remaining answers are solutions, rather than steps to resolving the problem.

5. **Answer: D.** The correct solution would be to reduce the temperature in the closet. Humidity, like temperature, must be maintained with specified ranges. If it runs too high, the equipment may fail due to excessive moisture; however if it's too low, static voltages can cause erratic operation.

6. **Answer: A.** The total length of a segment should not exceed 100 meters. Reducing the client-to-wall outlet length to 3m is the only answer that reduces the total segment length so that it's within specification. Reducing the hub-to-patch panel length to 3m provides a segment length of 103 meters. Reducing the patch panel-to-wall outlet length to 87m provides a segment length of 102 meters. Reducing the client-to-wall outlet length to 7m provides a segment length of 102 meters.

7. **Answer: B.** The netstat –a command can be used to display the current connections and listening ports. The Ping utility is used to test connectivity between two devices on a TCP/IP network. Telnet is an application-level protocol that allows a virtual terminal session on a remote host. The Tracert utility allows a path to be traced between two hosts.

8. **Answer: B.** The addition of a separate air conditioner and UPS will regulate temperature in the room as well as maintain server power. The key point in the scenario is the temperature in the room. At 70 degrees, the server is likely to behave abnormally. Note that the humidity, at 45 percent, is the borderline. Low levels of humidity cause static to increase, which may cause intermittent operation of the server.

9. **Answer: C.** The advantage of an SPS is that it's relatively inexpensive. A minor disadvantage is the time required to switch over to the battery backup. In newer models, this time is typically less than 5 ms. Note that a full cycle of 60 Hz current requires 16 ms to complete, so the SPS switches well within a single cycle time. The power supplies in servers and PCs have large filter capacitors that generally continue to supply the server during the brief switch-over time.

10. **Answer: D.** An Uninterruptible Power Supply (UPS), while also switching to a battery, avoids the switch-over time that could be a trouble spot for networks using an SPS. Because a UPS is placed in series with the main power, there is no switch-over latency time. The UPS continues to supply power to the server without interruption.

11. **Answer: B.** The new (electric) ceiling fans are causing electromagnetic interference with the cabling located in the ceilings, which results in higher rates of data corruption.

12. **Answer: C.** Due to the placement of the cables, it's likely that there's electromagnetic interference caused by the lighting in the ceiling. The cable length has not exceeded the maximum, and neither Cat6 or Cat3 cable is explicitly required in this sort of situation.

13. **Answer: A.** A faulty connection from the WAP to the wired network is the first problem to check. Due to the fact that all the wireless clients are failing simultaneously, distance is probably not an issue.

14. **Answer: C.** The default gateway should match the same Class of network as the workstations for each respective network.

Objective 4.9

1. **Answers: A, B, C.** Calling another user who is either connected to the same segment or on a remote segment and asking him whether he can connect is a valid troubleshooting step in this scenario. Trying to connect to the server yourself to see whether there are any connectivity issues is also a valid troubleshooting step in this scenario. If the user is only having a problem connecting to a single system, there is little likelihood that there is a problem with the network card. Therefore, replacing the NIC in the system that is having the problem would not be a valid troubleshooting step.

2. **Answer: B.** The patch cable from NIC to wall outlet is the only part of the cable that hasn't been checked. The question doesn't indicate that all workstations or servers are affected; therefore it is not necessary to reinstall the NOS. Replacing the hub is extreme and premature. A large portion of the segment checked good, therefore it is not necessary to replace all cabling from NIC to hub.

3. **Answer: D.** It's consistent with the Network+ model used for determining the boundaries of a problem. The first step in the model is to determine whether a problem affects the entire network. It is the only approach in the answers that includes this step first.

4. **Answer: A.** It's the second step in the Network+ operator problem escalation approach. The first step in the approach has been completed when the co-worker tried printing from another workstation. Reinstalling the printer drivers for both workstations and replacing the print server are incorrect because they are solutions rather than steps in the escalation process.

5. **Answer: D.** The workstations are left unprotected against viruses. The network is vulnerable to viruses at each workstation. Antivirus software was installed on the server. Software can't be installed on cables.

6. **Answer: C.** The second step is now implemented by having the second operator enter a ping at the original workstation.

7. **Answer: A.** This is the first step in determining whether a problem is with the network system or with the operator.

8. **Answer: B.** A patch, or fix, is intended as an interim solution to a problem discovered in a software package or routine. It's normally revision controlled and may or may not be beneficial in all applications.

9. **Answer: D.** The next step is to test the new hub port to make certain it works properly.

10. **Answer: B.** Because the system errors are networkwide, it is likely that the cause of the problem in this scenario lies with the virus suite as it is installed on all computers. To troubleshoot such a problem, it would be a good idea to check for patches or updates on the vendor's website. A problem with a RAID array would affect only the server in which it is installed, not the entire network. Because the office suite was only installed on some of the systems, it can be eliminated as a problem because all the systems are affected. The virus software appears to be the cause of the problem, but re-installing it is unlikely to help.

11. **Answer: C.** In this scenario, your first step is to gather information by examining the server log files. Once you have the information, you can proceed to the rest of the troubleshooting process. Rebooting the server is unlikely to cure the problem. Before reinstalling the printer or printer software, the log files should be examined to see whether there are any problems reported in the server log files.

12. **Answer: B.** The idea is to determine whether you can duplicate a problem by placing a suspect machine in a known good setting. For example, assume a router is the suspect. You would remove it and place it in a mock network to see whether the problem surfaces after all other devices are eliminated as potential problems. If you replicate the problem under these conditions, you know the router is bad, and you can replace it with a good one.

13. **Answer: A.** The patch cable from NIC to wall outlet is the only part of the cable that hasn't been checked. The question doesn't indicate that all workstations or servers are affected; therefore it is not necessary to reinstall the NOS. Replacing the hub is extreme and premature. A large portion of the segment checked good, therefore it is not necessary to replace all cabling from NIC to hub.

14. **Answer: C.** Calling another user who is either connected to the same segment or on a remote segment and asking him if he can connect is a valid troubleshooting step in this scenario. Trying to connect to the server yourself to see if there are any connectivity issues is also a valid troubleshooting step in this scenario. If the user is only having a problem connecting to a single system, there is little likelihood that there is a problem with the network card. Therefore, replacing the NIC in the system that is having the problem would not be a valid troubleshooting step.

15. **Answer: D.** It's the second step in the Network+ troubleshooting model: Re-create the problem. Note that the first step is identified in the question as "collisions have increased." All the remaining answers are solutions, rather than steps to resolving the problem.

16. **Answer: A.** Antivirus software should be installed on all servers as well as on all workstations on the network. At least once a month, the vendor should be queried for the latest version of their software. This ensures that the coverage of the viruses the software detects remains up to date.

17. **Answer: C.** The first step is to identify the affected area.

18. **Answer: B.** Now that an action plan has been implemented, the next step is to test the results, to see if it worked.

A

CD Contents and Installation Instructions

The CD features an innovative practice test engine powered by MeasureUp™, giving you yet another effective tool to assess your readiness for the exam.

Multiple Test Modes

MeasureUp practice tests are available in Study, Certification, Custom, Missed Question, and Non-Duplicate question modes.

Study Mode

Tests administered in Study Mode allow you to request the correct answer(s) and explanation to each question during the test. These tests are not timed. You can modify the testing environment *during* the test by selecting the Options button.

Certification Mode

Tests administered in Certification Mode closely simulate the actual testing environment you will encounter when taking a certification exam. These tests do not allow you to request the answer(s) and/or explanation to each question until after the exam.

Custom Mode

Custom Mode allows you to specify your preferred testing environment. Use this mode to specify the objectives you want to include in your test, the timer length, and other test properties. You can also modify the testing environment *during* the test by selecting the Options button.

Missed Question Mode

Missed Question Mode allows you to take a test containing only the questions you have missed previously.

Non-Duplicate Mode

Non-Duplicate Mode allows you to take a test containing only questions not displayed previously.

Random Questions and Order of Answers

This feature helps you learn the material without memorizing questions and answers. Each time you take a practice test, the questions and answers appear in a different randomized order.

Detailed Explanations of Correct and Incorrect Answers

You'll receive automatic feedback on all correct and incorrect answers. The detailed answer explanations are a superb learning tool in their own right.

Attention to Exam Objectives

MeasureUp practice tests are designed to appropriately balance the questions over each technical area covered by a specific exam.

Installing the CD

The minimum system requirements for the CD-ROM are

- Windows 95, 98, Me, NT4, 2000, or XP
- 7MB disk space for testing engine
- An average of 1MB disk space for each test

To install the CD-ROM, follow these instructions:

NOTE

If you need technical support, please contact MeasureUp at 678-356-5050 or email them at support@measureup.com. Additionally, you'll find Frequently Asked Questions (FAQ) at www.measureup.com.

1. Close all applications before beginning this installation.
2. Insert the CD into your CD-ROM drive. If the setup starts automatically, go to step 5. If the setup does not start automatically, continue with step 3.
3. From the Start menu, select Run.
4. In the Browse dialog box, double-click Setup.exe. In the Run dialog box, click OK to begin the installation.
5. On the Welcome Screen, click Next.
6. To agree to the Software License Agreement, click Yes.
7. On the Choose Destination Location screen, click Next to install the software to C:\Program Files\Certification Preparation.
8. On the Setup Type screen, select Typical Setup. Click Next to continue.
9. After the installation is complete, verify that Yes, I want to restart my computer now is selected. If you select No, I will restart my computer later, you will not be able to use the program until you restart your computer.
10. Click Finish.
11. After restarting your computer, choose Start, Programs, MeasureUp, MeasureUp Practice Tests.
12. Select the practice test and click Start Test.

Creating a Shortcut to the MeasureUp Practice Tests

To create a shortcut to the MeasureUp Practice Tests, follow these steps:

1. Right-click on your Desktop.
2. From the shortcut menu select New, Shortcut.
3. Browse to C:\Program Files\MeasureUp Practice Tests and select the MeasureUpCertification.exe or Localware.exe file.
4. Click OK.
5. Click Next.
6. Rename the shortcut MeasureUp.
7. Click Finish.

After you have completed step 7, use the MeasureUp shortcut on your Desktop to access the MeasureUp practice test.

Technical Support

If you encounter problems with the MeasureUp test engine on the CD-ROM, please contact MeasureUp at 678-356-5050 or email them at support@measureup.com. Technical support hours are 8 a.m. to 5 p.m. EST Monday through Friday. Additionally, you'll find Frequently Asked Questions (FAQ) at www.measureup.com.

If you'd like to purchase additional MeasureUp products, telephone 678-356-5050 or 800-649-1MUP (1687) or visit www.measureup.com.